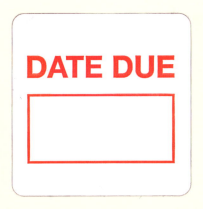

DATE DUE

AGING PRISONERS

Crisis in American Corrections

Ronald H. Aday

PRAEGER

Westport, Connecticut
London

Library of Congress Cataloging-in-Publication Data

Aday, Ron H.
  Aging prisoners : crisis in American corrections / Ronald H. Aday.
    p. cm.
  Includes bibliographical references and index.
  ISBN 0–275–97122–8 (alk. paper)—ISBN 0–275–97123–6 (pbk : alk. paper)
  1. Aged prisoners—United States.   2. Aged prisoners—Services for—United
States.   3. Aged offenders—United States.   I. Title.
HV9469.A553.2003
363'.66—dc21   2002070902

British Library Cataloguing in Publication Data is available.

Library of Congress Catalog Card Number: 2002070902
ISBN: 0–275–97122–8

First published in 2003

Praeger Publishers, 88 Post Road West, Westport, CT 06881
An imprint of Greenwood Publishing Group, Inc.
www.praeger.com

Printed in the United States of America

The paper used in this book complies with the
Permanent Paper Standard issued by the National
Information Standards Organization (Z39.48–1984).

10 9 8 7 6 5 4 3 2 1

Contents

Illustrations

Introduction

When I was a graduate student pursuing concentrations in gerontology and crime and corrections, the topic of aging prisoners became a natural fit for a dissertation topic. I interviewed my first group of aging prisoners in 1975 at a minimum-security special-needs facility in Oklahoma. Little did I know that some twenty-seven years later, I would still be pursuing a topic with the magnitude of societal interest that we find today. As I visit correctional institutions and talk with prison officials and other policymakers, the topic continues to be compelling. Over the years I have interviewed hundreds of aging prisoners and have heard stories about their crimes, families and friends, health issues, and adjustment to prison life. I hope that by relaying some of the stories and information that I have gathered will cause others to find this topic intriguing and worthy of pursuing.

A graying American population and a record number of inmates incarcerated in our jails and prisons are two of the major forces shaping the political and economic landscape of American society. In the next several decades it appears these two realities of American life will become even more pervasive and demand solutions. As we transition into the 21st century, we find ourselves exploring a new frontier, with the elderly serving as pioneers in our health-care system, churches, families, and prisons. A decade or so ago we would never have thought it possible that prison nursing homes would become a necessity. As Hooyman and Kiyak (1999, p. xiv) have so aptly stated, "aging is a complex and fascinating process." For one thing, aging brings about gradual change in all elements of society, both for the individual and for society. It is an arbitrary process of estab-lishing what is appropriate to or expected of people of various ages. In this case, how our society responds to the changes generated by the growing number of older offenders in the criminal justice system remains to be seen.

THE DEMOGRAPHIC TRANSITION

The world in 2002 had 420 million people over the age of 65 and, as a result, we are experiencing a traumatic age revolution. To think that 20 percent of all humans who have ever lived past the age of 65 are now alive is almost impossible to comprehend. The United States is also part of this unprecedented growth, and as we edge our way into the 21st century, pre-viously unimagined numbers of older people in American society have become a reality. Never before in our history have we had so many older citizens. Increases in the number and proportion of the older adult popu-lation, and the dynamic changes within the aging population itself, will rep-resent one of the most dramatic changes in American society. So profound is this demographic revolution that every aspect of social life and society is affected. The growth of the elderly population has significant economic im-plications for our various institutions and the public policymakers who are responsible for carving out a response to this demographic transition.

While we now have 35 million people aged 65 and older in the United States (Fowles & Greenberg, 2001), the baby boomers will solidify the aging revolution in America. This group born between 1946 and 1964 is 76 mil-lion strong, which is 70 percent more than were born during the preceding two decades (Shultz & Young, 1999). Baby boomers have now begun to enter their 50s and the first baby boomers will turn 65 in 2010. Future projections call for additional dramatic graying of America well into the 21st century. Although the boomers in their 50s are not considered old by chronological standards, they can be viewed as older adults with numerous physical and cognitive problems associated with the aging process that they begin to ex-perience by the age of 50. As life expectancy increases and baby boomers (nearly one-third of the U.S. population) work their way toward old age, the net result will affect all our social institutions. As this group continues to swell the ranks of the elderly population, increasing numbers of older adults are projected to come in contact with the criminal justice system.

PURPOSE AND FOCUS

The increase in the proportion of the elderly is having far-reaching ef-fects on all components of the criminal justice system. Almost 500,000 people age 50 and older are arrested every year in the United States (Uniform Crime Reports, 1998). Of these, 18 percent involve serious felonies such as murder, forcible rape, robbery, aggravated assault, burglary, larceny, motor vehicle theft, and arson. As an increasing number of our older population commit violent offenses, the likelihood an increasing number will enter prison becomes apparent. While crimes committed by older offenders run the gamut from disorderly conduct to homicide, current policy has little to say that adequately informs how the criminal justice system responds to this growing and diverse population.

As a result, the topics of aging, crime, and incarceration are increasingly demanding more serious scholarly attention. Correctional administrators and other policymakers need more information about important issues to respond effectively to the special needs of older offenders. They need accurate data and a comprehensive and informed dialogue that focuses on the major concerns of the rising number of older offenders, and adequately describes the diversity of the group as well. In the foreseeable future, policymakers will have to make decisions at every point from the time of apprehending older offenders to the time they are released. As Pollak (1941) so astutely observed approximately 60 years ago:

> Old criminals offer an ugly picture and it seems as if even scientists do not like to look at it for any considerable amount of time. . . . On the other hand, if the thesis of the interrelationship between age and crime is to hold, an investigation of all its implications has to yield results, and with the tendency of our population to increase in the higher age brackets, a special study of criminality of the aged seem to meet a scientific as well as a practical need. (p. 212)

If Pollak's view was accurate in 1941, it is even more so today. With the elderly prisoner population representing the fastest-growing age group in our prison system today, we have reached an important juncture in the fields of gerontology, criminology, and corrections.

The recent shift toward mandatory sentencing, the war on drugs, the violent nature of late-life offending, and the graying of America are the major turning points that unexpectedly escalated the need to address the issues discussed in this book.

The purpose of this book is to examine the empirical and theoretical problems of older adult crime. The book further explores the older inmate's adjustment to incarceration and the policies and programs currently installed to manage this special population. The book is designed to address significant research issues, provide theoretical explanations, and present illustrations of correctional programs. Perhaps this book can serve as a catalyst to promote future research, stimulate policy discussions, and provide an important step in meeting the many challenges facing policymakers, correctional officials, and other criminal justice personnel.

The field of aging is multidisciplinary in nature, and reaching some understanding of the concerns of the aging prison population will also require a broad approach. Thus, this book is intended for those in several academic fields and professionals responsible for providing care or establishing social policy for older offenders. Scholars and professionals in sociology, social work, psychology, counseling, recreational therapy, and nursing should find the information in these pages useful for evaluating the complex problems related to older offenders. Those in gerontology, criminal justice, criminology, and corrections will find the book to be a useful research tool or supplemental text for their students. As a relatively new topic, students should find the information useful as they plan for careers in various aspects of the criminal justice system. Criminal justice professionals— whether lawyers, judges, police officers, social workers, medical staff, probation and parole officers, or correctional staff and administrators—who work directly with older offenders should find the book relevant as they pursue ways to improve guidelines for working with the elderly prison population. Those responsible for the design and implementation of new facilities and programs should find the book especially helpful.

BOOK ORGANIZATION

The early chapters in this book raise a variety of questions on the nature and causes of elderly crime. Chapter 1 will present an overview of the aging population and some of the issues associated with aging in American prisons. Chapter 2 provides a point of departure for the examination of this topic by reviewing older offender crime trends and patterns. A historical review of previous research helps lay the groundwork for understanding current crime patterns among older adults. A few comparisons are also made between older male and female crime trends. Some criminal offenses are explored in order to give important insights into current crime trends and surrounding issues. In order to establish more efficient preventive strategies to reduce deviant behavior in old age, it is important to know that a significant number of older offenders commit violent crimes such as murder and sexual crimes. I hope that discussing these issues in some detail will encourage researchers to investigate the nature of these crimes more thoroughly.

Chapter 3 examines a variety of medical gerontological, psychological, and social theories to suggest some theoretical links between old age and crime. Although few of these theories have actually been tested with the elderly population, they will provide a useful contribution to the literature.

As the examination of the latter stages of life evolves toward greater academic maturity, it will be necessary to focus more specifically on theoretical explanations for changes in behavior associated with the aging process.
The discussion should point out the necessity for further theoretical development and complementary research. If nothing more, this chapter re-
inforces the complexities associated with the aging process and especially
the difficulties in understanding why first-time elderly offenders depart from
a lifetime of obedience to the law.

Chapter 4 addresses health-care concerns and offers essential data on
the health-care mandates and associated costs of providing health care for
an increasing number of aging inmates. Certainly providing health care in
a punitive environment is no easy task, and the issues discussed in Chapter 4 reinforce that fact. A comprehensive profile of older prisoners' health
provides several state comparisons, which offer a clearer picture of the older
offender's health problems. A variety of appropriate mental health concerns presented in this chapter add to the complexities of establishing
workable case-management strategies. Chapter 4 is particularly important
for policymakers, for it addresses some of the barriers to providing health
care to an aging population as well as inmate satisfaction with such care.

The effect of incarceration on the older inmate population is thoroughly
addressed in Chapter 5. Presented are some of the distinguishing differences
between offender types and how each might influence coping strategies. The
chapter provides a comprehensive overview of the negative consequences
that long prison sentences frequently bring to the individual inmate and their
relationships on the outside. How older offenders cope with a variety of losses
and the prospects of dying in prison are important topics for social service
professionals. Identifying some of the important components (religious activities, work, friendships) essential to socially constructing a positive prison
life provides useful information for establishing programming policies.

A topic of special importance for correctional officials and policymakers
is touched on in Chapter 6. For some years, states have been involved in remodeling old hospitals or building new facilities designed for the geriatric
offender. Chapter 6 explores the continuing debate on where best to house
aging inmates. The environmental theory suggests that as inmates age in
place it becomes paramount to design facilities that will provide an optimum
social and physical environment. Several geriatric facilities and programs are
presented as models for the correctional field. Chapter 6 identifies the importance of the relationship between older offenders and the prison environment, which more frequently is becoming their permanent home.

Chapter 7 focuses exclusively on the older female offender and the special needs generated by her inherent uniqueness. It is important to ac-

knowledge not only the differences in women's major health concerns, but also the differences in the shortcomings of the prison programming designed for them.

The examination of the health utilization and status provides new and insightful information for those responsible for managing the older female offender population. Coping with declining health and the consequences of long-term confinement on relationships both inside and outside the prison are issues that merit further exploration. Since research on older female offenders is scarce, it is also important to conduct further research on this small but growing segment of the prison population.

Chapter 8 reviews the policies implemented by the police, the courts, prisons, and alternatives to incarceration. While the literature presents mixed views on the creation of a geriatric justice system, substantial findings suggest that the elderly offender is treated exceptionally in a variety of criminal justice situations. Identifying current policies and making recommendations for the future will generate further debate on these issues. It is hoped that Chapter 8 will generate additional research that will advance knowledge on the topic of older offenders.

ACKNOWLEDGMENTS

I am grateful to the many individuals who contributed to the successful completion of this book. In particular, I would like to thank those who reviewed the manuscript and whose invaluable suggestions greatly improved the final draft. To the many inmates who gave me the opportunity to visit with them about some very difficult issues, I am indeed grateful. Finally, a special thanks goes to Praeger editor Suzanne Staszak-Silva, who always lifted my spirits with her cheerful e-mail and kept me going on this project.

REFERENCES

Fowles, D.G., & Greenberg, S. (2001). A profile of older Americans. Washington, DC: Administration on Aging.
Hooyman, N., & Kiyak, H.A. (1999). Social gerontology. Boston: Allyn & Bacon.
Pollak, O. (1941). The criminality of old age. Journal of Criminal Psychopathology, 3, 213–235.
Sültz, H.A., & Young, K.M. (1999). Health care USA: Understanding its organization and delivery. Gaithersburg, MA.: Aspen Publishers.

Chapter 1

Studying Older Offenders

For the first time in American history, we are faced with the dilemma of an aging prison population. Older offenders who commit violent crimes and are sentenced to long periods of imprisonment has become an astonishing fact since the early 1990s. This emerging problem will only be exacerbated in the future as an increasing number of aging inmates find their way into correctional settings. This problem coupled with the explosion of the general prison population, AIDS among the prisoners, and the complications associated with housing a growing number of mentally ill inmates have significantly challenged our correctional system. New aging issues, including, among others, dementia, cancer, stroke, and incontinence, and other chronic conditions such as arthritis and hypertension, which are frequent symptoms of this population, are further taxing many economically strapped prison systems.

Both state and federal correctional systems and politicians responsible for making and funding our current policies are confronted with a number of serious issues and research questions that must be addressed. I pose ten of the more common concerns currently being raised by legislators and criminal justice officials: (1) Should an elderly person with no previous criminal convictions be given special consideration by the police or courts? (2) Where do we safely house the increasing number of aging inmates? (3) Should we change our sentencing structure to reflect probable years remaining in the offender's life? (4) What research is needed that might prove helpful for correctional officials to better respond to the needs of the aging inmate? (5) As a society, how much do we want to spend on long-term incarceration? (6) Should rehabilitative programs be implemented in correctional settings for aging inmates, and to what extent? (7) How do we assist older offenders to ensure a successful transition into and out of prison? (8) How can we better project the economic impact of an aging prison population? (9) What type of end-of-life care should correctional systems provide for aging inmates who will certainly die in prison? (10) Should state and federal politicians revisit the mandatory sentencing policies now in place? This list, while not exhaustive, provides a cross section of the concerns that have surfaced since the early 1990s.

These and other pending challenges focused greater attention, as a result, on elderly crime and in particular the dramatic growth in the number of aging inmates since 1990. Researchers examined, for example, offending patterns, age and sentencing guidelines, ailing elderly inmates, health care costs and policies, and end-of-life issues. The print media around the country also began to address with greater frequency the new concerns that older offenders present to the criminal justice system. Some articles addressed the health-care needs of the aging population, the cost of life without parole, and the economic impact that caring for the growing number of aging inmates will have on state budgets. The difficulty that prosecutors and judges face when determining an elderly offender's criminal responsibility is also frequently mentioned.

Perhaps the most interesting aspect of the problem of elderly crime and resultant graying of our nation's prisons is the fact that researchers and the media were predicting this new challenge for well over a decade. As early as 1982 elderly crime was a major focus of one segment of 60 *Minutes* and elderly inmates in prison was also the focus of ABC's 20/20, some ten years later. Also in 1982 a National Elderly Offender Conference was held to explore the problem of elderly crime and incarceration. In 1985 interested researchers, practitioners, and educators established the Society for Interdisciplinary Research on Elderly Offenders (SIREO) to promote the study of elderly offenders. While this organization failed to maintain its functional status and momentum for any extended time, it contributed greatly to the literature and emerging policy debate in the 1980s.

The establishment of the Coalition for Federal Sentencing Reform in the late 1990s further illustrates the impact of the graying of America's prisons is having on current public debate. Formed by the National Center on Institutions and Alternatives in 1996, the coalition examined the unprecedented increase of elderly inmates in both federal and state prisons. The coalition, with the collaboration of the Heritage Foundation, convened national conferences and other work groups to address the issues surrounding the increase in elderly inmates. The goal of the coalition is to encourage federal legislation aimed at the supervised release of elderly nonviolent inmates and to reduce sentencing guidelines at the federal level. The Southern Legislative Conference, a regional body of the National Council of State Governments, also explores ways to reduce the number of older offenders making their way into jails and prisons. State and federal legislators alike began to realize that we can no longer afford to incarcerate so many sick, elderly inmates.

As scholars initially examined the rise of elderly crime, they made numerous policy recommendations, which, for all practical purposes, went unheeded until the early years of the 21st century. For legitimate reasons, criminal justice officials became preoccupied with the general increase in crime, enforcing drug laws, and accomodating more youthful offenders. Although we could easily have predicted the growth of the aging population, it was impossible to predict that state legislatures would continue to pass tougher and tougher mandatory sentencing laws. These enactments continued as the baby boomers made the transition into older adulthood. As a result, we were ill prepared for the "aging epidemic" in almost every component of the criminal justice system.

GRAYING OF AMERICAN PRISONS

The number of geriatric inmates in many state and federal prisons rose steadily after the early 1980s. Chaneles (1987) predicted that, by the year 2000, we would have approximately 125,000 incarcerated inmates age 50 or over residing in U.S. prisons. (The count actually took about two years longer to near that figure.) Correction officials were advised by researchers that as the number of elderly people in America's general population increased, so too would the number of elderly inmates. Their numbers jumped substantially in the 1990s, both in absolute terms and as a proportion of states' prison populations. The statistics reported on January 1, 2001, in *The Corrections Yearbook* indicated that there were over 1.3 million inmates confined to state and federal prisons nationwide, including the District of Columbia. Of these, 113,358 prisoners were over the age of 50, which represents a tripling of the 33,499 who were over age 50 recorded in 1990. After 1995, this population grew by about 10,000 per year, and it can be safely stated that, as of January 1, 2002, there were about 125,000 prisoners age 50 and over. This age group comprises 8.2 percent of the total inmate population, up significantly from the 4.0 percent reported in 1990. Approximately one-half of this group of inmates is over the age of 55 (American Correctional Association, 2001). Of the 145,416 prisoners housed in the Federal Bureau of Prisons, 16,066 or 11.0 percent, were 50 years of age or over (*Corrections Yearbook*, 2001).

Convergence of Trends

According to the Georgia Department of Corrections (1999), a variety of related trends have contributed to the graying of American's prison population: (1) the increasing number of older adults in the general population and increase in arrests of elderly citizens for serious crimes; (2) the massive increase in prison capacity in the 1990s (7 percent annually); (3) a fundamental national shift toward a more retributive and punitive response to crime; (4) the severe curtailment of discretionary early release from prison; and (5) the increase in the incarceration rate from 344 per 100,000 in 1993 to 461 per 100,000 in 1998, an increase of 30 percent.

Thus, the dramatic and unprecedented growth in state and federal prison populations since 1980 was driven by increases in both the proportion of convicted offenders who were sentenced to prison terms and the length of such terms (Silverman & Vega, 1996). In the 1980s a fundamental shift toward a more retributive and punitive response to crime occurred. As offenders committed serious crimes, they were more frequently confronted with mandatory minimum periods of imprisonment and extended prison terms without benefit of parole. In other words, new laws increased the flow of inmates into the prison system, and simultaneously reduced the number who can leave. As long as the general toughening of the public's attitude toward crime persists and legislatures respond with longer prison sentences, the number of older inmates serving life sentences will increase, posing a significant challenge for correction officials.

Truth in Sentencing

Most experts agree that the growth in the older prison population is not due to an elderly crime wave. According to the U.S. Department of Justice, the trend results more directly from "three strikes" and truth-in-sentencing laws (Edwards, 1998). Truth-in-sentencing laws recently enacted contributed significantly to the increase in inmates serving lengthy sentences. Ditton and Wilson (1999) report that prisoners released in 1996 served on average thirty months in prison or jail, or 44 percent of their sentences. This same report revealed that well over half of the state prison systems in the early 21st century required offenders to serve 85 percent of the prison sentence. Nearly 7 in 10 violent offenders served under the 85 percent requirement. Overall, truth-in-sentencing laws have added fifteen months to time served for violent offenses. In addition, fourteen states have abolished parole board release for offenders altogether, and a few other states have abolished parole board release for certain violent or felony offenders.

Georgia is one of several states with a "two strikes and you're out" law. This law requires that anyone convicted of any of seven serious violent felonies must serve a minimum of ten years in prison without parole. Any sentence handed down by the court beyond ten years is also pardon-proof. If an offender were convicted of a second "deadly sin" he/she would automatically receive a mandatory sentence of life without parole. Enacted in the mid 1990s, "two strikes" laws were already having a significant effect on long-term incarceration within ten or twelve years. Within twelve years of the enactment of the Georgia law, more than 3,000 offenders were sentenced to a minimum sentence of ten years without parole. Mandatory sentencing reduced the potentially parolable inmate population from 96 percent of all inmates in 1996 to 68 percent within two years (Georgia Department of Corrections, 1999). In addition, effective January 1, 1998, the Georgia Parole Board instituted a policy requiring all inmates convicted of twenty violent crimes not covered under the "two strikes" legislation to serve a minimum of 90 percent of their court-imposed sentence. As a result, those inmates who fall under the parole board's 90 percent policy will serve 2.3 years longer in prison than inmates sentenced for the same crime prior to the implementation of the 90 percent policy. These legislative reforms drove prisoner populations to historic highs.

Some states found the increase in the geriatric inmate population to be far greater than they anticipated. For example, Florida housed 1,350 inmates 50 years of age or older in the state's prison system in 1988. That same year, corrections officials estimated that number would increase to 3,094 by the year 2000 (Dugger, 1988). By 1998 the number had already ballooned to 4,403 inmates, a 195 percent increase in a decade and already exceeding the 2000 projection. As of January 1, 2002, Florida reported 6,172 inmates who are 50 years of age or older, a figure that comprised about 8 percent of its total prison population (*Florida Department of Corrections annual report*, 2002). According to Florida correctional officials, the older inmate population is expected to comprise 14 percent of Florida's total inmate population by the year 2011.

Increase in Long-Term Inmates

Since 1980 long-term incarceration has become a major contributor to the explosion of the American prison population. Problems have arisen in defining this prison population because there is no uniform agreement about what constitutes "long-term." Definitions vary substantially over time and place. What constitutes long-term can range from five years to more than ten (Silverman & Vega, 1996). Whatever the minimum amount of time required to qualify as a long-termer, older inmates serving long sentences require more attention than they did because of their greater numbers, and the demand will increase because of declining health and other problems of adjustment to the later stages of life. Long-term inmates as a group appear to be getting older because the average age of long-term offenders admitted into prison has risen.

Table 1.1 presents data from the year 2000 on the three long-term populations and those over the age of 50 by state. A review of this data provides an alarming pattern. Twenty-nine states reported that at least 20 percent or more of the total (in-count) prisoner population consisted of natural lifers (life with any parole possibilities), lifers (serving life with possible parole), and inmates sentenced to twenty or more years in prison. Four states (Alabama, Arkansas, Oklahoma, and Tennessee) reported that about 40 percent of their total prison fell in one of these three categories. Alabama led the way with 47 percent in the long-term inmate category. The trend toward longer prison terms is illustrated by the fact that there were 17,280 natural lifers, 84,918 lifers, and 189,990 inmates serving twenty years or more. Another 3,533 prisoners were serving time on death row during the same period. As a whole, these groups constitute 24 percent of all inmates in state and federal prisons (*Corrections Yearbook*, 2000). The average percentage of inmates serving twenty years or more remained steady from the early 1990s to 2000, the overall number of long-term inmates increased dramatically during the same period.

Several states also experienced large increases in the number of inmates age 50 and over. From 1995 to 2000, there was an overall increase of 38 percent for inmates in this age category. In several other states, the older inmate population grew even faster. For example, Texas, Louisiana, and Mississippi saw their older inmate population double from 1995 to 2001. In 2000 Texas led the nation with 13,064 older inmates, followed by California with 12,426. Ironically, these two states housed approximately 25 percent of the inmates in this age category that year. As Table 1.1 indicates, fourteen states had at least 8 percent of their prison population over the age of 50. Five years earlier only three states had so many inmates over 50 (*Corrections Yearbook*, 1996).

In a report released in 1999, the Texas Department of Criminal Justice provided projections of its elderly population, which it defines as 55 years of age and above (Fabelo, 1999). The elderly population in Texas represents a growing percentage of the prison population in Texas. In 1998 there

Table 1.1
Comparison of Selected Long-Term Prison Populations

	Grand Total	Over Age 50	% Over Age 50	Natural Lifers	Lifers	20 Years or More	% Life and 20
AL	29,633	1,925	6.3	1,249	3,188	6,977	38.5
AK	4,173	361	8.7	27	208	257	11.8
AZ	26,641	2,377	8.9	106	852	1,999	11.1
AR	12,449	870	6.8	410	689	4,625	44.8
CA	162,765	12,426	7.6	2,621	23,020	6,698	19.8
CO	16,878	1,417	8.4	258	566	2,380	18.9
CT	18,659	849	4.5	177	225	1,197	8.4
DC	10,328	611	5.9	0	1	2	0.0
DE	5,874	326	5.4	178	214	271	10.9
FL	71,319	5,873	8.2	3,049	4,485	9,026	23.2
GA	43,936	3,426	7.8	221	5,954	6,044	27.8
HI	5,053	458	8.9	24	215	236	9.3
ID	5,260	508	9.6	71	352	298	13.7
IL	45,281	2,392	5.3	1,088	14	9,619	23.7
IN	20,125	1,636	8.1	54	206	6,300	32.6
IO	7,856	468	5.8	512	0	1,452	24.5
KS	8,344	727	8.6	0	755	2,350	36.8
KY	15,082	1,156	7.7	16	709	2,006	18.1
LA	34,954	2,787	8.0	3,585	0	4,597	23.4
ME	1,738	179	10.3	38	13	0	0.0
MD	23,145	1,509	6.5	181	1,916	4,888	30.1
MA	11,209	1,274	11.1	700	873	253	15.9
MI	48,028	4,436	9.2	2,600	1,711	4,562	18.5
MN	6,238	389	6.1	21	331	501	13.4
MS	20,304	1,171	5.8	694	1,455	2,568	20.9
MO	27,914	2,054	7.3	621	37	2,948	18.0
MT	3,105	250	8.1	22	30	790	27.3
NE	3,814	294	7.6	174	70	592	21.7
NV	9,860	1,099	10.8	321	1,287	423	22.0
NH	2,282	277	12.1	56	96	265	18.3
NJ	28,907	1,854	6.4	10	1,104	3,348	15.4
NM	5,338	399	7.5	0	480	185	12.5
NY	70,197	5,111	7.3	74	12,757	6,730	27.9
NC	31,534	2,258	7.2	201	3,229	6,504	32.5
ND	1,161	63	5.4	6	25	74	8.9
OH	45,833	4,338	9.5	81	4,512	11,579	35.3
OK	23,181	2,072	8.9	341	1,259	5,163	29.1
OR	11,478	1,078	9.3	84	499	1,154	14.9
PA	36,607	3,653	9.9	3,629	0	1,324	13.5
RI	3,291	239	6.9	17	153	266	12.6
SC	21,793	1,333	6.1	342	1,558	4,137	27.7
SD	2,592	202	7.7	142	0	260	15.3
TN	22,166	1,514	6.8	168	1,414	4,689	28.3
TX	149,519	13,064	8.7	0	7,589	45,172	35.3
UT	5,664	490	8.5	8	58	1,213	22.1
VT	1,782	122	6.7	6	5	64	4.1
VA	30,186	2,688	8.0	396	1,502	8,254	30.0
WA	14,915	1,352	9.0	398	433	1,532	15.7
WV	3,856	372	9.6	207	308	422	32.9
WI	20,787	1,382	6.6	64	888	3,610	21.9
WY	1,657	183	10.9	150	29	133	18.6
FBOP	145,416	16,066	11.0	0	3,297	11,026	9.8
	1,379,695	113,358	8.2	25,398	90,571	193,514	25.5

Note: 0 = not reported;

Source: *Corrections Yearbook* (2000); Criminal Justice Institute, South Salem, NY.

were 4,779 inmates age 55 or older in Texas prisons, representing 3.7 percent of the prison population. This figure compares to 2,567 four years earlier. Like numerous other states, the elderly inmate population has increased more rapidly than any other age group. The increase is mainly attributed to an increase in admissions of elderly inmates to prison that has outpaced the increase for other age groups. Between 1994 and 1998, admissions to prison for offenders age 55 and older increased 55 percent compared with an overall increase in admissions of 24 percent. It was also reported that elderly inmates are admitted to prison with longer sentences than offenders in other age groups, resulting in relatively longer periods to serve in prison. In 1998 the average sentence at admission to prison for older offenders was 11.6 years, compared with 8.1 years for the average sentence for all admissions overall. Growth in admissions and longer sentences are the two factors that account for the accelerated growth in the elderly population in Texas. Prison officials expect this acceleration to continue well into the 21st century. The elderly population is projected to increase by 121 percent between 1998 and 2008. If these projections hold true in just a few years, Texas will be responsible for maintaining over 10,000 elderly inmates (55 and older) with health problems common in persons ten years older than 55 (Fabelo, 1999).

As early as 1987, Florida had incarcerated approximately 4,000 inmates who were serving life without parole (Malcolm, 1988). In 2001 Florida was holding 3,049 natural lifers, 4,485 lifers, and 9,026 inmates serving twenty years or more. This constitutes 25 percent of Florida's total prison population of 65,122 (*Corrections Yearbook*, 2001). In response, one of its prisons, which houses over 600 inmates, has already evolved into an institution serving almost exclusively elderly inmates. With its bulging elderly prison population, it is evident that Florida will continue to convert existing facilities or build new ones to accommodate the special needs of an older inmate population.

California instituted an indeterminate term of twenty-five years to life for offenders with two or more prior convictions for violent offenses. In addition, California's three strikes law has already put more than 13,000 three-time felons behind bars as of 2001. The greater probability of longer sentences and greater use of habitual offender statutes mandating life without parole and minimum sentencing and restricting automatic good-time credits mean that these offenders—who constitute the bulk of the recently incarcerated—have a greater likelihood of growing old in prison. The number of prisons in California grew from twelve in 1983 to twenty-six in 1993 with seven more approved for construction in the late 1990s (Pelosi, 1997).

In the early 21st century, 6.9 percent of California's 160,687 inmates were over 50, and Tofig (1997), for one, expected the number in that age group to increase. A recent study (Beiser, 1998) estimated that the number of Californian inmates over 50 could climb as high as 125,000 by the year 2020.

Evidence that the nation's prison population is experiencing a graying trend has been demonstrated by a number of state reports and other research. A number of states have commissioned studies to investigate and make policy recommendations to meet the coming crisis. Other states admit that the graying of the prison population is creating a significant problem for housing, and programming and contributes to rising prison health-care costs as well. Some state legislatures are now examining the strict sentencing guidelines, which, in part, have contributed to the problem of increasing numbers of elderly inmates. Nevertheless, since stricter sentencing measures remain popular, most states are simply holding firm and bracing for an increase in the number of older prison inmates.

Figure 1.1
And on it goes . . .

Cartoon courtesy Sandy Campbell, *The Tennessean*, April 10, 1994.

DEFINING THE OLDER OFFENDER

The selection of age 65 as the demarcation between middle and old age is an arbitrary one, patterned after social legislation of the late 19th and early 20th centuries. This contemporary definition of old age has been used primarily for social purposes to determine the point of retirement and to establish eligibility of older persons for various entitlements. In fact, the age of 65 as a marker of old age does not serve well in demarcating changes in general health functioning, mental capacity, or psychological or physical endurance (Butler, Lewis, & Sunderland, 1998). Although chronological age is a valuable predictor of "oldness," it is frequently an inaccurate indicator of a person's physical and mental status, and caution should be used not to place too much emphasis on chronological age alone in making policy decisions.

Aging is a most complex process and varies considerably with an individual's genetic makeup, lifestyle, and social environment. It is a known fact in the medical community that any given population will have wide variations in the onset of aging effects. Prison populations are really no different. Older inmates will display heterogeneity similar to that of the population at large, with some inmates being physically "old" at age 50 and others remaining "young" in mind and body at age 60 and over (Flynn, 1992). Planning and programming for the older offender present many challenges for prison and jail administrators, who are hampered by the lack of a common definition of who an older offender is (Morton, 1992).

The inability to agree on what constitutes an elderly offender is one of the most troublesome aspects of comparing research outcomes from various studies (Forsyth & Gramling, 1988). A review of the literature finds that previous researchers have defined elderly inmates as those 65 years (Forsyth & Grambling, 1988) of age and older, some 60 (Kratcoski, 1990), some 55 (Goetting, 1992; Long, 1992; Roth, 1992), and many 50 (Aday, 1994; Anderson, 1997; Flynn, 1992). The majority of the studies, however, have used age 50 or 55 as the chronological age at which one becomes an older offender.

In a national survey of state correctional departments, I found that 50 years of age is the most common criterion for old age that correctional officials utilize (Aday, 1999). This study reported that correctional officials commonly agree that the typical inmate in his 50s has the physical appearance and accompanying health problems of someone at least ten years older. House (1990, p. 398) supports this view when he states that "the lowest socioeconomic stratum manifests a prevalence of chronic conditions at ages 45–55 that is not seen in the highest socioeconomic stratum until after age 75." Morton (1992) further stipulates that age 50 is the ideal starting point to initiate preventive health care and the taking of other appropriate measures to reduce long-term medical costs for older inmates. Finally, *The Corrections Yearbook* includes in its annual profiles of older inmates those who are 50 or older.

Caution should be used when using chronological age exclusively to define the onset of old age. As in the general population, some people are considered old at 50 or 60 because of chronic conditions while others may be quite young from a health standpoint at 70 or 80. While the declining health of many inmates substantiates the phrase "old before their time," other inmates may remain in reasonably good health well into their 60s or 70s. According to Flynn (1992), the major issue for researchers is not so much a matter of identifying and verifying the exact chronological cutoff point as it is a matter of achieving a consensus in the field for comparative research and planning purposes.

OLDER INMATE DIVERSITY

The majority of older offenders age 50 and over currently housed in state and federal prisons are non-Hispanic whites. The older prisoner population does, however, include a disproportionate number of African Americans (Krebs, 2000). Southern states typically incarcerate a greater proportion of African Americans than states in other regions of the country. For example of the 4,054 older inmates incarcerated in Georgia prisons, 51 percent are African American with 48 percent white and 1 percent Native American (Georgia Department of Corrections, 1999). The average age of incarcerated inmates age 50 and over is 57 years. Although the number of older females is also increasing, the overwhelming majority (95 percent) of older prisoners are male. Only about one-third of older inmates are married (Aday, 1994; Goetting, 1983). A substantial number of older offenders have sparse educational backgrounds; only about 20 percent have completed high school (Aday, 1994; Douglass, 1991). A substantial number are unskilled laborers, and 28 percent of the older inmate population in Georgia, for example, was unemployed at the time of arrest. Another 18 percent were considered incapable of holding a job when arrested. When coupled with the fact that a significant number of elderly prisoners are likely to have histories of poor health and a high incidence of alcohol abuse, it is evident that this prison population is highly vulnerable to early aging.

OLDER INMATE TYPES

The need to identify the older inmate as a special category within the inmate population has been suggested frequently (Aday, 1994; Chaiklin, 1998; Flynn, 1992; Krebs, 2000). The inconsistencies of previous research make it difficult to accurately describe the older offender population. The lack of consensus on a criterion for the age at which a prisoner becomes old has contributed to the difficulty. The use of small, nonrandom samples also creates a barrier to establishing a national profile of older offenders. Let me first discuss general categories of older offenders in prison before addressing the issue of criteria in more depth.

We do know that there are distinct differences in the criminal histories of older offenders. As Chapter 2 will describe, traditionally two types of older inmates have been distinguished: "first-time" or "new elderly" offenders and those with multiple incarcerations, who are frequently referred to as "career" or "chronic" offenders. The chronic offender or multiple recidivist may spend a significant amount of his or her life revolving in and out of prison. Typically the crimes committed would mirror those of a younger offender. New elderly offenders are those who are incarcerated for the first time late in life. As a whole, this group is more likely to have committed a violent crime (murder or sexual offenses) against another person. Goetting (1983) further developed this typology to include two additional categories. A third group included inmates who in fulfilling life sentences have simply grown old in prison. Goetting referred to this group of individuals incarcerated at an early age as "old timers." Finally, a fourth group has been distinguished: short-term first offenders who were incarcerated during their middle years and turned 55 while in prison. I have proposed that in all four groups, the aging prisoner often represents a special population in health-care needs, problems of individual adjustment to institutional life, and problems of family relationships posing special difficulties to the prison system regarding custody, rehabilitation, and parole (Aday, 1994).

It has been estimated that somewhere between 40 and 45 percent of older offenders were serving time for first offenses (Beck, 1997; Goetting, 1983). Goetting, in her national sample of 288 inmates age 55 or older, found that 45.6 percent were career criminals or multiple recidivists. Although the other two categories reported by Goetting are relatively small (lifers = 2.32 percent; short-term first offenders = 10.68 percent), these two categories can be expected to increase significantly because of new sentencing practices and demographic trends. More inmates are receiving life without parole at a young age and they too will eventually grow old in prison. The number of the baby boomers turning 50 will swell the category of short-term first offenders in that age group. The fact that two-thirds of older inmates age 55 and older have been incarcerated for less than five years supports this prediction (Beck, 1997).

WHO ARE THE OLDER ADULTS?

Since aging is the result of a complex interaction of several factors, some of which are heredity, socioeconomic status, social environment, and lifestyle, older people exhibit great diversity. As more people survive into their senior years and spend longer periods of time in old age, the older population become more diverse and can be characterized and compared across a variety of important variables, including gender, marital status, education, living arrangement, and income. As the older population itself ages, older women increasingly outnumber older men. This contributes to the fact that about three-fourths of older men are married, and more than half of older women are widowed. Older adults live in a variety of settings throughout the country, with the greatest numbers found in California, New York, Illinois, Florida, Ohio, Pennsylvania, Michigan, New Jersey, and Texas. Most older adults live in households in the community and the majority of men live with their spouses. While a substantial number of older adults are considered poor, the percentage of older people below the poverty level has been declining. Less than 15 percent now fall in that category. The majority of the elderly depend on Social Security for more than half their income and about one-third rely on it for more than 80 percent of their income (Social Security Administration, 1999). Slightly more than half today's older population graduated from high school, but that figure is expected to increase in future cohorts of older adults (AARP, 1999).

WHAT HAPPENS AS WE AGE?

It is critical that those working in the criminal justice field have some understanding of the normal aging process as they develop and implement programs and policies. Physical and mental health changes affected by the aging process have important implications for police apprehension and appropriate sentencing. Properly assessing the functioning ability of older inmates throughout their incarceration is also essential. Overlooking the diversity of older inmates and accompanying needs may very well result in serious legal implications for many prison systems (Morton, 1992).

As people age, natural physiological changes occur, although changes may vary from one older adult to another. The elderly experience fewer acute illnesses than younger persons and have a lower death rate from them. Health conditions are frequently more likely to be chronic illnesses or diseases that are long-term or permanent, progressive, and typically incurable. Such chronic conditions may result in residual disabilities that require long-term management (Hooyman & Kiyak, 1999). Chronic diseases are linked to normal aging and are therefore typically illnesses of middle and later life. Current data for the U.S. population show that among individuals age 22–44, 15 percent had some form of disability. The figure increased to 36 percent among middle-aged adults between 55 and 64 and to 72 percent among those 80 and older (LaPlante, Carlson, Kaye, & Bradsher, 1996). More than 80 percent of persons age 65 and over have at least one chronic illness, and multiple conditions are common (National Center for Health Statistics, 1993). Of those age 65 and older experiencing chronic conditions, 7 in 10 had multiple ailments (Hooyman & Kiyak, 1999).

Chronic problems are often accompanied by continuous pain or distress. National surveys have reported that almost 40 percent of older persons with chronic diseases report limitations in their ability to perform basic activities of daily living (Guralnick & Simonsick, 1993). The likelihood of being disabled by chronic diseases increases significantly with age. According to Ebersole and Hess (1998), the most common chronic conditions among older adults are arthritis (48 percent), hypertension (37 percent), hearing impairments (32 percent), heart disease (30 percent), orthopedic impairments (18 percent), cataracts (17 percent), sinusitis (14 percent), diabetes (10 percent), and tinnitus (8 percent). The incidence of chronic disorders varies with ethnicity (House, 1990). For example, arthritis and hypertension are more common among blacks than whites, whereas the reverse is true of hearing impairments and heart disease.

Chronic Health Conditions

Degenerative arthritic and rheumatic disorders are the most common of the chronic illnesses that affect the mobility of the elderly (Ebersole & Hess, 1998). Degenerative disorders of joints and connective tissue occur throughout the body. Such disorders cause pain, depression, immobility, and functional and self-concept disturbances. A common type of joint disease is osteoarthritis. This progressive disease is the most common of the arthritic disorders, and 90 percent of older adults show some evidence of it (Ebersole & Hess, 1998). The patient's joints become stiff and painful, which restricts movement.

Chronic respiratory disorders such as bronchitis, emphysema, and fibrosis are particularly common in older men, but they are increasing significantly in women, presumably because of their greater exposure to cigarette smoke. Chronic obstructive pulmonary diseases (such as bronchitis, emphysema, and asthma) are the fourth leading cause of death in the 65-and-over age group (National Center for Health Statistics, 1993). Behaviors associated with fatigue, confusion, persistent cough, fever, and general chest discomfort may indicate infection.

Other chronic diseases are also quite prevalent among the older adult population. Cardiovascular diseases such as diseases of the heart, hypertension, stroke, and arteriosclerosis are common, for example. Hypertension, or high blood pressure, has been found to be the major risk factor in the development of cardiovascular complications. The rates of high blood pressure are higher among African Americans than whites. The elderly also frequently develop chronic conditions of the gastrointestinal system, affecting the esophagus, stomach, intestines, colon, liver, and biliary tract. As a result, older adults are more likely to experience atrophic gastritis, which is a chronic inflammation of the stomach lining.

The incidence of cancer tends to increase with age. Among those age 65 years and older, approximately 20 percent die from cancer, especially cancer of the stomach, lungs, intestines, and pancreas. Lung cancer has its highest incidence in men age 65 and over, and it is frequently associated with smoking (Hooyman & Kiyak, 1999). Cancer of the colon is more common in women than in men, whereas rectal cancer is more frequent in men than in women. Women also face risks of breast and cervical cancers that increase with age. Diagnosing cancer in old age is often more difficult than at earlier life stages, because of the masking effects of other chronic diseases.

Kidney functions deteriorate with age. As a result, the ability to filter liquid products decreases by approximately 50 percent in the elderly. Compounding this problem, bladder function and efficiency also declines with age. The capacity of the bladder may be reduced by as much as 50 percent in some persons older than age 65. In addition, an enlarged prostrate gland is common in males over the age of 60. The enlarged gland and the decreased bladder capacity result in increased frequency of urination, difficulty in starting and stopping the stream, and greater potential for bladder infections in elderly males.

Sensory Decline

Loss of sensory functioning as we age, although gradual, accumulates to substantially reduce the vividness of the environment in which we live. Deterioration associated with sensory deprivation in the elderly can be attributed to the loss of sensory acuity and can be aggravated by living in a highly restrictive environment such as prison. Add poor vision and poor hearing the restrictions of decreased energy and chronic disorders, and the reasons for mental and emotional deterioration become obvious.

The decreased sense of smell and taste with aging frequently affects the elderly appetite. External factors such as smoking and medications may also contribute to taste and smell deterioration. Some older people compensate for losses in taste sensitivity by increasing their salt intake. Weight loss may become a problem, especially for older males, who frequently lose interest in eating. Also, with diminished salivary gland response, dry mouth, and diminished muscle strength, elderly persons are more vulnerable to choking.

Touch sensitivity also deteriorates with age. An important aspect of the decline in touch sensation is the fact that older people are less able to discriminate among levels of perceived pain. As a result, older people may exhibit nonverbal signs of discomfort (e.g., restlessness, withdrawal, or reduced level of activity) rather than complain about pain. The elderly also have decreased sensitivity to both heat and cold. With decreased subcutaneous fat tissue and sweat gland activity, the elderly do not adapt well to environmental extremes.

Vision and hearing are both critical links to the world around us. Although vision is important for negotiating the physical environment, hearing is vital for communicating with the social environment. Vision problems increase with age and cataracts may form. Hearing loss disrupts a person's understanding of others and even the recognition of one's own speech. A common hearing problem is the degeneration of the auditory nerve, which decreases the ability to hear high-frequency tones and discriminate between consonant sounds. Tinnitus, a high-pitched ringing in the ears that is particularly acute at night or in quiet surroundings, may appear. The elderly with hearing loss may become withdrawn and irritable and frequently are less communicative.

Cognitive and Emotional Disorders

Correctional facilities in the United States currently house more mentally ill individuals than hospitals and mental institutions do. Approximately 210,000 persons with severe mental illnesses are incarcerated in federal and state jails and prisons (Chaiklin, 1998). In addition to experiencing the effects of normal aging, many of the aged suffer from specific mental or emotional disorders of various severities. The prevalence of psychiatric disorders among older persons who are living in the community is estimated at anywhere from 15 to 25 percent, the exact figure depending on the population and categories of disorders examined (Hooyman & Kiyak, 1999). The incidence of mental health problems among individuals aging in prison is considered higher (Beck & Maruschak, 2001).

An important emotional manifestation of old age is rage aimed at the uncontrollable forces that confront older adults, as well as rage at the indignities and neglect of a society that once valued them. The belief that older people are likely to be cantankerous, ornery, irritable, or querulous may arise from a realistic reaction of some older adults to a careful review of their actual situation. Much of the rage is in response to inhumane treatment or anger toward significant others who have disappointed them. Some older people may also rage against the inevitable nature of aging and death, or at least in coming to terms with them (Butler, Lewis, & Sutherland, 1998).

Depression is the most frequent mental health problem in the elderly, and it increases in incidence with age (Eliopoulos, 1997). According to Alexopoulos (1995), about 2 percent of the population over 65 meet the DSM-IV criteria for major depressive disorder, but the prevalence of clinically significant depressive symptoms is 15–20 percent among community-residing elders (Reynolds, Small, Stein, & Teri, 1994). Since depression presents itself in many forms, it often goes unrecognized because its symptoms may be mistaken for physical illness, the effects of polypharmacy, or dementia. Depression has also been correlated with stroke, hearing loss, and pain. Frequently, medications add to or initiate depression as well (Ebersole & Hess, 1998).

Anxiety disorders remain one of the most common psychiatric conditions in the elderly, and as many as 18 percent of those over age 65 suffer from them (Flint, 1994). Such disorders can be manifested in various ways, including somatic complaints, rigidity in thinking and behavior, pacing, fantasizing, confusion, and increased dependency. In contrast with fear, anxiety tends to occur without apparent conscious stimulus. Adjustments to physical, emotional, and socioeconomic limitation in old age, and the new problems of aging that are frequently encountered, add to causes of increases in anxiety.

It is estimated that 4 million older adults suffer from some form of dementia (Eliopoulos, 1997). Dementia, also referred to as organic brain syndrome or senile dementia, applies to a variety of conditions that are caused by or associated with damage of brain tissue. Brain damage leads to impaired cognitive function and in more advanced stages to impaired behavior and personality. Although not part of normal aging, the likelihood of experiencing dementia does increase with advancing age. Alzheimer's disease is the most common irreversible dementia in late life, accounting for about 60 percent of all dementias (Hooyman & Kiyak, 1999).

It is estimated that the prevalence of paranoia ranges from 5 to 10 percent in the older adult population (Ebersole & Hess, 1998). Older adults' mistrust of the world can be viewed as a common reaction to the loss of control of their daily lives. Sensory losses, illness, and disability increase insecurity and misperception. Paranoia is sometimes induced by alcoholism or medications such as antidepressants. The inability to correctly evaluate the social milieu because of isolation or degrees of cognitive disturbance contributes to paranoia and feelings of suspicion among the elderly (Blazer, 1995).

SUMMARY

If current trends continue, increases in the costs of housing and caring for elderly offenders will represent a substantial portion of most corrections departments' budgets in the near future. With a predicted rise in the number of offenders who are older, sicker, and serving longer sentences, coupled with institutions' stretched resources, many believe our corrections departments are facing an inevitable crisis. Age is considered one of the biggest issues that will continue to affect corrections and correctional health care in the future. As an increasing number of prisons with non-commutable sentences are housed in the nation's prisons, correctional health-care policy and practice will focus more on the needs of the geriatric prison population.

Despite the fact that policymakers are well aware of the changing inmate population, little systematic planning has been conducted to address the multitude of attendant issues. While we have in place sporadic facilities and programs designed especially for aged and infirm inmates, most criminal justice institutions and organizations are still operating without a comprehensive plan to respond adequately to the pending crisis. As more cohorts enter the latter stages of life, the age revolution will significantly affect all facets of the criminal justice system. In particular, our institutions will face a tremendous challenge by the year 2020 as they bulge at the seams with older adults. Care for an increasing number of older inmates will dramatically strain health-care services as well as prison medical costs. Under current sentencing policy, new facilities will have to be built and creative programs implemented. Policymakers will have to address the special needs of inmates who will spend the remainder of their lives in prison as well as of those who will be released in old age with few employable skills.

REFERENCES

Aday, R. H. (1994). Golden years behind bars: Programs and facilities for the geriatric inmate. *Federal Probation, 58*(2), 47–54.

Aday, R. H. (1999). *Responding to the graying of American prisons: A 10-year followup*. Unpublished report. Murfreesboro: Middle Tennessee State University.

Alexopoulos, G. S. (1995). Mood disorders. In H. Kaplan & B. Sadock (Eds.), *Comprehensive textbook of psychiatry* (pp. 112–133). Baltimore: Williams & Wilkins.

American Association of Retired Persons (AARP). (1999). *A profile of older Americans*. Washington, DC.

American Correctional Association. (2001). *Directory of adult correctional facilities*. Lanham, MD.

Anderson, D.C. (1997, July 13). Aging behind bars. *New York Times Magazine, 146*, 23–33.

Beck, A. J. (1997). Growth, change, and stability in the U.S. prison population, 1880–1995. *Corrections Management Quarterly, 1*(2), 1–14.

Beck, A. J., & Maruschak, L. M. (2001). Mental health treatment in state prisons, 2000. Washington, DC: U.S. Department of Justice.

Beiser, V. (1998, March 7). Aging behind bars. *The San Mateo Times*, p. 7.

Blazer, D. G. (1995). Anxiety disorders. In W. B. Abrams, M. H. Beers, & R. Berkow (Eds.), *The Merck manual of geriatrics* (pp. 219–237). Whitehouse Station, NJ: Merck Research Laboratories.

Butler, R. N., Lewis, M., & Sunderland, T. (1998). *Aging and mental health*. New York: Macmillan.

Chaiklin, H. (1998). The elderly disturbed prisoner. *Clinical Gerontologist, 20*(1), 47–62.

Chaneles, S. (1987, October). Growing old behind bars. *Psychology Today, 21*, 46–51.

Corrections yearbook. (1996). South Salem, NY: Criminal Justice Institute.

Corrections yearbook. (1998). South Salem, NY: Criminal Justice Institute.

Corrections yearbook. (2001). South Salem, NY: Criminal Justice Institute.

Ditton, P.M., & Wilson, D. J. (1999). *Truth in sentencing in state prisons*. Washington, DC: U.S. Department of Justice.

Douglass, R. L. (1991). *Oldtimers: Michigan's elderly prisoners*. Unpublished report. Michigan Department of Corrections. Lansing, Michigan.

Dugger, R. L. (1988). The graying of American prisons: Special care considerations. *Corrections Today, 50*(3), 26–30, 34.

Ebersole, P., & Hess, P. (1998). *Toward healthy aging*. St. Louis: Mosby.

Edwards, T. (1998). *The aging inmate population: SLC special series report*. Atlanta, GA: The Council of State Governments.

Eliopoulos, C. (1997). *Gerontological nursing*. Philadelphia, PA: Lippincott.

Fabelo, T. (1999). *Elderly offenders in Texas prisons*. Austin, TX: Criminal Justice Policy Council.

Flint, A. J. (1994). Epidemiology and comorbidity of anxiety disorders in the elderly. *American Journal of Psychiatry, 151*, 640–649.

Florida Department of Corrections annual report. (2002). Tallahassee, FL: Florida Corrections Commission.

Flynn, E. E. (1992). The graying of America's prison population. *The Prison Journal* (1–2), 72, 77–98.

Forsyth, C. J., & Gramling, R. (1988). Elderly crime: Fact and artifact. In B. McCarthy & R. Langworthy (Eds.), *Older offenders: Perspectives in criminology and criminal justice* (pp. 3–13). New York: Praeger.

Georgia Department of Corrections. (2001). *Georgia's aging inmate population.* Atlanta, GA.

Goetting, A. (1983). The elderly in prison: Issues and perspectives. *Journal of Research in Crime and Delinquency, 20*, 291–309.

Goetting, A. (1992). Patterns of homicide among the elderly. *Violence and Victims, 7*, 203–215.

Guralnik, J. M., & Simonsick, E. M. (1993). Physical disability in older Americans. *Journal of Gerontology, 48*, 3–10.

Gurian, B. S., & Miner, J. H. (1991). Clinical presentation of anxiety in the elderly. In C. Salzman & B. D. Lebowitz (Eds.), *Anxiety in the elderly* (pp. 252–270). New York: Springer.

Hobbs, F. B., & Damon, B. L. (1996). *65 + in the United States.* Report no. P23–190. Washington, DC: Bureau of the Census.

Hooyman, N., & Kiyak, H. A. (1999). *Social gerontology.* Boston: Allyn & Bacon.

House, J. (1990). Age, socioeconomic status, and health. *Milbank Quarterly, 68*, 383–411.

Kratcoski, P. (1990). Circumstances surrounding homicides by older offenders. *Criminal Justice and Behavior, 17*, 420–430.

Krebs, J. J. (2000). The older prisoner: Social, psychological, and medical considerations. In M. B. Rothman, B. D. Dunlop, & P. Entzel (Eds.), *Elders, crime and the criminal justice system* (pp. 207–228). New York: Springer.

LaPlante, M., Carlson, D., Kaye, S., & Bradsher, J. (1996). *Families with disabilities in the United States.* San Francisco: University of California, San Francisco, Disability Statistics Rehabilitation Research and Training Center, Institute for Health and Aging.

Long, L. M. (1992). A study of arrests of older offenders: Trends and patterns. *Journal of Crime and Justice, 15*, 157–175.

Malcolm, A. H. (1988, December 24). Aged inmates pose problem for prisons. *The New York Times*, p. 1.

Morton, J. B. (1992). *An administrative overview of the older inmate.* Washington, DC: U.S. Department of Justice.

National Center for Health Statistics. (1993). Current estimates from the national health interview survey: U.S. *Vital and Health Statistics*, series 10 (p. 176). Washington, DC.

Pelosi, A. (1997). Age of innocence: A glut of geriatric jailbirds. *The New Republic, 216*(18), 15–18.

Reynolds, C. F., Small, G. W., Stein, E. M., & Teri, L. (1994, February). When depression strikes the elderly patient. *Patient Care, 14*, 85–102.

Roth, E. B. (1992, July–October). Elders behind bars. *Perspectives on Aging, 21*, 25–31.

Silverman, M. & Vega, M. (1996). *Corrections: A comprehensive view*. New York: West.

Social Security Administration. (1999). *Income of the population 55 years or older*. Washington, DC: Office of Research and Statistics.

Sultz, H. A., & Young, K. M. (1999). Health care USA: Understanding its organization and delivery. Gaithersburg, MA: Aspen.

Tofig, D. (1997, February 18). Aging behind bars: Connecticut's prison house. *The Hartford Courant*, p. A1.

U.S. Bureau of the Census. Population projections of the U.S., by age, sex, race, and Hispanic origin data: 1950 to 1998. *Current Population Reports* (pp. 25, 42). Washington, DC.

Chapter 2

Old Age and Crime

In all societies, chronological age is considered to be important because it provides certain clues to the current phase of the individual's life cycle and, in turn, prompts certain behavioral expectations. More specific to our purposes is the fact that different age periods reveal quantitative differences in the structure of criminality. Criminal behavior has always been predominantly associated with the younger generation, and researchers and policymakers deem the crimes of youthful offenders more serious and dangerous for the fabric of society than crimes committed by older people. In recent years, however, the role of the elderly in the criminal justice system has emerged as an issue of increasing importance.

While in the past we were more accustomed to seeing the elderly as victims, increasing attention is now being given to the elderly as perpetrators of crime. In fact, one of the most intriguing trends in the field of criminology and corrections in the past decade has been the dramatic increase in attention to older offenders (Anderson, 1997; Kratcoski & Babb, 1990; Morton, 1993; Rothman, Dunlop, & Entzel, 2000; Smyer, Gragert, & LaMere, 1997). Common portrayals of the elderly offender in the media have been the "victimless" felon writing bad checks, driving under the influence, engaging in disorderly conduct, or shoplifting in order to survive or provoke attention. Lately, however, the elderly are committing more serious offenses that were at one time confined almost exclusively to the young.

Although the norm has been a decline in deviant behavior among the majority of the elderly population, an investigation of criminality in the later years of the life cycle has become an important objective for a variety of reasons. In addition to the obvious growth of the older population, Flynn (2000) has identified several factors demonstrating the necessity of exploring elderly crime and older offenders. First, elder crime needs to be thoroughly examined to fully develop a descriptive profile of the older prisoner. Such an analysis of the career crime patterns of the older offender can serve as a point of departure for pinpointing any distinguishing characteristics that might have an impact on eventual institutional adjustment. For example, examining differences in social, personal, and crime characteristics between first offenders and repeat offenders can provide useful information for prison officials establishing appropriate policies. Second, a better understanding of criminal activity in later life can lead to an increased understanding of the special needs of an aging population as a whole. Only by investigating the nature of elderly crime can we fully understand the causes, whether they are underlying structural problems within society or specific problems associated with the aging process or perhaps a combination of both. Third, if we are to develop public policies for controlling criminal activities in later life, empirical evidence is necessary for the purpose of establishing successful policies and procedures for implementing them. And fourth, research findings and theoretical developments from the the study of elder crime patterns can lead to further insights into the age and crime controversy. With a greater understanding of elder crime patterns, proactive community-based programs might reduce violent crimes within families.

This chapter will provide an overview of crime patterns of the older offender. I will address (1) a historical overview of elderly crime patterns, (2) an examination of *Uniform Crime Reports* data, (3) an analysis of contemporary crime trends in later life, including gender differences, (4) the role that drugs and alcohol play in criminal behavior, and (5) an analysis of patterns of criminal activity in later life: shoplifting, sexual offenses, homicide.

A HISTORICAL VIEW OF OLDER OFFENDERS

While infrequent, research on the criminal activity of older offenders is not a recent phenomenon. Researchers have investigated crime patterns related to old age for most of the 20th century. Duncan recorded one of the first studies mentioning the old offender in 1930. Duncan's attempt to analyze age and crime relationships studied prison records of those incarcerated in the Texas penitentiary from 1906 to 1924. Duncan concluded that while the crime rate begins to decline after the age of 40, advancement in years is not proof that crime will disappear. Although the overall crime rates of those from ages 50 to 59 were slightly less than one-third of their predicted share of prison inmates, Duncan reported that violent crimes were a frequent occurrence among older criminals.

Historically, studies have delineated two distinct types of elderly offenders: first offenders, or those committing a crime for the first time in their life, and chronic offenders, who have committed multiple offenses during their lifetime. Schroeder (1936) provided pioneer research in the crimes of each type with a group of 486 criminals, half younger than 40 and half 40 years or over, ranging from 15 to 64 years of age. He discovered that persons who commit crime after 40 years of age represent two distinct groups. One group tended to commit crimes of violence such as murder and sexual crimes while the other group was more likely to commit white-collar crimes such as fraud. In the first two types of crimes, he found that violent offenders tend to be relatively free from early records of delinquency and crime. In the second group, the criminal behavior tends to be a continuation of a pattern established at an earlier age.

Pollak (1941) also published significant early work pertaining to criminality and the aging process. He hypothesized that the decrease in criminality with age differs by type of crime. In order to support his hypothesis, Pollak investigated the persistence of criminal activity such as homicide, aggravated assault, sexual offenses, and violation of liquor laws among those between the ages of 50 to 70. He concluded that general descriptions, case studies, and prison statistics furnished the following facts about the criminality of the aged: (1) a general decline of the crime rate with advancing years, (2) a high incidence of first offenders among older criminals, (3) relative frequency of certain types of crime among the older criminal population, and (4) characteristic strains of criminal behavior and specific groups of victims. For Pollak, these facts led to the conclusion that criminality of the aged had a unique pattern of its own.

Using comparative statistics, Fox (1946) examined the variables of race, age, and intelligence quotient as they related to respective crimes. Using major categories such as homicide, burglary, and larceny, Fox found that older men differed significantly from younger male criminals in their tendency to be drunk and disorderly, to break state securities laws, and to conspire to obstruct justice or to commit crime. Fox further concluded that younger men tended to select the cruder methods of stealing, whereas older men's thefts were more involved in business and politics. Crimes of dissipation, such as those involving sex, alcohol, and drugs, appeared to be more frequent among the older group. Moberg's (1953) research tended to support Fox's earlier findings. He found among the aged criminals there was a high incidence of first offenders, and certain types of crimes tended to predominate, such as drunkenness, sex offenses, embezzlement, and fraud, while crimes that involve physical violence were relatively infrequent. Moberg also gave attention to the variations in criminal behavior by age and especially sexual crimes committed in old age.

Adams and Vedder (1961) reported a psychological basis for homicide, manslaughter, and sex crimes among the elderly prison population. In reviewing the records of prisoners committed to prison over a twelve-year period, the authors found a higher incidence of convictions for assault among offenders aged 50 and older. The authors distinguish between economic crimes (which represent an inability to legally meet subsistence needs) and crimes of violence (a psychological reaction to physical deterioration). In this regard, aged inmates were viewed as a unique group of offenders experiencing physical and mental deterioration who react to their perceived devalued status with antagonism and aggression. Thus, the authors cite socioeconomic pressures as causative of mental and physical distress that find an outlet in crimes of violence.

Cromier (1971) also reported significant differences between offenders who had no previous criminal record and those of the same age with a history of criminality. The differences were particularly evident in the types of criminal offenses and the offenders' social values and personality. Cormier found that older first offenders were more likely to have committed homicide in a well-defined social relationship (such as marriage) and committed sexual offenses during the libidinal crisis of middle age or later. Offenses against property proved to be the outstanding crime for those who started criminal activities before the age of 25.

In surveying state prisons, Krajick (1979) reported that violent crimes committed by elderly inmates were usually against a family member or a close friend or acquaintance. In agreement with earlier research, Krajick noted that older first offenders commit crimes of passion, which are linked to the status deprivation that frequently accompanies old age. The deprivation is characterized by economic devaluation, boredom, rigidity in attitudes, and increased emotional instability. Teller and Howell (1981) also found that first offenders were more likely to be sentenced for crimes against persons than repeat offenders were. As other studies found, Teller and Howell found elderly criminal behavior directed against family members and close acquaintances. In addition, first offenders reported that they committed their crimes spontaneously and did not consider themselves criminals. In contrast, multiple recidivists reported that they generally planned their crimes and viewed themselves as criminals.

In 1984 I conducted research that found that 58 percent of the total sample were chronic or multiple offenders (Aday, 1984). About one-half the sample of 94 offenders were incarcerated for the first time after age 50. Of the crimes committed, 67 percent were crimes of violence against another individual. A breakdown of crime distribution between chronic and first offenders revealed that murder and sex offenses were the most common for both groups. However, 80 percent of offenders arrested for the first time were convicted of crimes of violence compared with only 58 percent of those classified as multiple offenders.

Using a sample of persons age 55 and above who were arrested in Flint, Michigan, over a four-year period, Brahce and Bachand (1989) also produced distinct groups of habitual and nonhabitual offenders. Of the 491 arrested subjects, 88 percent were males and 11 percent were females. The authors' analysis revealed that 83 percent of the males and 95 percent of the females in the sample showed no previous arrest history. In contrast to prison studies, this study found that few elderly offenders were most likely to be arrested for less serious offenses such as misdemeanors, alcohol-related offenses, and property crimes. The career or habitual criminal subgroup who had been arrested an average of 16.8 times were far more likely to be arrested for violent crimes such as murder, rape, robbery, burglary, and aggravated assault.

Fry (1987) identified specific patterns for the older first offender. He reported that this subgroup could be characterized as (1) violent offenders sentenced for a crime that involved a family member; (2) white-collar property offenders, likely sentenced for fraud after years of successful business experience; (3) drug offenders, more likely to be sentenced for the sale of drugs with no record of prior or current drug use; and (4) alcohol offenders, most likely sentenced to prison for vehicular manslaughter.

This historical review reveals that, as a whole, the crime patterns among older offenders have remained rather consistent though the years. In keeping with previous findings, more recent estimates reveal that approximately 45 percent of elderly inmates are first offenders (Goetting, 1984; McShane & Williams, 1990; Rothman, Dunlop, & Entzel, 2000). First offenders are also more likely to be sentenced for crimes against persons than are chronic offenders. Violence accounts for 42.6 percent of all crimes committed by those 55 or older, compared with a rate of 28.5 percent for violent crimes committed by those between the ages of 45 and 54 (Beck, 1997). In sum, sentencing for new crimes is especially high among older offenders as these late-life felons tend to be incarcerated for crimes such as rape, murder, and child molestation.

UNIFORM CRIME REPORTS

The most widely accepted legal topology is the crime classification produced by the Federal Bureau of Investigation's *Uniform Crime Reports* (UCR). The UCR data are published annually by the FBI and consist of crimes known to the police rather than actual crimes committed. Under the UCR topology, a general distinction based primarily on the perceived severity of the offenses is made between index crimes and non-index crimes. Index Crimes, frequently a major focus of research, include the following legally defined offenses: murder and nonnegligent manslaughter, forcible rape, robbery, aggravated assault, burglary, larceny/theft, motor vehicle theft, and arson.

The limitations and shortcomings of the UCR as a source of research data have been thoroughly documented. According to Sapp (1989), the major cautions in interpreting UCR data are the following: (1) The UCR is not a complete report of crimes committed. It includes only "selected" crimes and then includes only those occurrences that are known to the police. (2) Participation in the UCR is entirely voluntary and there is no way of mandating reporting. (3) Jurisdictional differences exist in definitions of offenders, and variable interpretations affect the data. (4) Drastic changes in numbers or rates of crime may occur because of changes in reporting methods and communications of known offenses. (5) Reporting is a political process that can have a drastic effect on the data. Such limitations may be magnified when looking at age data on arrests. Still, Miethe and McCorkle (1998, p. 5) argue that "if the goal of a crime typology is to reduce complexity without distorting differences within and between categories, the UCR classification is a clear improvement over the other legal typologies." In spite of the various weaknesses of the UCR, our most comprehensive knowledge about the older offender comes largely from it.

ESTABLISHING ELDERLY CRIME TRENDS

During the past three decades, there has been a significant increase in research in the prevalence of criminal activity among older adults. As in the case of elderly victimization, some scholars reported what they thought to be significant increases in elder crime ranging from minor offenses such as vandalism, drunkenness, shoplifting, and driving offenses to more violent crimes like personal violence and property offenses. The media that found this notion intriguing helped fuel this distorted view. As researchers examined crime data more closely, little evidence was found to support earlier predictions (Cullen, Woziniak, & Frank, 1985; Long, 1992; Steffensmeier,

1987). In retrospect, authors have attributed the notion of a "geriatric crime wave" to an excessive preoccupation with the increasing elderly population. In other words, it was assumed that the growth of the elderly population would naturally lead to increased criminal activity among this age group.

Small increases in the raw numbers of elder arrests can also seem large when expressed in percentage changes (Flynn, 2000), a problem now encountered when reporting increases in female criminality. For example, relying on UCR data, Shichor and Kobrin (1978) note that during the eleven-year period from 1965 to 1974 arrests of the elderly for major crimes increased 43 percent as a proportion of all age group arrests. The authors further reported that elderly arrests for major crimes increased 220 percent in absolute number of arrests. They also concluded that arrests of younger groups most prone to criminal behavior remained relatively constant throughout the eleven-year period, while arrests of the elderly were increasing by over 40 percent over the 11-year period.

To provide a more balanced view, several recent studies have objectively examined arrest data to analyze patterns and changes in arrests of older offenders. Cullen, Wozniak, & Frank (1985) are among the first authors to examine the notion of the rise of a "new elderly criminal." Following the methodological framework employed by Steffensmeier (1978) in his assessment of changes in the pattern of female lawlessness, these authors examined the empirical adequacy of the view depicting the elderly as joining the ranks of serious offenders at an unprecedented rate. Data from the UCR were utilized as the measure of crime, and the author studied crime patterns over a fifteen-year period (1967–1982). Arrest data were examined for the offenses included in the FBI's "Crime Index," which includes murder, rape, robbery, aggravated assault, burglary, larceny theft, and auto theft. They argue three basic points in opposition to a "geriatric crime wave." First, while their analysis does reveal large increases in percentage terms, the reported raw figures are relatively small. For example, rapes rose by 200 percent and robbery by 130 percent between 1967 and 1982. However, in actual numbers this represents an increase of only 74 arrests for rape and 86 arrests for robbery. Second, the basic crime pattern remained relatively consistent during the period studied. At every year studied, larceny theft constituted the most frequent offense among the elderly. An increase in violent crimes such as burglary and robbery is not evident. Finally, the authors conclude that by examining the changes that occurred in crime rates for all age categories, elderly crime rates did not increase substantially faster than the crime rates for the rest of the population. The authors concluded that any growth could be attributed to elderly population increases rather than to a fundamental alteration in crime patterns.

Table 2.1

Number and Percentage of Arrests for Index Crimes Within Each Age Cohort, 1975–2000

	Number of Crimes Committed						%
	1975	1980	1985	1990	1995	2000	Change*
All Ages							
Violent Crime							
Murder	19,526	18,745	15,777	18,298	16,701	8,709	−55
Rape	21,963	29,431	31,934	30,966	26,561	17,914	−18
Robbery	129,788	139,476	120,501	136,300	137,811	72,320	−44
Agg. assault	202,217	258,721	263,120	376,917	438,157	316,630	60
Total	370,453	446,773	431,332	562,481	619,230	415,573	10
Property Crime							
Burglary	449,155	475,639	381,875	341,192	292,315	189,343	−57
Larceny theft	958,938	1,128,823	1,179,066	1,241,236	1,164,375	783,082	21
Auto theft	120,224	129,783	115,621	168,338	149,053	98,697	−17
Arson	—	18,459	16,777	14,974	14,965	10,675	−42
Total	1,528,317	1,751,704	1,693,339	1,765,740	1,620,704	1,081,797	−03
Age 50 and Over							
Violent Crime							
Murder	1,543	1,265	1,125	824	733	476	−69
Rape	491	844	1,370	1,288	1,336	1,000	51
Robbery	975	1,280	1,271	1,023	1,198	1,043	6
Agg. assault	13,487	15,321	14,336	16,323	20,471	17,813	24
Total	16,238	18,706	18,102	19,458	23,748	20,332	20
% distribution	(4.5)	(4.1)	(4.2)	(3.5)	(6.8)	(4.9)	
Property Crime							
Burglary	3,249	4,198	4,006	3,298	3,515	3,404	4
Larceny theft	38,139	55,560	61,622	56,467	42,708	33,076	−13
Auto theft	982	1,315	1,447	1,234	1,352	1,298	24
Arson	—	680	787	502	483	391	−42
Total	42,370	61,073	67,075	60,999	47,575	38,169	−10
% distribution	(2.9)	(3.5)	(3.9)	(3.5)	(3.0)	(3.5)	
Age 65 and Over							
Violent Crime							
Murder	320	248	226	188	149	96	−70
Rape	55	108	225	227	235	168	67
Robbery	155	151	223	110	149	87	−43
Agg. assault	2,087	2,424	2,442	2,741	3,510	2,632	20
Total	2,617	2,931	3,116	3,266	4,043	2,983	12
% distribution	(.7)	(.7)	(.7)	(.6)	(.7)	(.7)	
Property Crime							
Burglary	398	527	508	434	431	388	−2
Larceny theft	8,566	12,857	15,265	15,003	9,722	5,137	−40
Auto theft	123	264	199	174	143	125	1
Arson	—	84	90	84	84	49	−41
Total	5,057	9,087	13,732	15,695	10,380	5,699	−36
% distribution	(.6)	(.8)	(.9)	(.9)	(.6)	(6)	

*1975–2000.

Note: Arson not reported prior to 1975.

Source: *Source of Criminal Justice Statistics* 1975, 1980, 1985, 1990, 1995, and 2000. U.S. Department of Justice. Bureau of Justice Statistics, Washington, DC: USGPO.

Likewise using UCR data, Steffensmeier (1987) reviewed the patterns of arrest from 1964 to 1984 for offenders aged 65 and older. He also investigated changes in the magnitude and seriousness of elderly crime patterns by comparing crime rate increases or decreases with those of other age groups. Using demographic age-standardization techniques, he found that the overall arrest rate for older people remained about the same over the twenty-year period. However, there were changes in arrest rates for some offenses. For example, arrest rates for older people had declined significantly for such offenses as public drunkenness, disorderly conduct, gambling, and vagrancy, but rates had increased for alcohol-related offenses (DWI and public drunkenness) and larceny theft. Steffensmeier concluded that his analysis of actual crime levels and crime trends did not support any evidence of a "geriatric crime wave."

Sapp (1989) analyzed the trends and patterns of arrests of those aged 55 or over. Results of the UCR data indicate that while the elderly population is increasing, the actual percentage of all arrests of the elderly is declining. From 1972 to 1981, the total number of arrests for all ages and all offenses increased by 53 percent, but arrests of elderly offenders decreased by 3 percent during the same time period. Although the numbers and percentage of elderly offender arrests both declined for all crimes, Sapp reported an increase for the Index Crimes reported in the UCR. For example, violent offenses declined slightly, but property offenses increased significantly during the ten-year period.

Another time-series study utilizing UCR data for the years from 1972 to 1989 is worthy of mention (Long, 1992). Using arrest data to analyze patterns and changes in the arrest of offenders aged 55 years and older, Long noted a decrease of 30 percent in arrest patterns for this age group. In terms of the percentage of all arrests accounted for by the older offenders, the decrease was from 6.2 percent of all arrests in 1972 to only 2.6 percent in 1989. It is significant to note that this decrease occurred while the percentage of older persons in the population increased by 27 percent. When considering Index Crime data, this decline in arrests of the elderly does not hold. Index Crimes accounted for 6.4 percent of all elderly arrests in 1972 but increased to 17.5 percent of all elderly arrests in 1989. After accounting for the 27 percent increase of the elderly population during this seventeen-year period, an overall increase of 50.6 percent was computed for both Index and Non-Index Crimes. Much of this increase was attributed to the increase in property offense arrests.

Table 2.1 provides a summary of the changes in arrests patterns for Index Crimes in the UCR between the years 1975 and 2000. The analysis reveals that while there has been a general increase in arrests over this twenty-

five-year period for the population as a whole, numerous violent and property crimes have declined significantly since the late 1980s. A review of
the crime patterns for those aged 50 and over seems to reveal increases for
most Index Crimes. Of course, much of the increase can be attributed to
the actual growth in numbers of individuals aged 50 and over in our population. As Table 2.1 reveals, violent Index Crimes accounted for 4.9 percent of all arrests in 2000 for those over age 50 compared with 4.5 percent
some 25 years earlier. While the actual number of arrests for those over age
65 increased somewhat, percentage distribution of arrests for this age category remained stable. These results are similar to those found by other researchers. The data presented here show no real evidence of a "geriatric
crime wave."

According to UCR data, the total number of arrests in the United States
has remained rather stable for most of the previous decade. In 1989 a little over 11.2 million persons were reported arrested. This number remained
constant until 1995, when 11.4 million arrests were recorded. By 1997 total
number of arrests had dipped to 10.5 million, and in 1998 the number of
reported arrests decreased again to 10.2 million. This decline constitutes
an 8 percent decrease from 1989 arrest data. Accounting for this recent
decline in arrests has been the primary reduction of both property and violent offenses. In 1989 there were 537,084 reported arrests for various vi-

Table 2.2

**Gender Differences in Number and Percentage of Arrests for Index Crimes
for Persons Age 50 and Over (1989–1998)**

	Number of Arrests				
	1989	1992	1995	1998	% Change
Males					
50–54	165,967	187,216	191,994	194,912	+ 15%
55–59	124,264	108,284	102,562	98,742	– 20%
60–64	68,482	66,391	58,843	51,319	– 25%
65+	69,177	72,343	62,893	53,325	– 28%
Total	410,601	434,238	416,292	398,298	– 03%
Females					
50–54	28,535	33,325	34,416	38,805	+ 26%
55–59	17,289	17,800	16,469	17,457	NC*
60–64	11,528	11,168	9,196	8,300	– 28%
65+	14,525	15,551	12,649	10,302	– 29%
Total	71,877	77,844	72,730	74,864	+ 04%

Source: U.S. Department of Justice, Criminal Justice Statistics 1989, 1992, 1995, and 1998 (Washington, DC: Government Printing Office).

*No change

Table 2.3
Gender Differences in Number of Arrests for Violent Crimes for Persons Age 50 and Over (1989–1998)

| | Number of Arrests | | | | | | | | % Change | |
| | 1989 | | 1992 | | 1995 | | 1998 | | | |
	M	F	M	F	M	F	M	F	M	F
Murder	770	130	765	240	644	89	477	85	-38%	-34%
Rape	1,310	6	1,497	11	1,328	8	1,135	10	+2%	+40%
Robbery	934	64	1,150	93	1,104	94	855	102	-5%	+37%
Agg. Assault	14,351	1,657	16,896	2,146	18,993	2,592	16,115	2,456	+11%	+32%
Other Assault	25,133	3,823	29,219	5,186	33,909	5,555	41,955	6,519	+40%	+41%

Source: U.S. Department of Justice, Criminal Justice Statistics 1989, 1992, 1995, and 1998 (Washington, DC: Government Printing Office).

Table 2.4
Gender Differences in Number of Arrests for Property, White-Collar, and Selected Drug- and Alcohol-Related Crimes for Persons Age 50 and Over (1989–1998)

| | Number of Arrests | | | | | | | | % Change 1989–1998 | |
| | 1989 | | 1992 | | 1995 | | 1998 | | | |
	M	F	M	F	M	F	M	F	M	F
Burglary	2,969	506	3,171	459	2,994	521	2,800	590	-05%	+14%
Larceny theft	32,153	22,367	33,866	22,710	26,646	16,062	23,372	13,167	-27%	-41%
Auto theft	1,296	115	1,330	131	1,232	120	1,167	163	-10%	+29%
Arson	448	79	449	89	394	88	345	99	-23%	+10%
Forgery	1,215	429	1,593	607	1,629	655	1,527	726	+20%	+40%
Fraud	14,899	4,766	10,076	6,001	9,246	6,272	8,630	6,052	-42%	+21%
Drugs	14,192	2,212	15,554	2,439	20,779	3,016	23,676	3,855	+40%	+42%
DWI	98,398	9,997	96,751	10,742	82,850	9,827	79,778	10,686	-18%	+06%
Liquor laws	9,995	1,268	11,555	1,242	14,958	1,510	11,915	1,365	+16%	+07%
Drunkenness	67,037	4,210	58,859	4,006	46,622	3,426	45,493	3,762	-32%	-11%

Source: U.S. Department of Justice, Criminal Justice Statistics 1989, 1992, 1995, and 1998 (Washington, DC: Government Printing Office).

olent crimes, and this number stood at 481,278 in 1998, a 10 percent reduction. Property crimes show an even greater decline of 28 percent (declining from 1,808,414 arrests to 1,292,825). The larceny theft category comprised most of the arrests and hence influenced the overall decline in property offenses. During the same period, aggravated assaults did show a very slight increase of 1 percent. Other increases were shown for curfew and loitering law violations (50 percent), other assaults (18 percent), and drug abuse violations (2 percent).

OLDER MALE/FEMALE CRIME TRENDS

There has also been a gradual decrease in arrest patterns for most crimes committed by adults aged 50 and over during this same period. As a whole, this group continues to maintain the lowest overall crime rate of all adult age groups. In 1989, the 482,162 arrests of those over the age of 50 constituted 4.2 percent of all arrests reported by UCR. In 1998 UCR reported a slight decrease, with 473,162 overall arrests for this age group. This number constituted 4.3 percent of all reported arrests, showing little change from the figure reported a decade earlier. Table 2.2 illustrates, however, that while arrests have declined for most age groups, there has been a significant increase in criminal activity among the 50–54 age category. This may give some glimpse of future crime patterns, as the number of baby boomers who reach age 50 continues to increase. Over a ten-year period, the number of arrest among males in this age category increased by 15 percent and females, with smaller raw numbers, increased some 26 percent. While this table shows that most age groups over age 50 saw significant declines, overall older females did exhibit a minor increase of 4 percent for all female offenders 50 years and older.

Approximately 15 percent of those arrested at age 50 and over involve serious felonies such as murder, forcible rape, robbery, aggravated assault, burglary, larceny, motor vehicle theft, and arson. Violent crimes made up 2,656 (3.3 percent) of all arrests for those aged 50 and over. Specific Index Crimes have shown a gradual increase in certain violent and property crimes, especially when controlling for gender. As Table 2.3 demonstrates, females have shown increases during the past decade for rape, robbery, and aggravated assault. Although the percentages are significant, actual numbers reveal only slight increases. Arrests for murder declined significantly for older males and females. There was a pronounced increase in arrests for aggravated assault for both males (11 percent) and females (32 percent). Other assaults have increased more pronouncedly, with both males and females showing a 40 percent increase.

Table 2.4 reveals similar patterns in property crime rates among older males and females. Again, older males show more declines than their female counterparts. Older males and females both indicate a notable decline in larceny theft. Females dropped from 22,367 arrests in 1989 to 13,167 a decade later, representing a 41 percent reduction. On the other hand, males showed a 25 percent decline with 31,153 reported arrests in 1989 and 23,372 in 1998. However, larceny theft was the leading cause of arrest and, overall, property crimes constituted 13,167 arrests, which make up 18.7 percent of the total crimes committed by older females. Older males' arrest rates were also much lower for larceny theft than for other property crimes.

Other property, white-collar, and selected drug- and alcohol-related crimes for persons aged 50 and over are also shown in Table 2.4. As noted in this table, female arrests have increased for most categories with the exception of larceny theft and drunkenness. Older males' rates of alcohol-related arrest have declined significantly, while drug arrests have increased dramatically. There has also been a significant decline in males arrested for larceny theft and fraud. However, when the actual population increases are factored in, the upward arrest trends are not earthshaking. While the elderly population 65 years and older increased by 12 percent between 1990 and 2000, increases in arrest trends have been limited to a few specific crimes. Of course, the age 50 and over population has increased dramatically with the influx of baby boomers into this age category.

ALCOHOL AND DRUG ABUSE AND CRIME

It is a well-established fact that drug and alcohol abuse contributes significantly to the crime patterns in the United States. The 1997 Survey of Inmates in State and Federal Correctional Facilities found that 83 percent of the state prisoners reported past drug use, and 57 percent reported using drugs in the month prior to their offense. The combined use of alcohol and drugs accounted for 18 percent of rapes and sexual assaults, 24 percent of the aggravated assaults in which the offender was drinking, 36 percent of robberies, and 15 percent of the simple assaults involved a drinking offender (U.S. Department of Justice, 1998). The Department of Justice reported other studies of alcohol use by convicted offenders indicating that approximately 35 percent of the over 5 million adults in prisons, jails, on probation or parole supervision were under the influence of alcohol when they committed the offenses leading to their convictions.

The literature suggests some significant relationships between drug and alcohol abuse and criminal activity among females. Analyzing Bureau of

Justice Statistics, Beck (1997) reported that 84 percent of female inmates had previously used drugs. It is estimated that 33 percent of all incarcerated women prisoners have a enough of a drug problem to warrant treatment. The majority of women arrested, regardless of the charge, test positive for at least one illicit drug (McQuiade & Ehrenreich, 1998). A national survey reported that approximately 54 percent of female prisoners had used drugs in the month before incarceration, 65 percent reported regular use, and 53 percent were under the influence of drugs or alcohol at the time of arrest (Snell & Morton, 1994).

Research has also suggested a link between the type of drug used and the type of crime committed. Heroin and narcotics usage is more frequently linked to prostitution and property crimes, whereas crack cocaine appears to be linked to violent crime and drug dealing (Inciardi, Lockwood, & Pottieger, 1993). A national study revealed that nearly one out of four females reported committing their crimes to get money for drugs, and more than a third were under the influence of drugs when they committed their crimes. Similarly, a California study found over one-third of the women sampled indicated a drug-related motivation for crime (Bloom, Chesney-Lind, & Owen, 1994).

When violent crimes occur, research has found a high probability that either the victim, the perpetrator, or both are intoxicated (Warner & Leukefeld, 2001). Research findings, however, are mixed on the role that drugs plays in violent crimes. Snell and Morton (1994) reported that female inmate drug users differed from nondrug users in that users were less likely to be in prison for violent crimes. Other studies have found that drugs played a more significant role in women's violent offenses (Cox, 1982; Greenfield & Snell, 1999). A study of female homicide offenders conducted by Spunt and associates found that drugs played an important role in their criminal activity. Approximately 90 percent of the sample had used alcohol, 76 percent had used marijuana, and 54 percent had used powdered cocaine. About one-third had used alcohol, marijuana, or both regularly, and approximately 25 percent reported using cocaine regularly.

Research has also found that offenders on probation, in local jails, and in state prisons were all about equally likely to have been drinking at the time of their offenses (Logan, Walker, & Leukefeld, 2001). Male probationers in the study were more likely than female probationers to report alcohol use at the time of their offenses. Findings from this study also found that about one-half of all probationers had engaged in arguments with their families or friends while drinking and approximately one-third had engaged in a physical fight with someone after drinking. According to probationers' reports, convicted males in local jails were more likely than convicted females to report alcohol use at the time of their offenses.

Studies have also found links between criminal activity, alcoholism, and drug abuse and homelessness. A study (Douglass & Hodgkins, 1991) conducted in Detroit found African American homeless persons to have served time in jail (55 percent to 33 percent) or in federal or state prison (30 percent vs. 12 percent). Other studies conducted in Detroit and New York also reported that about 25 percent of older women had a history of imprisonment, which was approximately half the prevalence of older men (Cohen, Ramirez, Teresi, Gallagher, & Sokolovsky, 1997; Cohen & Sokolovsky, 1989). Although not all homeless persons are problem drinkers or drug users, studies have found higher rates of lifetime histories of alcohol abuse or dependence among homeless age 50 or older (DeMallie, North, & Smith, 1997). Certainly, there appears to be a causal relationship between alcohol abuse and those living on the streets and deviant or criminal activity.

As Table 2.4 indicates, DWI arrests for older males have recently declined while female arrests were up only slightly between 1989 and 1998. In spite of the decline in alcohol-related crime among older adults, alcohol-related crime and drunkenness still account for a substantial number of elder arrests. Drug abuse among the older population has increased significantly, and some older drug abusers are involved in a variety of criminal activities (Flynn, 2000). Drug abuse has contributed to an increase in the number of older males and females incarcerated in state and federal prisons. In particular, the federal prison system is currently housing a growing number of older drug offenders.

PATTERNS OF ELDERLY CRIME

Homicide

Older offenders who commit homicide have not received much attention in the homicide literature. Studies of elderly offenders has primarily focused on white-collar offenders, organized crime, and perpetrators of multiple street crimes (Gilbert, 1990). Media reports of elderly persons committing homicides point to the increasing need for examining more closely the type of homicide committed by older adults, the relationship of the victim to the perpetrator, and the general impact on the overall homicide rate.

Several studies have examined unjustifiable homicides committed by older persons. Examining nationwide data reported in the FBI's *Supplemental Homicide Reports* for 1980, Wilbanks and Murphy (1984) compared nonelderly (18–59) and elderly (60 and over) homicide offenders. Elderly and nonelderly offender rates were correlated with the demographic variables of age, sex, and race rates for fifty states. It was found that the elderly offender rate varied widely, from Delaware, South Dakota, North Dakota, Vermont, and New Hampshire, with rates of 0.00, to Tennessee with 3.49, Hawaii with 3.51, Arkansas with 3.79, South Carolina with 4.33, and Alabama with 5.09. While the older offender rate varied across jurisdictions, the authors reported that the rate was strongly and positively correlated with the homicide rate for younger offenders in the same states.

It was also noted that the elderly are far less likely (7.7 percent compared with 16.5 percent) to be involved in homicides against strangers than are the nonelderly. In addition, when compared to nonelderly black offenders, elderly black offenders are more likely to be involved in intraracial homicides. On the other hand, there were no reported differences between elderly and nonelderly white offenders in participation in intraracial homicides. Another pattern reported in this study revealed that approximately a third of the very old (those 74 and over) were more likely to kill someone within his or her own age category.

Hucker and Ben-Aron (1984) cited the inability to control emotions and affections as contributing to assaultive behavior by elderly offenders. They studied violent offenders referred to a psychiatric assessment unit, which separates elderly criminal behavior from other geriatric aberrant behavior. The authors compared three types of criminal offenders. Two groups of violent offenders, elderly and nonelderly, were matched on the charges of murder and assault. The third group consisted of nonviolent elderly charged with a nonaggressive sex offense. The nonelderly group was composed of individuals aged 30 and younger, while the elderly offenders were all aged 60 and older.

From comparisons between the groups, the authors were able to conclude that there is some variation in elderly offenders by type of crime committed. In addition, comparisons between the violent elderly and nonelderly revealed major differences in choices of weapon, circumstance, locale, and prior history. The elderly group was more inclined to use firearms, whereas the nonelderly's weapon of choice was a knife. Domestic quarrels were more frequently reported among the elderly offenders than among the nonelderly. Delusional behavior also accounted for a significant number of violent crimes by the elderly. For the elderly, deadly crimes of violence generally occurred in the home of the victim or that of the offender. On the other hand, younger offenders committed their violent offenses in a variety of environments. Elderly offenders were less likely to have committed previous crimes (Hucker & Ben-Aron, 1984).

It was further hypothesized that the reason is that they are not as strong as younger persons. The elderly are more likely (78 percent versus 63 percent) to use a firearm. The author proposed that it is unlikely that an older, presumably weaker, person would attack a younger person with a knife, stick, or a blunt instrument that could possibly be seized and used by the intended victim. The truth of the author's conjecture was evident in my interview with an 85-year-old inmate convicted of killing his 21-year-old son, the youngest of twelve children (Aday, 1993, p. 77):

> My wife and I weren't making ends meet. I asked my son one morning if he would help us. "No," he said. "Well," I said, "you'll just have to leave." My son became abusive, choking and hitting me.... I said, "Boy, you get out of here." He said, "I ain't going nowhere, but you're going somewhere." "I went into the bedroom and brought back a gun. I shot him twice.... I meant to kill him."

This illustrates one scenario in which the elderly become victims of younger, stronger family members and use proactive measures including deadly force to control their social situation.

Other studies have focused more specifically on the nature of the social relationships between older offenders and their homicide victims. Kratcoski (1990) investigated 179 unjustifiable homicides committed by offenders age 60 or older in Cleveland, Detroit, and Cincinnati. Data for the years 1970 through 1985 were gathered from a variety of sources, some of which were case files available in the coroners' and prosecutors' offices and police files. The majority of offenders in this cross-sectional sample were males (82 percent) and African Americans (72 percent). The ages of the sample ranged from 50 to 83 (mean age was 67) and the vast majority of the offenders were retired, unemployed, or on welfare at the time the homicide event took place. Mostly unskilled or semiskilled, their education level was predominately high school or some evidence of attending high school. The following is a summary of the results reported by Kratcoski (1990):

- The victim and assailant were known to each other in 89 percent of the cases. In 25 percent of the cases, one spouse was killed by the other.
- The vast majority of homicides involving the elderly (81 percent) occurred as a result of a quarrel.
- Because of the close relationships, 74 percent of the homicide incidents occurred in the home, 12 percent at the workplace of the victim, 5 percent on the street, 4 percent in hospitals, and 5 percent in jails or other public buildings.
- Alcohol was involved in 44 percent of the homicide cases in this sample. Of those who were under the influence of alcohol at the time of the homicide, 46 percent had a history of alcohol abuse.

- Four of the elderly offenders were declared not guilty by reason of insanity and several were placed in mental hospitals for the homicide offenses.
- In thirty-seven cases, the assailants never went to trial for the homicide offense. Case records also revealed that four offenders were receiving psychiatric counseling at the time of the offense and another seven had been under psychiatric care during an earlier point in their lives.

Research supports the notion that homicide generally occurs between members of the same sex, and nearly all such crimes involve men. Relatively few women commit homicide, and when they do, their victims are almost always men (Goetting, 1992). For some, the stresses of later life, particularly physical illness, exacerbate an already tense and unhappy marriage. Old age is not necessarily a time of dignity, peace, and passive acceptance of one's lot in life. Some older people get drunk and disorderly, fight with their neighbors, and deal with problems of illness, poverty, and loneliness in socially unacceptable ways (Alston, 1986). In such cases crimes of passion often occur. Frequently, the perpetrator is unhealthily dependent on the victim or vice versa, the perpetrator is in a disturbed psychological state, and the family is socially isolated. I provide an illustration for this type of homicide below (Aday, 1995, p. 78):

> When I came out of the hospital after several operations, a long-time acquaintance of mine was staying with my wife. When I came in he was in my home and I shot him.... I shot him four times. It was early in the morning and he was still in bed. My wife had just gone to work. I had never been locked up before in my life and have always been a hard worker. I just turned myself in and didn't harm anyone else.

It is evident that as the range of social interaction shrinks with advancing age, interpersonal primary relationships become intense, with a resulting increase in opportunities for conflict. Added to this potential violence is the significant proportion of elderly offenders who, with a prior history of violent behavior, continue to exhibit violent tendencies within the family at a later age.

For many older persons, dependency on a spouse or close acquaintances increases at the time when the spouse and friends are less likely to be able to assist the elderly persons because of their own personal aging and other medical, emotional, or financial problems. At times, a violent act toward a spouse or close friend may be motivated by frustration or resentment toward that person. Caring for another person over an extended period of time can become a real burden, and the associated stress can result in physical abuse.

Occasionally, a violent act may be triggered by pity, as in the nationally noted Florida case of the offender who killed a spouse suffering from an incurable illness: Roswell Gilbert was found guilty of first-degree murder for the "mercy killing" of his wife of fifty-one years who suffered from Alzheimer's disease and a painful bone ailment (Wilbanks, 1985). Gilbert received a life sentence for the killing, of which he must serve at least twenty-five years. It was determined that Gilbert premeditated the shooting of his wife and took time to reload before shooting her a second time. It was also determined that his wife was not bedridden nor in an advanced state of Alzheimer's. It was concluded Gilbert had also failed to explore other alternatives, such as placing her in a nursing home or hiring a private nurse.

In other cases, the violent act is a severe manifestation of the type of reaction the person had always relied upon to solve problems or frustrations (Kratcoski, 1990). The number of elderly offenders with a prior history of violence and weapons offenses would suggest that patterns of violent behavior learned earlier in life remain present and manifest themselves in violence within the family at a later age (Kratcoski & Walker, 1988). Homicide incidents tend to occur during or after a quarrel, in a spontaneous rather than a planned manner, with the male most frequently the aggressor. The victim can be the instigator of the violence by provoking the aggressor verbally or by being the first to act with physical aggression.

Sexual Offenses

Little has been written about the elderly sexual offender. This may reflect the view that old age is inevitably accompanied by a decrease in sexual desire and functioning (Clark & Mezey, 1997). The public generally wants to disassociate itself from sexual deviants and the "dirty old man" child molester. However, a significant number of older inmates are incarcerated for committing sexual offenses such as rape, pedophilia, and exhibitionism. Crime statistics show that those over age 50 accounted for 10 percent of all sexual offenses, excluding forcible rape (Federal Bureau of Investigation, 1999). This percentage held steady throughout the 1990s. Of those arrested for forcible rape, 4.5 percent were 50 years of age or older. Florida, Georgia, Wisconsin, Tennessee, and Ohio report that anywhere between 25 and 35 percent of offenders over the age of 50 are incarcerated for sexual offenses. Although older adult males are by no means overrepresented, the older sex offender presents some special problems to both the social services and the criminal justice system (Watson, 1989). For example, sex offenders are sentenced to long terms and frequently exhibit symptoms of depression and guilt for their actions. Family relations may also be strained resulting in a lack of community support.

It has been reported that the elderly sex offender differs from younger sex offenders in several ways. For example, while pedophiles are typically older men, rapists are generally more likely to be young, violent offenders (Knopp, 1984). Other research has found that between 12.5 percent and 14.4 percent of child sex offenders over the age of 60 referred to forensic services were discovered to have organic brain disorders (Henn, Herjanic, & Vanderpearl, 1976; Hucker & Ben-Aron, 1984). Declines in mental and physical functioning associated with aging are also likely to be experienced more frequently and have been postulated as potential triggers for sexual offending (Goodwin, Cormier, & Owen, 1983). The meaning of the offense and the outcome of the criminal justice process are likely to be different for the elderly offender, who may be protected from arrest by his or her prestige or by immediate family members who are sheltering themselves from shame.

Sexual offenses committed by older offenders frequently involve child victims. I found that nearly one-third of Tennessee's older inmates incarcerated for sex crimes were convicted of child molestation or incest (Aday, 1994a). The offender often knows the victim, who is, more than likely, a stepdaughter or even a grandchild living in close proximity. Such is the case described below in the words of an elderly inmate (Aday, 1994a, p. 83):

> You know kids can ask a lot of questions.... My five-year-old granddaughter wanted to see my private parts. Like a fool, I let her. When she went to the doctor for her annual checkup, she told him that she seen and played with my private parts. She wasn't harmed in any other way.... Know why I'm here, I feel a lot of shame.

In the case described below a combination of factors contributed to sexual battery. Again, the older offender describes this situation (Aday, 1994a, p. 83):

> There were 15 people living in our three-bedroom house. These were friends of the family out of work. Three females between the ages of eight and ten were looking for affection. I touched their private parts.... I know the charges were justified. I took a plea bargain so the kids wouldn't have to go to court.

In this case the inmate felt his age, open-heart surgery, and heavy medication contributed to his behavior. Living in close proximity with a number of small children provided easy opportunity for such behavior. The new elderly offender was 69 years old when the event took place. He claimed to be impotent at the time of the crime.

Research has been conducted on a group of thirty grandfathers ranging in age from 49 to 74 and serving prison sentences for sexually abusing forty-four of their grandchildren (Stevens, 1995). In its analysis of data from inmate case files at the Ohio Department of Corrections Rehabilitation central office, this study provides information about the offender, victim, and offense. The vast majority of the offenders were white (77 percent) and the majority were married and living with their spouses. Most of the older offenders in this sample did not graduate from high school.

In one-third of the cases drug or alcohol use is mentioned as a possible contributor to the sex crimes. Twenty offenders, in this case, were charged with rape, three with gross sexual imposition, and three with rape and gross sexual imposition. Only five of the older offenders had a previous arrest for a sex offense, and five had a previous arrest for a violent crime other than a sex offense. Six of the grandfathers had been incarcerated before the present imprisonment. It can be concluded from this small sample that sex offenders were more likely to commit their sexual offenses in their own home. Fifteen of the victims were abused in the perpetrator's own home and ten were molested either in a mutual home or the young victim's place of residence.

Of the forty-four victims, thirty-eight were girls and six were boys. The victim's ages ranged from 4 to 13 with the average age being 8.5 years. In 30 percent of the cases, the grandfather was living with the victim. In eleven cases, the sexual abuse continued from one to three years, and in six cases the abuse continued for more than three years. This study also indicates that the amount of force and types of threats or coercion used were quite significant. Physical force included such activities as pushing, holding down, and striking. A combination of these activities was used on ten of the victims. Coercion and verbal threats were used on ten other youthful victims.

Finally, in an attempt to describe more fully the characteristics of the elderly child sex offender and their offenses, Clark and Mezey (1997) obtained access to case notes of thirteen sex offenders between the ages of 65 and 89. Four of the subjects had previous convictions for sexual offenses, two of them against children and two against adults. Of the two cases involving children, one included indecent assaults on children four years prior to the current offenses and the other was for indecent exposure to children forty years earlier. Thirty-eight percent of the men faced charges for the sexual abuse of family members and 62 percent offended against children who were outside the family, but with whom they were acquainted. None of the offenses involved children unknown to the offenders. One-third had offended across two generations, involving both granddaughters and grandsons. Two of the offenders were diagnosed as being moderately depressed, but none of the subjects showed any evidence of mental illness. None of the men had ever received treatment for his sexual offending behavior.

The research presented here reveals that these crimes represent the most serious forms of sexual abuse. Certainly, grandfathers and other older sex offenders should be recognized as serious offenders who may possibly repeat their crimes when released. Treatment for older sex offenders should be encouraged and careful supervision should be practiced when a sex offender is released. The U.S. Department of Justice has indicated that convicted sex offenders are 7.5 times as likely as other ex-convicts to be rearrested for sexual misbehavior (Krane, 1999). As a result, parole boards treat sex cases cautiously, regularly denying release to infirm elderly offenders.

It is currently unknown whether some older offenders commit sexual crimes for the first time in later life or whether it is a behavior that has been previously acted out but went unreported. One of the oldest incarcerated offenders, at age 95, Ellef Ellefson was serving time in 2001 at the Jackson Correctional Institute on charges of sexual assault on a child. Ellefson was 86 when he was convicted of this particular crime. Records provided by the Wisconsin Department of Corrections show Ellefson also took indecent liberties with a minor in 1937. Between that time and his current sentence he was convicted four other times. Some would argue that he was actively engaging in lewd and lascivious behavior more frequently than his apprehension record would indicate. The large number of sex offenders among those incarcerated over the age of 50 shows the need for additional research to determine the extent of these predatory patterns.

Shoplifting

In the 1980s there was a significant increase in shoplifting first offenses by individuals over the age of 60 (Moak, Zimmer, & Stein, 1988). In order to establish a profile of shoplifters, Feinberg (1984) interviewed a sample of 191 senior shoplifters in Broward County, Florida. Elders in the sample ranged in age from 58 to 89. While most were in their sixties, some 42 percent were over the age of 70. Conclusions from the study dispelled a number of prevalent myths about elderly shoplifters. The following characteristics of shoplifting were reported.

- They are typically first-time law violators who have led constructive lives.
- Few have any knowledge of the criminal justice system, and are anxious, embarrassed, and contrite.
- Most are married and have an active social support system.
- They did not steal because they are lonely, isolated, or craving attention.

- Most are of better than average socioeconomic status.
- Most are stable members in their community and had lived there many years.
- Very few suffer from a recent loss of a spouse, close friend, or relative.
- They are as likely to feel optimistic as they are to feel pessimistic.
- Elderly males slightly outnumbered elderly females.
- The average theft tends to involve merchandise of little value.

Feinberg (1984) concludes that the elderly who steal are not indigent and the majority have adequate financial resources. They typically owned their own home, are high school graduates, and had retired from white-collar or professional occupations. Since most shoplifters took clothing articles such as shirts, blouses, and cosmetics, Feinberg concluded that the elderly do not engage in this form of criminal activity for subsistence purposes.

Other studies demonstrate considerable diversity within the phenomenon of shoplifting (Klemke, 1992). Most criminal activities show significant patterns in when they are most likely to occur in the life cycle. A recent national report found that the 52 percent of shoplifters were between the ages of 18 and 30. Another 45 percent were between the ages of 31 and 65 and only 3 percent of the shoplifters were 65 years of age or more (Shoplifters Alternative, 1996). Klemke (1992) also reported that numerous earlier studies conducted prior to 1980 confirmed that young persons were much more likely to be apprehended for shoplifting than were older people. This statistic was particularly descriptive of males. Female apprehensions remained quite high until age 55 and then declined.

Older individuals are apprehended frequently in supermarket shoplifting. About 15 percent of the 9,832 apprehensions from 391 supermarkets were 50 years of age or older (Griffin, 1988). Klemke (1992) reviewed apprehensions made in a multistate department store chain in 1989 and 1990. Apprehensions gradually decreased after the peak in the 11–15 age group, and approximately 10 percent were 50 years of age or older. The latter age group contained equal numbers of each gender. Only about 5 percent of the 7,434 those apprehended were over the age of 60.

Because elderly shoplifters are usually not motivated to steal by economic hardship, shoplifting, for some, may be symptomatic of a psychiatric disorder arising from social isolation. Late-onset kleptomania (individuals who engage in nonsensical shoplifting of items they neither want nor need) is considered rare among the elderly population (McNeilly & Burke, 1998). Models of kleptomania have reported rates of depression and social isolation as high as 80 percent among those who engaged in nonsensical shoplifting (Yates, 1986).

Why people shoplift remains an open question. One group contends that shoplifters suffer from low frustration tolerance, poor self-images, or recent traumatic experiences. Others assert that no pathological state contributes to shoplifting. They argue that shoplifting is shaped by the same economic forces that drive other crimes—the desire for an item, the lack of money, the need for excitement, or an unexplained urge. While the process of aging may exaggerate many of these possible causes, more extensive research is needed to fully understand the motivations for elderly shoplifting.

SUMMARY

Historically, crime patterns among those in the later stages of life have revealed two types of older offenders. One group is composed of repeat or chronic offenders who have engaged in criminal activity for the majority of their lives. The other group includes individuals who commit more violent crimes, generally against family members or personal friends and acquaintances. In keeping with past crime trends, today approximately one-half of older offenders who find their way into prison are classified as new offenders.

This chapter stressed the importance of examining these late-life crime patterns. In particular, it is evident that older first offenders are committing crimes of violence leading to long sentences. If we are to reduce the number of older offenders finding their way into the criminal justice system, it is imperative that we investigate more thoroughly the motivations for criminal activity in old age, especially for first offenders. Although crime statistics reveal a gradual decline in overall criminal activity, certain offending patterns are still very troublesome. For example, older female crime rates has increased for most crime categories, and the crimes committed among middle-age women are frequently violent in nature. However, when the actual raw numbers are examined, there is little cause for concern for a geriatric crime wave among female offenders.

Overall, crime trends in the 1990s revealed a gradual decline in the number of arrests for most older offender age categories. A comparison of arrest rates between 1989 and 1998 shows that only offenders in the 50–54 age category reported any increase. The declines of 24 percent in arrests of those aged 55 and over have come while the actual number of older adults in that age category increased. This fact suggests that it is highly unlikely criminal activity will explode as the aging population continues to increase. In particular, criminal behavior appears to be less likely for those 65 and older. Of course, there are few crimes committed by seniors over the age of 85, the fastest-growing group of elderly.

REFERENCES

Adams, M. E., & Vedder, C. (1961). Age and crime: Medical and sociological characteristics of prisoners over 50. *Journal of Geriatrics, 16*, 177–180.

Aday, R. H. (1984). Old criminals. In E. Palmore (Ed.), *Handbook on the aged in the United States* (pp. 295–310). Westport, CT: Greenwood.

Aday, R. H. (1994a). Aging in prison: A case study of new elderly offenders. *International Journal of Offender Therapy and Comparative Criminology, 38*(1), 79–91.

Aday, R. H. (1994b). Golden years behind bars: Programs and facilities for elderly inmates. *Federal Probation, 58*(2), 47–54.

Alston, L. T. (1986). *Crime and older Americans.* Springfield, IL: Charles C. Thomas.

Anderson, D.C. (1997, July 13). Aging behind bars. *The New York Times Magazine, 146*, 23–33.

Beck, A. J. (1997). Growth, change, and stability in the U.S. prison population, 1980–1995. *Corrections Management Quarterly, 1*(2), 1–14.

Bloom, B., Chesney-Lind, C., & Owen, B. (1994). *Women in California prisons: Hidden victims of the war on drugs.* San Francisco: Center on Juvenile and Criminal Justice.

Brahce, C. I., & Bachand, D. J. (1989). A comparison of retiree criminal characteristics with habitual and nonhabitual older offenders from an urban population. *Journal of Offender Counseling, Services and Rehabilitation, 13*, 45–59.

Clark, C., & Mezey, G. (1997). Elderly sex offenders against children: A descriptive study of child sex abusers over the age of 65. *Journal of Forensic Psychiatry, 8*(2), 357–369.

Cohen, C. I., Ramirez, M., Teresi, J., Gallagher, M., & Sokolovsky, J. (1997). Predictors of becoming redomiciled among older homeless women. *Gerontologist, 37*, 67–74.

Cohen, C. I., & Sokolovsky, J. (1989). *Old men of the Bowery.* New York: Guilford.

Cox, J. (1982). *Self-perceptions of health and aging of older females in prison: An exploratory group case study.* Unpublished doctoral dissertation, Southern Illinois University, Carbondale.

Cromier, B. M. (1971). Behavior and aging: Offenders aged 40 and over. *Laval Medical Journal, 42*, 15–21.

Cullen, F. T., Wozniak, J. F., & Frank, J. (1985). The rise of the elderly offender: Will a "new" criminal be invented? *Crime and Social Justice, 23*, 151–165.

DeMallie, D. A., North, C. S., & Smith, E. M. (1997): Psychiatric disorder among the homeless: A comparison of older and younger groups. *Gerontologist, 37*, 61–66.

Douglass, R. L., & Hodgkins, B. J. (1991). Racial differences regarding shelter and housing in a sample of urban elderly homeless. In S. M. Keigher (Ed.), *Housing risks and homelessness among the urban elderly* (pp. 78–93). New York: Haworth.

Duncan, O. D. (1930). An analysis of the population of the Texas penitentiary from 1906–1924. *American Journal of Sociology, 36*, 770–789.

Federal Bureau of Investigation. (1989). *Uniform crime reports*. Washington, DC: U.S. Government Printing Office.

Federal Bureau of Investigation. (1992). *Uniform crime reports*. Washington, DC: U.S. Government Printing Office.

Federal Bureau of Investigation. (1995). *Uniform crime reports*. Washington, DC: U.S. Government Printing Office.

Federal Bureau of Investigation. (1999). *Uniform crime reports*. Washington, DC: U.S. Government Printing Office.

Feinberg, G. (1984). White haired offenders: An emergent social problem. In W. Wilbanks & P. Kim (Eds.), *Elderly criminals* (pp. 83–108). Lanham, MD: University Press of America.

Feinberg, G., & McGriff, M. D. (1989). Defendant's advanced age in a prepotent status in criminal case disposition and sanction. *Journal of Offender Counseling, Services and Rehabilitation. 13*, 87–123.

Flynn, E. E. (2000). Elders as perpetrators. In M. B. Rothman, B. D. Dunlop, & P. Entzel (Eds.), *Elders, crime and the criminal justice system* (pp. 43–86). New York: Springer.

Fox, V. (1946). Intelligence, race, and age as selective factors in crime. *Journal of Criminal Law, 37*. 150–151.

Fry, L. J. (1987). Older prison inmate: A profile. *Justice Professional, 2*(1), 1–12.

Gerwerth, K. E. (1988). Elderly offenders: A review of previous research. In B. McCarthy & R. Langworthy (Eds.), *Older offenders: Perspectives in criminology and criminal justice* (pp. 14–34). New York: Praeger.

Gilbert, E. (1990). *The social ecology of elderly homicide*. Unpublished doctoral dissertation, Tallahassee, Florida State University.

Goetting, A. (1984). The elderly in prison: A profile. *Criminal Justice Review, 9*(2), 14–24.

Goetting, A. (1992). Patterns of homicide among the elderly. *Violence and Victims, 7*, 203–215.

Goodwin, J., Cormier, L., & Owen, J. (1983). Grandfather–granddaughter incest: A trigenerational view. *Child Abuse and Neglect, 7*, 163–170.

Greenfield, L. A., & Snell, T. L. (1999). *Women offenders*. Washington, DC: Bureau of Justice Statistics.

Griffin, R. (1988). *25th Annual Report: Shoplifting in supermarkets*. Van Nuys, CA: Commercial Service Systems.

Grosswirth, M. (1981, November). "When grandma is a thief." *50 Plus, 4*, 74–77.

Henn, F. A., Herjanic, M., & Vanderpearl, R. H. (1976). Forensic psychiatry: Profiles of two types of sex offenders. *American Journal of Psychiatry, 133*, 694–696.

Hucker, S. J., & Ben-Aron, M. H. (1984). Violent elderly offenders: A comparative study. In W. Wilbanks & P. K. Kim (Eds.), *Elderly criminals* (pp. 69–82). Lanham: Maryland University Press.

Inciardi, J., Lockwood, D., & Pottieger, A. (1993). *Women and crack-cocaine*. New York: Macmillan.

Klemke, L. W. (1992). *The sociology of shoplifting: Boosters and snitches today*. Westport, CT: Praeger.

Knopp, H. F. (1984). *Retraining adult sex offenders: Methods and models*. Orwell, VT: Safer Society Press.

Krajick, K. (1979). Growing old in prison. *Corrections Magazine, 5*(1), 32–46.

Krane, J. (1999). Why old sex offenders are still dangerous. <www.apbnews.com/cjsystem/behind_bars>.

Kratcoski, P. C. (1990). Circumstances surrounding homicides by older offenders. *Criminal Justice and Behavior, 17*, 420–430.

Kratcoski, P. C., & Babb, S. (1990). Adjustment of older inmates: An analysis by institutional structure and gender. *Journal of Contemporary Criminal and Justice, 6*. 139–156.

Kratcoski, P. C., & Walker, D. B. (1988). Homicide among the elderly: Analysis of victim/assailant relationship. In B. McCarthy & R. Langworthy (Eds.), *Older offenders: Perspectives in criminology and criminal justice* (pp. 62–75). New York: Praeger.

Logan, T. K., Walker, R., & Leukefeld, C. (2001). Substance use and intimate violence among incarcerated males. *Journal of Family Violence, 16*, 93–104.

Long, L. M. (1992). A study of arrests of older offenders: Trends and patterns. *Journal of Crime and Justice, 15*, 157–175.

McNeilly, & Burke, W. J. (1998). Stealing lately: A case of late-onset kleptomania. *International Journal of Geriatric Psychiatry, 13*(2), 116–121.

McQuiade, S., & Ehrenreich, J. H. (1998). Women in prison: Approaches to understanding the lives of a forgotten population. *Affilia: Journal of Women and Social Work, 13*, 233–247.

McShane, M. D., & Williams, F. P., III. (1990). Old and ornery: The disciplinary experiences of elderly prisoners. *International Journal of Offender Therapy and Comparative Criminology, 34*(3), 197–212.

Miethe, T. D., & McCorkle R. (1998). *Crime profiles: The anatomy of dangerous persons, places, and situations*. Los Angeles: Roxbury.

Moak, G. S., Zimmer, B., & Stein, E. M. (1988). Clinical perspectives on elderly first-offender shoplifters. *Hospital and Community Psychiatry, 39*(6), 648–651.

Moberg, D. (1953). Old age and crime. *Journal of Criminal Law, 43*, 773–782.

Morton, J. B. (1993, February). Training staff to work with elderly and disabled inmates. *Corrections Today, 55*, 44–47.

Pollak, O. (1941). The criminality of old age. *Journal of Criminal Psychopath, 3*, 213–235.

Rothman, M. B., Dunlop, B. D., & Entzel, P. (2000). *Elders, crime and the criminal justice system*. New York: Springer.

Sapp, A.D. (1989). Arrests for major crimes: Trends and patterns for elderly offenders. *Journal of Offender Counseling, Services and Rehabilitation, 13*, 19–44.

Schroeder, P.L. (1936). Criminal behavior in the later period of life. *American Journal of Psychiatry, 92*, 925–928.

Shichor, D., & Kobrin, S. (1978). Note: Criminal behavior among the elderly. *Gerontologist, 18*, 213–218.

Shoplifters Alternative. (1966). *Why do shoplifters steal?* Jericho, NY: Shoplifters Anonymous.

Smyer, T., Gragert, M.D., & LaMere, S.H. (1997). Stay safe! Stay healthy! Surviving old age in prison. *Journal of Psychosocial Nursing, 35*(9), 10–17.

Snell, T.L., & Morton, D.C. (1994). *Women in prison.* Washington, DC: Bureau of Justice Statistics.

Steffensmeier, D.J. (1978). Crime and the contemporary woman: An analysis of changing levels of female property crime, 1960–1975. *Social Forces, 57*, 566–584.

Steffensmeier, D.J. (1987). The invention of the "new" senior citizen criminal. *Research on Aging, 9*(2), 281–311.

Stevens, G.F. (1995). Grandfathers as incest perpetrators: Dirty old men or predatory offenders? *Journal of Crime and Justice, 18*, 127–141.

Teller, F.E., & Howell, R.J. (1981). Older prisoner: Criminal and psychological characteristics. *Criminology, 18*(4), 549–555.

U.S. Department of Justice, Bureau of Justice Statistics. (1998). *Sourcebook of criminal justice statistics.* Washington, DC: U.S. Government Printing Office.

Warner, B.D., & Leukefeld, C.G. (2001). Rural–urban differences in substance use and treatment utilization among prisoners. *American Journal of Drug and Alcohol Abuse, 27*, 65–82.

Watson, M. (1989). Legal and social alternatives in treating older child sexual offenders. *Journal of Offender Counseling, Services and Rehabilitation, 13*, 141–147.

Wilbanks, W. (1985). The elderly offender: Relative frequency and pattern of offenses. *International Journal of Aging and Human Development, 20*(4), 269–281.

Wilbanks, W., & Murphy, D.D. (1984). The elderly homicide offender. In E. Newman, D. Newman, and M. Gewirtz (Eds.), *Elderly criminals* (pp. 79–92). Cambridge, MA: Oelgeschlager, Gunn & Hain.

Williams, G.C. (1989). *Elderly offenders: A comparison of chronic and new elderly offenders.* Unpublished master's thesis. Middle Tennessee State University, Murfreesboro.

Yates, E. (1986). The influence of psychosocial factors on nonsensical shoplifting. *International Journal of Offender Therapy and Comparative Criminology, 30*, 203–211.

Chapter 3

Explaining Crime in Old Age

The process of aging has been portrayed as a constant succession of transitory stages. Unfortunately, gaps exist in our knowledge of what happens during these life stages and, in particular, between adolescence and old age. These are precisely the years during which one fulfills most of one's ambitions, assures the continuity of life, or fails badly in one's individual and social aspirations. It is also a period when old age itself brings new challenges and problems. As people live longer, they demand that their health care and their social lives reflect the improvements and variety enjoyed by the general population. However, many of the aged in our society become frustrated socially, economically, and psychologically and have difficulty coping with environmental changes over which they have no control. Frequently the journey to old age fails to meet expectations and the resulting frustration may exhibit itself in delinquent behavior.

This chapter provides an overview of the causes of crime among the older adult population. I will present positions that theorists have taken on how age influences criminal behavior and on descriptions of the behavior associated with the aging process. The chapter will include biological and medical explanations of criminal behavior as well as the roles of alcohol, gender, and personality and other mental disorders. I also give significant attention to social explanations for criminal behavior in the latter stages of life. These explanations will include the most predominant criminological and gerontological theories. This chapter is not exhaustive, but I hope it provides an impetus for criminologists and gerontologists to further explore crime causality in the later years.

THEORY AND CRIME

The search for causes of crime at any age has been long and arduous, and much still remains to be done. Philosophers, lawyers, social theorists, physicians, anthropologists, psychoanalysts, psychologists, biologists, and sociologists have all examined crime from the viewpoint of their respective disciplines for centuries. Crime is a complicated and multidisciplinary issue, and criminology has responded with very many theories. A review of the literature on old age and crime, however, reveals a distinct dearth of systematic studies of crime causation in later life. Research on the topic has largely been descriptive with little attempt to provide theoretical perspectives to account for criminal behavior among the elderly. To date theories of criminality have primarily focused on the behaviors of younger delinquents (Burton, Evans, Cullen, Olivares, & Dunaway, 1999).

Some argue that general theories of crime do not satisfactorily account for special subgroups of criminals such as elderly criminals. New perspectives are needed to more specifically understand elderly offender patterns and to explore disparate findings on demographic and other offender characteristics in a more coherent framework. In particular, since crime occurs infrequently among older adults, its infrequency requires further explanation (Flynn, 2000). For example, is deviant behavior attributable to the changes associated with the aging process and the lack of coping resources? To what degree do mental disorders and other life changes contribute to criminal activity in later life? Do older offenders commit crimes late in life for economic reasons, as younger offenders do? Why do some older offenders continue crime careers while others cease criminal activity?

When addressing the reasons why elderly people engage in criminal behavior, it is important to take into consideration patterns of offenses. For example, the social or personality factors that pointed elderly offenders with long criminal histories in criminal directions when they were young are presumably the same ones that influence those behaviors today (Balazas, 2001). Career criminals do exist, and even though they may frequently get caught, they continue to find criminal behavior more rewarding than conforming to societal norms. Some chronic offenders may also undergo some degree of institutionalization and find prison life to be more reassuring than life's challenges on the outside. Numerous inmates have indicated to me that they have committed crimes in order to reenter a prison setting offering such amenities as food, shelter, and health care and a familiar way of life (Aday, 1994).

In contrast, other offenders commit crimes for the first time at an advanced age. Research has concluded that elderly first offenders constitute a most unusual group in that they have lived most of their lives as law-abiding, contributing members of society (Feinberg, 1984; Flynn, 2000; Long, 1992). Except for their criminal behavior, they are ordinary elderly persons who have led a conforming existence throughout their lives. Feinberg suggests that one would expect these average elderly citizens to personify normative standards, especially with regard to rules, which they themselves created as part of conventional society. Providing explanations for why model elderly citizens engage in criminal activity late in life is a complicated issue, as the literature attests (Kratcoski & Pownall,1989).

To date, few theories have focused specifically on older persons and why they engage in lawbreaking activities. Those few theories do identify the same causes and correlates of crime as do more general theories of criminal activity (Kercher, 1987). The explanations for crime in old age are not nearly as extensive or as elaborately explained (Akers, La Greca, & Sellers, 1988; Alston, 1986; Feinberg, 1984; Malinchak, 1980). According to Kercher, these explanations are not actually theories but would be better termed speculations. He contends that most previous attempts to explain criminal behavior among older persons have been limited in the number of independent variables examined and the logic used to form reasonable hypotheses.

Certainly, when applying theoretical models of criminal activity to behavior in the latter part of the life course, it is necessary to give consideration to offender characteristics. Offenders past the age of 65 may engage in criminal activities for very different reasons than younger offenders do. For example, some elderly offenders who commit criminal acts for the very first time may do so because of anxiety disorders or other physical or mental factors associated with old age. It is also important to acknowledge gender differences when explaining criminal activity among older adults. While opportunity and socialization have been mentioned as two strong explanations of female criminality, the recent emergence of feminist criminology has provided alternative suggestions (Pollock-Byrne, 1990).

THE INFLUENCE OF AGE ON CRIME

Numerous studies have proposed sociological explanations of the observed relationship between age and crime (Greenberg, 1985; Hirschi & Gottfredson, 1983; Piquero & Mazerolle, 2001). Most explanations have focused on the transition between adolescence and adulthood, when involvement in many forms of crime peaks and then begins to decline. It has been suggested that criminality is conditioned by age, with youth and young adulthood being the periods when criminality reaches its peak.

Hirschi and Gottfredson (1983) insist that behavior analogous to crime declines with advancing age. Their observation directs theoretical attention to the entire life span, not to only one part of it. They further note the correlation between age and rule breaking in prison. Other research has also reported that the most adequately established correlate of misconduct among prison inmates is age (MacKenzie, 1987). It should be pointed out that the age of maximum criminality varies somewhat with the type of crime. As biological maturity is achieved, there is a pronounced decline in most forms of criminality, and with old age murder, forcible rape, and robbery virtually disappear (Flynn, 2000).

Interest in the persistence of criminal careers of street offenders has increased (Miethe & McCorkle, 1998). This movement has focused new attention on crime desistance or the termination of criminal careers. Most of the research on the later stages of criminal careers has focused on the failure to desist, or recidivism. Because most studies of recidivism are motivated by interest in parole prediction or other policy questions (Shover & Thompson, 1992), there are few theoretical explanations of desistance. Although it is considered an important issue, criminologists are primarily interested in the causes of crime rather than crime cessation (Uggen & Piliavin, 1998). Making causal inferences about criminal activity is frequently seen as more rewarding for theory and policy when compared with desistance research. Another view is that many age-related biopsychosocial factors (employment status, intelligence, economic opportunities) thought to be related to criminal participation contribute to crime desistance as well (Gove, 1985; Long, 1992).

Several explanations have been advanced to explain the well-documented decline in criminality during the latter stages of life (Fattah & Sacco, 1989). One view suggests that with advancing age there is a tendency to make a transition toward conformity. Psychological evidence showing that rebellious and antisocial tendencies decline with age supports this hypothesis (Eliopoulos, 1997). Further support for the hypothesis comes from an empirical study of maturational reform (Jolin, 1985). Jolin concluded that male career criminals who have refrained from criminal activity apparently go through a midlife transition much the same way as law-abiding males. Jolin found that, after a midlife assessment, ex-offenders changed attitudes and values as well as their course of behavior. The study further disclosed that the most notable external change occurring was the transition from criminal to noncriminal behavior.

The decline in physical strength and agility, endurance, enterprise, and initiative has also frequently been linked to a reduction in criminal activity with advancing age (Fattah & Sacco, 1989). Previous research has supported the view that the weakening body becomes incapable of those crimes in which physical strength and skill is paramount (Beirne & Messerschmidt, 1995). Hirschi and Gottfredson (1983) note that some crimes surface only when the strength necessary to inflict injury or coerce others has been attained. It has been suggested that the same crimes are likely to disappear when this strength has been lost or weakened as a result of age or other physical decline. Other research has also introduced mobility as being significant to the type of criminal pattern in which an older person might engage. For example, persons committing crimes against property exhibited the highest mobility, while crimes against the public order, petty crimes, and crimes against persons require less mobility, in descending order (Carlie, 1970; Piquero & Mazerolle, 2001).

Rowe and Tittle (1977) suggested four variables (social integration, moral commitment, deterrence, and motivation) to explain the diminution of criminality with age. The authors contend that these variables do not affect crime in a direct manner. The statistical results indicated a negative relationship between age and criminal behavior, which was attributed to generational differences and partly to life cycle changes. The authors contend that complex interactions between of two or more of these variables can affect age and crime relationships. For example, a high degree of moral commitment may increase with age, but conformity may result only when it is tied to significant sanctions.

The notion that increased integration results in a decline in criminal activity has received prior support from Hagan (1993) and Hirschi & Gottfredson (1995). These studies found such variables as family background, civil status, and employment as possible determinants of continued criminality in later life. As people mature, they are more likely to become socially integrated and settle into predictable niches and an organized social life. The more involved people become, the more likely they are to take their identities from associations within the community as a whole and from the roles they perform.

Finally, Shover (1985) contends that aging offenders gradually become aware of the finality of death. In essence, potential offenders begin to view time as a diminishing resource and become increasingly unwilling to risk spending their remaining years in prison. They view disengaging from a criminal career as preferable to the effort of maintaining a successful criminal career. As they grow progressively weary, the daily routines of managing criminal involvement become tiring and burdensome to aging offenders (Shover & Thompson, 1992). While aging offenders struggle with everyday boundary maintenance, they find contentment and peace of mind in living a straight life. Aging offenders achieve psychological and social equilibrium by lowering their material aspirations and finding interest in more traditional goals.

GENDER AND CRIME

Although we will discuss more fully women and crime in Chapter 7, several fundamental questions should be posed here when discussing gender and crime. (1) How do we explain why females engage in crime? (2) Are the causes of female criminality distinct from or similar to causes of male criminality? (3) How can we explain the variance in the rate of crime between males and females? Although a number of theorists have applied traditional social theories to explain differences between the genders in their chosen types of crime, others have suggested that a "gendered" theory is more suitable for explaining differences between male and female offending (Steffensmeier & Allan, 1996). Criminologists do agree, however, that the gender gap in crime is universal, as we saw in Chapter 2.

From the 1960s to 2000 we can say, however, that female criminality in general steadily increased. In 1963, almost 12 percent of all arrests were women. Some forty years later the percentage had increased to over 20 percent (Small, 2000). Any number of explanations has been offered to explain why women continue to commit crimes at a steady rate. Opportunity theorists would attribute the increase in female criminality to women's achieving greater equality with men. The opportunity theory holds that women are actually no more or less likely to abide by the law than men. Steffensmeier & Allen (1998) have argued that as more women enter the labor force, they will have more opportunities to commit the type of employment-related crimes typically committed by their male counterparts. Like males, some women will take advantages of these opportunities and others will not (Simon & Landis, 1991).

Other theorists have argued that masculinity theory can demonstrate links with female criminality as women become more liberated and take on male characteristics of being aggressive. Small (2000), for example, summarizes arguments that as women become masculinized, their rates of offending for both property and violent offenses will converge with male rates of offending. The prediction is that as male and female social roles merge, the rates of offending will become comparable. Another position reviewed by Small is that as women become more economically independent, they will engage in fewer crimes, particularly those of passion against their spouse or lovers, as they become less dependent. Others have suggested that the increase in some types of female criminality result from the continued marginality of women in society (Boritch & Hagan, 1990; Simpson & Ellis, 1995). This argument holds that older women are committing crimes for the necessities of life. This reasoning could explain shoplifting and other petty property crimes.

Broidy and Agnew (1997) argue that strain theory may help provide insight into the relation between gender and crime. Recent research has shown that females as well as males are susceptible to a variety of frustrations that correlate positively with criminal behavior. These authors' notion of strain theory goes beyond the classic view that strain occurs as a result of the failure to achieve valued monetary success. Agnew's (1992) version of strain theory recognizes that there are several sources of strain, including the loss of positive influences like friends and romantic partners and the presence of negative stimuli like excessive demands and verbal, sexual, and physical abuse. Since the majority of older women's arrests are for property offenses and violent crimes, Agnew's broader version of strain theory can prove useful in explaining deviant behavior in this group. Armed with a lifetime of negative experiences, older women or men may reach a breaking point at which they react against individuals or the system that has been victimizing them.

BIOLOGICAL AND MEDICAL EXPLANATIONS

Historically, the theories explaining later life criminality were largely biological. Among a group of older criminals, Adams and Vedder (1961) observed a phase of "unadjustment" followed by a permanent "maladjustment." They attributed this criminal behavior partly to the "conscious or subconscious" realization of physiological impotence. Winfree and Abadinsky (1996) have also given special attention to the variations in criminal behavior by age. They feel that older sex offenders have been viewed as suffering from weakened inhibitions. Additional biological research and theory has stressed the importance of biochemical factors such as dietary and hormonal imbalances and physiological factors such as brain abnormalities and dysfunction (Gove, 1985).

Elderly criminal behavior is often associated with some type of organic brain disease accompanying the aging process, such as cerebral arteriosclerosis or senile dementia. The pathological changes produced by such disorders are believed to weaken an individual's inhibitions or cause delusions that lead to episodes of violence or deviant sexual activity (Gewerth, 1988). For example, a chronic brain syndrome that includes a loss of inhibitions may result in illegal sexual behavior, such as exhibitionism or child sex abuse (Clark & Mezey, 1997). Crimes may also result from the need to compensate for feelings of rejection, impotence, or unattractiveness (Whiskin, 1968). Some older men have fantasies of rejuvenation based on their contact with young children (Butler, Lewis, & Sunderland,

1998). It has been reported that men who molest children in old age are compensating for physiological impotence (Goodwin, Cormier, & Owen, 1983). Other older males may display a greater degree of rigidity, suspiciousness, and quarrelsomeness with consequent aggressiveness (Rodstein, 1975). In one study of 27 cases involving older offenders, approximately half were diagnosed as having neurospychiatric disturbance, and sex offending was common among male first-time offenders (Wong, Lumsden, Fenton, & Fenwick, 1995).

Hypoglycemia may also be related to criminal behavior among the older population. Blood-sugar levels below an acceptable range can impair brain functioning. The result can be confusion, anxiety, anger, and aggression (Glick, 1995). Researchers have noted a link between hypoglycemic reactions and sexual offenses (Virkkunen, 1986). Prison inmates generally report higher levels of hypoglycemia than the noninmate populations. Certainly, investigating the link between hypoglycemia and the older offender would be beneficial, especially since a significant number of later offenders commit sexual offenses.

Numerous biosocial researchers have also studied the relationship between hormonal levels and aggressive as well as criminal behavior. Research has linked androgen, the male sex hormone, and testosterone levels to antisocial, aggressive, and violent behavior. Samples from prison inmates have indicated higher levels of testosterone among the men who committed violent crimes (Kreuz & Rose, 1972). Other research suggests that older men become less criminal as they age because testosterone levels decline as they progress through the life cycle (Gove, 1985).

ALCOHOL AND CRIME

The abuse of, dependency on, or addiction to alcohol affects an estimated 15 percent of the older population (Eliopoulos, 1997). This disease can seriously threaten the physical, emotional, and social health and well-being of the older adult. A majority of older alcoholics are chronic alcohol abusers who have used alcohol heavily throughout their lives. Older persons tend to be unable to tolerate alcohol and become intoxicated from lower dosages. Other complications result from mixing alcohol with prescription and over-the-counter drugs. The abuse of alcohol can be manifested in a variety of ways, which can be confused with other disorders such as insomnia, irritability, anxiety, and confusion. Alcohol abuse has been linked to greater physical and mental deterioration.

There is evidence that alcohol use will probably increase in the future from a cohort effect. The reason that the current older population has a relatively low rate of alcohol consumption is that they are a light-drinking generation, but current middle-aged and young adults have a higher rate of alcohol consumption (Miller, Belkin, & Gold, 1991). Most of the factors deemed important explanatory elements for any age group, such as drugs and alcohol, poverty, and the environment, also apply to those who commit crimes later in life. Prevailing theories suggest that many older adults drink in response to the material and emotional stresses associated with aging issues such as illness, bereavement, poverty, and social isolation (Meyers, 1984). In many instances, alcohol abuse emerged as a problem late in the lives of older offenders, when excessive drinking was used as an escape mechanism to make more tolerable the difficulties associated with individual aging, illness, or loss of loved ones (Kratcoski & Pownall, 1989).

Numerous studies have explored the relationship between criminal activity and alcohol abuse. In particular, alcohol abuse is a problem frequently associated with violent offenses by the elderly (Jennison, 1984). Violent crimes among older problem drinkers increase with. Other research has reported a significant correlation between alcohol abuse and violent offenses (Paradis, Broner, Maher, & O'Rourke, 2000). These authors found that almost half their sample reported a history of alcohol abuse and the majority were charged with violent crimes. Ham (1976) reported that over 63 percent of his sample of state prison inmates over 50 years of age were in prison for some form of homicide. Based on prison records of Ham's sample, all the murders committed involved heavy drinking. Research also reveals that a high incidence of alcoholism and unstable social relationships are descriptive of elderly inmate populations in general (Aday & Rosefield, 1992; Krajick, 1979; Kratcoski & Pownall, 1989). These studies, along with those of nonprison populations (Jennison, 1984; Kercher, 1987, Meyers; 1984), aid in documenting an obvious pattern in elderly crime in which a significant number of older offenders have drinking problems, which contribute, in some fashion, to their criminal activity. While these studies conclude that violent crimes committed by older offenders are associated with a history of excessive drinking and with the consumption of alcohol immediately prior to the crime, further research is needed.

PERSONALITY DISORDERS AND OTHER MENTAL DISORDERS

The offenses of older people are often attributed to mental disturbances associated with aging, and there is an increase in prisoners with prior mental hospitalization. Chaiklin (1998) has suggested that some crimes committed by the aged may be attributed to the process of deinstitutionalization. A recent study, which classified criminal offenders by type of mental disorder, determined that 67.1 percent of all inmates antisocial personalities (Hodgins & Cote, 1990). The authors estimate that schizophrenia accounts for 6.3 percent, manic-depression 1.6 percent, disorders from drug use 18 percent, depression 8.1 percent, and alcohol abuse 33.1 percent. A review of twenty studies of the relationship between psychosocial problems and crime found great variation in the degree and type of disorders said to be prevalent among incarcerated offenders. The studies categorized from 0.5 percent to 26 percent of all inmates as psychotic, 2.4 percent to 28 percent as mentally subnormal, 5.6 percent to 70 percent as psychopathic, 2 percent to 7.9 percent as neurotic, and 11 percent to 80 percent as suffering from mental disorders associated with alcoholism or excessive drinking (Prins, 1980). According to Jemelka, Rahman, & Trupin (1993), there is a general lack of agreement on the formal definition of mental disorders and there are variations in the manner in which inmates are classified, diagnosed, and tested. It can be tentatively concluded from such studies that a significant number of convicted felons suffer from mental impairment of one type or another.

Some psychological explanations of crime and other forms of deviant behavior stress the importance of various personality factors and traits in an attempt to explain why some people become chronic offenders. Personality theories, in general, stress that certain characteristics predisposes individuals to criminal behavior. When combined, these traits make up what some psychologists term the criminal personality (Glick, 1995). The *Diagnostic and Statistical Manual of Mental Disorders* (American Psychiatric Association 1994 [*DSM-IV*]) defines personality traits as "enduring patterns of perceiving, relating to, and thinking about the environment and oneself, and are exhibited in a wide range of important social and personal contests. It is only when personality traits are inflexible and maladjustive and cause either significant impairment in social or occupational functioning or subjective distress that they constitute a personality disorder."

One type of personality disorder that is of particular interest to criminologists is the antisocial personality disorder. It is of interest because the essential feature of this disorder is a history of continuous and chronic antisocial behavior that may also be criminal. Glick (1995) estimates that 3 percent of the U.S. male population has antisocial personality disorder. The following serve as examples of behavior for those with antisocial personality disorder: failure to accept social norms with respect to lawful behavior as indicated by repeated thefts, illegal occupations, multiple arrests, felony convictions, repeated physical fights or assault, failure to honor financial obligations, disregard for the truth, and recklessness (*DSM-IV*).

It has been suggested that while sociological and cultural theories are more useful for explaining early delinquency, psychiatric explanation might be more enlightening when it comes to explaining late-life criminality (Fattah & Sacco, 1989). For some time now psychiatrists have suggested that brain damage, cerebral disease, and traumatic brain injuries might be associated with disturbances of behavior that are criminal in nature. Others are convinced, however, that most offenses of old age are expressions of beginning senile dementia or the development of a mental condition not yet apparent. Numerous case studies have suggested the important role of dementia as a factor in criminal activity in later life. Two retrospective case studies reporting court liaison referrals in inmates over the age of 60 have found rates of dementia ranging from 19 percent to 30 percent (Heinik, Kimhi, & Hes, 1994; Rosner, Wiederlight, Harmon, & Cahan, 1991). Also, clinical interviews found dementia in 21 percent of a small sample of 28 inmates 65 years of age and older (Barak, Perry, & Elizur, 1995). It should be pointed out that these and other studies have been limited by the lack of standardized diagnostic tools and by sample selection bias.

More specifically, clinical studies report a very high incidence of organic brain disease among elderly sex offenders (Clark & Mezey, 1997, Henn, Herjanic, & Vanderpearl, 1976). Another study found organic brain disorders present in 13 percent of child sex offenders over the age of 60 referred to forensic services (Hucker & Ben-Aron, 1984). Losses associated with normal aging have been postulated as a potential trigger for sexual offending (Goodwin, Cormier, & Owen, 1983). It has been suggested that elderly sex offenders have "a long lasting Achilles heel normally held in check by compensatory satisfactions or pressures but liable to re-emerge in times of stress, and that old age, ill health and disability may lead to such impulses manifesting themselves" (Fazel & Jacoby, 2000, p. 201). Other issues surrounding the elderly male's loss of masculinity may also be important. The need to compensate for the loss of the outward symbols of masculinity such as work, physical health, and sexual activity could also contribute to an explanation of why men with previously unblemished records commit sexual crimes in old age.

Chronic brain syndrome may be associated not only with a loss of inhibitions, resulting in illegal sexual behavior such as exhibitionism, but in rigidity, suspiciousness, and quarrelsomeness with accompanying aggressiveness. Feelings of despair and undue dependence on family and social agencies may lead to violent and aggressive acts against family members.

Loss of status and breakdown of authority, at times with paranoid reactions, may also lead to physical assaults on family members (Rodstein, 1975).

Personality traits commonly associated with acts of violence against others may persist or even become pronounced in old age. Tendencies toward aggression do not completely disappear with advancing age. Some individuals may become more quarrelsome, more irritable, more suspicious, and more mistrustful in their later years. In a variety of personal circumstances, the elderly are likely to suffer from intense frustration and great emotional tensions. As Richman (1982) has suggested, with increasing decline comes a decreased tolerance for frustration and a decreased capacity to delay the discharge of impulses.

Other clinical studies have found a significant relationship between mental disorders and violent crime. A recent study reported that 28 percent of elderly jail detainees had a history of previous psychiatric hospitalizations (Paradis et al., 2000). Forty percent were diagnosed with psychotic disorders, including schizophrenia and paranoid psychosis. Others were diagnosed with adjustment disorders such as organic brain syndrome and dementia. Of this sample of 83 older offenders above the age of 62, 68 percent had been charged with violent felonies. Of these, 25 percent were charged with murder, attempted murder, or manslaughter. In particular, the authors found that patients who reported paranoid delusions were statistically more likely to be charged with a violent crime. Goetting (1992) also found that 61 percent of her sample of elderly arrested for homicide were diagnosed with psychotic symptoms at the time they were apprehended.

Some have suggested that the crime of shoplifting may be symptomatic of a psychiatric disorder (McNeilly & Burke, 1998; Moak, Zimmer, & Stein; 1988; Yates, 1986). Although late-onset kleptomania (individuals who engage in nonsensical shoplifting of items they neither want or need) is considered rare among the elderly population, it has been effectively used as an appropriate diagnostic tool (McNeilly & Burke, 1998). The *DSM-IV* diagnostic criteria for kleptomania include recurrent failure to resist impulses to steal objects not needed for personal use or for the monetary value. Significantly high depression scores, and an actual or anticipated loss within close temporal proximity to the theft, have been reported among shoplifters (Cupchik & Atcheson, 1983; Moak et al., 1988). Etiological models of kleptomania have reported rates of depression and social isolation as high as 80 percent among those who engage in nonsensical shoplifting (Yates, 1986).

For example, Moak et al. describe a 70-year-old woman who was referred to a community mental health center under court order after her second arrest in one year for shoplifting. She reported an urge to shoplift while in crowded stores since the death of her husband ten years earlier. She entered stores without the intent to shoplift, but once inside, she found herself driven to examine things that she did not need while thinking "I should have that" and "I ought to do it." The woman had no history of violating the law. She worked part-time and managed her own home. However, she was still experiencing acute grief and depression from the death of her husband.

Koenig, Johnson, Bellard, Denker, & Fenlon (1995) reported in their sample of ninety-five older male inmates residing in a federal correctional facility that over half were diagnosed with a variety of psychiatric disorders, including major depression, dysthymia, panic, generalized anxiety, antisocial personality disorders, and posttraumatic stress disorders. Inmates with psychiatric disorders were no more likely than other inmates to be recently incarcerated or to be serving a first prison term. Older offenders with a previous history of alcohol or drug abuse were at greater risk of having a current psychiatric disorder.

In examining motives for criminal activity, Taylor and Parrott (1988) found two-thirds of the older offenders between 55 and 64 years old and over three-quarters of those over 65 were without an address and living with few social supports. In this sample of older offenders, 37 percent had a major functional psychosis. Wong, Lumsden, Fenton, and Fenwick (1995) discovered in a maximum security hospital that about 75 percent of the elderly offenders were admitted in their 20s or 30s and were detained into old age because of a single incident of violence. The majority of this group suffered from schizophrenic illness. This group profile clearly contrasted with the first-time offenders nearing old age. Wong et al. found that new elderly offenders over the age of 50 suffering from various mental disturbances commit fewer violent offenses than those in the younger group. However, they noted that sex offenses and brain disorders were common in male first-time offenders among the subgroup of new elderly offenders.

CONTROL THEORIES

Although control theories have typically been applied to other delinquent populations, some have been introduced as theoretical explanations for crimes by older offenders (Akers, La Greca, & Sellers, 1988; Burnett, 1989; Greenberg, 1985; Long, 1992; Malinchak, 1980). Akers et al. state that social control theory offers reasonable explanations of deviance and crime among older offenders that are as coherent and relevant as they are for adolescents. They argue that the concepts and propositions of social control theory are abstract enough not to be age-specific. In addition, adolescence and old age have commonalities in behavior that show promise in accounting for substance abuse, crime, and milder forms of deviance among the elderly.

The most influential control theory of deviance was social bonding theory originally formulated by Hirschi (1969). Akers et al. (1988) found reason to believe that social bonding theory can explain conforming and nonconforming behavior of older people. While the social processes of younger and older populations may not be identical, stronger bonds should produce greater conformity in any segment of society. Thus, the more integrated or bonded with society, the less likely the elderly person will be to engage in criminal activity and the more likely to continue to adhere to society's norms. However, the specific kinds of attachments, commitments, and involvements of the elderly may be different from those of young people. For the elderly, attachment would more than likely be a spouse, adult children, siblings, or elderly peers. Also for the elderly, commitment would be more closely tied to past and present achievements. While the elderly may maintain future aspirations, their identities and reputations are generally already established. Thus, an older person's commitment to conformity would be widely influenced by the desire to protect an established reputation.

Various forces of social integration would also contribute to conformity and should produce constraints on criminal activity among the elderly. The more likely the elderly are to be involved in hobbies, family activities, volunteer services, senior center activities, church activities, and work, the less likely they will be to engage in deviant behavior. For Akers et al., the weaker the bonds of attachment, involvement, commitment, and beliefs, the greater the probability that criminal offending will occur. On the other hand, the more integrated or bonded the elderly person, the more likely he or she will refrain from criminal activity. Since previous research has only weakly supported Akers et al.'s theory, further exploration is needed.

Feinberg (1984) has inferred that the elderly engage in criminal behavior because they frequently exit several roles simultaneously: physical disabilities, retirement, change in residence, death of a spouse, and so on. The loss of social roles separates them from mainstream society and, forced to cope with life changes, they evolve a new identity. Contributing to the identity crisis at the end of the 20th century were a rapidly changing society and the emergence of new moralities. Using Walter Reckless's (1967) social control theory, Feinberg contended that certain inner and outer containments for the elderly are weakened. Reckless conceives of inner containment as consisting of (1) a favorable self-image, (2) an awareness of being interdirected, (3) a high level of status frustration, (4) a strong set of internalized morals and ethics, and (5) a well-developed superego. Feinberg argues that the role losses that the elderly suffer result in lowered self-esteem and it is this lack of an adequate social structure and support system that leads to a lack of direction and continuity.

Concomitantly, the elderly may also experience weakening of Reckless's outer containments: (1) a broad role structure, (2) a set of reasonable limits and responsibilities, (3) opportunities for status achievement, (4) cohesion, including joint activity and integration with other elderly and nonelderly in society, and (5) a strong sense of belonging.

Breakdowns in inner and outer containment are then viewed as either causing or facilitating elderly persons to become involved in such crimes as shoplifting. For the elderly, such a deviant activity would not normally require an apprenticeship or the acquisition of new skills. Such behavior can also be integrated into one's normal daily activities. Many older people may shoplift out of economic necessity and may not view such behavior as illegal (Feinberg, 1984). Unfortunately, Feinberg failed to provide any additional research data to support his social control theory.

ANOMIE AND STRAIN THEORY

Social disorganization and various strain theories have evolved from various theoretical and research traditions (Akers, 1994). The general view is that the less solidarity, cohesion, or integration within a group or community, the higher the rate of criminal activity. Typically, theories of social disorganization, anomie, and strain theories have focused specifically on delinquent crime, criminal gangs, and deviant activities in disadvantaged lower-class and ethnic groups. Some research literature in these traditions, however, have studied the elderly.

The elderly share many characteristics of a well-defined subculture. As a subculture, the elderly maintain some unique norms (patterns of expected behavior) that distinguish them from the wider culture. The elderly's shared losses in societal status (career, loss of spouse, and other role changes) bind them together. As a whole, society offers few opportunities to socialize people into the newly devalued status. Consequently, the elderly often find themselves isolated and engaged in activities with little intrinsic meaning. Anomie, or feelings of powerlessness, meaninglessness, and normlessness, has been hypothesized as a predictor associated with the negative consequences of aging (Akers, La Greca, & Sellers, 1988).

Strain theories typically frame the criminality of older offenders in the context of living in a state of drift, relatively free of social controls and day-to-day responsibilities. According to strain theory, people are subjected to various stressors or outside pressures. Observing that many in the elderly population must survive on fixed incomes, despite increases in the cost of living, Malinchak (1980) argues that strain theory may prove useful for explaining specific types of crime engaged in by the older offender. As Akers et al. (1988) point out, it is possible to use anomie as an independent variable in the explanation of elderly deviance or crime.

Two areas in which there has been some attempt to relate deviant response to anomic strain among the elderly are alcohol or drug abuse and suicide. The most common explanation of late-onset alcoholism or problem drinking is that it is a response to stress, normlessness, alienation, and loss of external control (Atchley, 2000). Of course, as discussed in other chapters, problem drinking is frequently associated with other criminal behavior among older offenders. Elderly suicide, particularly among white males, can often be a result of life events such as illness and related pain, death of a spouse, or economic loss.

Another criminal activity of the elderly examined within the strain framework is stealing. Shoplifting is a frequent misdemeanor charge, and most shoplifters are white females (Barrow, 1996). Since older people are caught stealing lipstick, perfume, night creams, and cigars, it is difficult to develop a direct link between shoplifting and economic hardship. According to Barrow, shoplifting among the elderly represents the combined influence of stress, age, and merchandising. In addition, uncertainty about the future may compel some elderly to shoplift in order to conserve money for anticipated expenses. Moving from a greater to a reduced fixed income creates in some older people a concern about the future and a compulsion to conserve. In other words, many older people may steal to ease fears about their financial status in the future. Villa, Wallace, & Markides (1997) have suggested that many older people are living beyond their pensions and, with rising prices and fixed income, they are experiencing greater economic pressures.

Others may engage in shoplifting to get attention, and stealing may reflect feelings of deprivation in human relationships. In addition to the economic issues, the elderly are faced with numerous emotional losses. For example, children, grandchildren, and other family members may be thousands of miles away. Spouses and close friends may die, leaving the elderly survivors feeling deprived and isolated. For older people who feel neglected by their children, stealing may be a way of getting attention. Subconsciously, elderly shoplifters may want to be caught or at least noticed (Dullea, 1986).

The theoretical link between life events, anomie, and criminal activity needs to be examined more comprehensively. We have yet to fully test an anomie/strain theoretical model as it applies exclusively to the elderly. It is merely conjectured that the central concepts of normlessness and alienation and the stressors of important life events could be combined with strain models to produce a coherent anomie perspective on elderly deviance (Akers, La Greca, & Sellers, 1988). Other anomie concepts would also appear to be directly applicable. For example, Akers and Cochran (1985) mention external locus of control as an indicator of perceived powerlessness, especially for the elderly, who frequently fear becoming dependent on others. Strain theory explanations for elderly crime and deviance appear similar to those for adolescents. This theory, like social bonding, offers coherent explanations that are as relevant to the elderly as to other age groups.

SOCIAL LEARNING THEORY

Social learning theory focuses on individual, learned behaviors and reciprocal interaction with the social environment. Numerous criminologists have indicated the importance of learning theory as an explanatory tool for understanding crime (Akers, 1994; Beirne & Messerschmidt, 1995). While Akers's social learning theory is intended to be a general theory of crime, the perspective has been applied to a specific criminal and deviant behaviors of both youthful and adult populations. Akers (1973) applies the general principles of social learning to white-collar, professional, organized, and violent crimes as well as drug use, suicide, and mental illness. The principles of social learning theory are (1) how a person first engages in a deviant act, (2) how that person progresses to more frequent engagement, (3) the events that reinforce the act, and (4) the content of the conditions favorable to the act. In short, an individual is exposed to classifications of behavior as good or bad, right or wrong. The more a person holds positive valuations on a behavior, the more likely that person will be to conform to such behavior.

Although social learning theory has not been fully tested nor widely accepted (Beirne & Messerschmidt, 1995), it has some merit for explaining recurring engagement in criminal activity over the life course. Learning theory should be relevant to any age group, including the elderly population. As Akers, La Greca, & Sellers (1988) have suggested, "social learning theory is a dynamic process of acquiring and maintaining conforming and deviant behavior patterns without specific reference to or limitation by age, sex, or other socio-demographic variables" (p. 40).

Certainly, rewards and costs attached to behavior are equally important for all age groups. When the model is applied to elderly offenders, some of the empirical measures have to be modified to make them more applicable (Akers et al., 1988). Career criminals have had such behaviors reinforced. They continue to engage in a pattern of criminal activity even though they know the likelihood of returning to prison. Close association with law-violating peers and friends should be as important for the older offender as it is for juveniles. Those who are involved in crime and other forms of deviant behavior after entering the elderly years are apt to have established such patterns earlier in life. However, new behavior patterns are frequently assumed later in life. In particular, drug trafficking has become a more frequent activity among older offenders. The question remains whether this has been a lifelong pattern or whether the person was apprehended for the first time in old age.

Considerable support has emerged for the social learning model when applied to elderly drinking behavior (Akers et al., 1988). While the theoretical model has been largely tested on youthful samples, a matter researcher preferences, have influenced this trend rather than a lack of relevance during the later stages of life. One would expect that a social learning model would be empirically supported by data from elderly criminal behavior. The theory would predict that older offenders who associated with other offenders are differentially reinforced for committing criminal acts. However, the explanatory power of the model may be different for new and for chronic elderly offenders.

DISENGAGEMENT THEORY

Some authors have applied the disengagement theory to delinquent behavior in later life. According to this theory, the elderly, especially males, become increasingly isolated from persons and formal organizations outside the home after they retire. Retirement may result in a period of disenchantment accompanied by a lack of identity (Atchley, 2000). In view of the very great significance of occupational status, retirement leaves the older male in a peculiarly functionless situation. As a result, feelings of uselessness and rejection can occur, and tensions between elderly spouses or companions can increase as they spend more time together (Kratcoski, 1990).

In some cases, older workers are forced to retire against their will because they are no longer employable and have outdated skills. In this case, difficulties related to disengagement may be particularly acute when an older person is compelled to leave the workforce. Mandatory disengagement may result in maladjustment and feelings of bitterness. Another possible emotional reaction to forced disengagement is a sense of rage at the seemingly uncontrollable forces as well as the frequent indignities and neglect of a society that once valued the older worker's productive capacities (Butler, Lewis, & Sunderland, 1998). Feelings of personal failure can manifest themselves in lashing out through aggressive violence. The description of some older people as cantankerous, ornery, irritable, or querulous can more easily be interpreted if sensitivity is given to the degree of outrage older people feel, consciously or unconsciously, at their situation. Not only is rage a common emotional reaction to the perceived inhumane treatment, but some older people also rage against the inevitable nature of aging and their general feelings of vulnerability.

Barrett (1972) attributes the need to maintain a certain status in old age as an important theoretical explanation of why delinquency may persist in old age. For Barrett, should the need for prestige remain high, older people may become delinquent, just like children and adolescents, to build a feeling of importance. The older criminal may become a forger or commit fraud to enhance a feeling of personal superiority from bilking another through cunning. According to Barrett (p. 130), "he may gamble, become a vandal, steal an auto or violate any number of statutes merely to satisfy his ego." Many older individuals become delinquent (just as children do) in their search for identity and companionship.

LABELING THEORY

Prejudice, stereotyping, and discriminatory behavior against the aged by the majority group often occurs in modern society. The aged have frequently been the butt of societal and personal labels. Labeling theory emphasizes that deviance must be viewed from the perspective of the audience. Labeling theory is concerned primarily with how some behaviors are labeled "deviant" and how being given such a label influences a person's behavior. From a sociological standpoint, deviance can be defined as conduct that is generally thought to require the attention of social control agencies, or, more specifically, behavior about which something must be done. Consequently, deviance is not a property inherent in certain forms of behavior; it is rather a property conferred upon those individuals by a wider audience. Thus, the critical variable in the study of deviance is the social audience rather than the individual persons, since it is the audience that eventually decides whether any given conduct will become a socially defined case of deviation.

Hence, the consequences of labeling have been generally viewed as negative in nature. For example, being labeled as deviant has negative concurrences because people labeled as deviant tend to see themselves as deviant. Taking on the deviant role leads them to continue their so-called deviant behavior. Getting labeled as a deviant or criminal leads others to view you in those terms, overlooking other more positive qualities or statuses. Once a person is typed, that person's acts are interpreted in accordance with the deviant status to which he or she has been assigned. Labeled people may no longer be treated as respectable community members; they may lose their jobs or be sent to a prison. Responses of this type often push labeled people further into the deviant activity. Older ex-convicts who have spent a substantial amount of their adult years in prison may not get legitimate jobs and may return to criminal activity as a means of coping.

Although labeling theory does not explain the causes of initial criminal activity, it does suggest that those who are powerless are more likely to be labeled and consequently may become chronic offenders into their later years in life. As older persons accept negative labeling, they are more likely to become inducted into a negative, dependent position. In the process of "role engulfment," the labels applied by others become part of the individual's personal identity or self-concept. As they learn to behave in ways that criminals are "supposed" to act, they perceive themselves in that role, and a negative spiral is set into motion. For the elderly, the labeling process can occur when someone who is about to retire starts to behave as others have defined the retired status: unproductive, useless, and inactive. The labeling process may become more pronounced when an older person is apprehended for committing a sexual crime and is labeled a pervert.

Certainly, labeling theory demonstrates that the process of societal reaction can actually amplify for the older chronic offender the very problems it seeks to eliminate. For example, societal reaction to deviance often tends to stigmatize those who deviate from the norm. Stigmatization is a way of spoiling a person's identity and making it difficult for him or her to be accepted back into society. It becomes even more difficult for the aging chronic offender who not only has to overcome the stigma of a criminal, but also the stigma associated with old age. The stigmatizing effect of the primary deviation is one of the most important factors in the occurrence of secondary deviation and is often used by researchers to explain cases of recidivism (Beirne & Messerschmidt, 1995). Older, uneducated offenders may have great difficultly hiding or correcting their stigma. Thus, the effects of stigma may partly depend on the institutional context in which it is conferred. Goffman (1961) reports that in "total institutions" where large numbers of like-situated individuals are cut off from the wider society for an extended time, it becomes increasing difficult to combat the effects of stigma. Aging chronic offenders with lower social status and perhaps a minority status will have few resources for counteracting a stigma. As a result, a negative label leads to further criminal activity and incarceration.

CONTINUITY THEORY

According to continuity theory, individuals tend to maintain a consistent pattern of behavior as they age. In other words, the aging person preserves typical ways of adapting to the environment in order to maintain inner psychological continuity as well as the outward continuity of social behavior and circumstances. This explanation argues that there is a genuine causal link between past and future criminal behavior. Basically, this perspective proposes that, with age, we become more of what we already were when younger. This link, commonly referred to as the state-dependent effect, suggests that the commission of criminal acts reduces inhibitions and strengthens motivation to commit crime (Paternoster, Dean, Piquero, Mazerolle, & Brame, 1997). Central personality characteristics become even more pronounced and core values even more salient with age. In early life, the self is established with feedback from others. This identity crystallizes and is resistant to subsequent change. Once the identity is established, the individual tends to interact with persons who support this self-view and to avoid or discount those who do not (Burnside & Schmidt, 1995).

When applied to criminal activity in old age, continuity theory may provide an explanation of the chronic offender who continues to commit crimes over the life course. Previous research has shown that the earlier a person is introduced into the criminal justice system, the more likely it is that he or she will become dependent on the penal institution for his or her needs and identity. To maintain a greater consistency in their lives, people are motivated to maintain their internal continuity as an effective means of meeting important basic needs. For example, an individual's identity may be shaped by criminal activity; and basic needs such as food, housing, and other necessities may met by participating in illegal activities. Various pressures and attractions move people toward external continuity as well. People are expected by others to present themselves in a way that is tied to and connected with their past role performances (Atchley, 1989). External continuity of relationships is motivated by the desire for predictable social support. Many older inmates have developed an inner circle of close friends who have accompanied them from prison to prison. External continuity is maintained when the older chronic offender preserves his or her interactions among those who affirm his or her view of self. Living and growing old in a familiar prison world helps older inmates maintain an inner strength and may very well minimize the effects of social and personal deficits as normal aging occurs.

SUMMARY

The complex nature of crime contributes significantly to the lack of a decisive criminal etiology. Few crimes can be traced to a single cause. Causes of crime are multiple, varied, and interwoven. Elderly criminality is difficult to explain because criminal behavior is an atypical activity among those who have reached the later stages of life. Some of the popular explanations of elderly crime are circular (Fattah & Sacco, 1989). Popular psychiatric explanations in particular, according to Fattah and Sacco, use the criminal behavior of the elderly individual to diagnose her or him as suffering from a mental disorder, and then use the disorder to explain the criminal behavior in question.

Another reason for the difficulties in explaining criminal activity is that crime is not a homogeneous category of behavior, and elderly criminals are not a homogeneous group. For example, different explanations may be for explain crime committed by multiple or repeat offenders than for criminal activity committed for the first time late in life.

One more fact to be aware of when trying to understand and explain criminality is the problem of adjustment. The psychological, physical, and social changes associated with old age mean that this period of life can be stressful. Crime, especially when it occurs for the first time late in life, may be a symptom of the fundamental changes associated with old age. Ways of coping with these changes will inevitably vary between one individual and another according not only to individual differences but also to the influence of the environment and the strength or weakness of support systems and resources.

In conclusion, it can be safely stated that the lack of knowledge limits the explanations that can be provided for the patterns of criminal involvement among the elderly. Scholars have suggested that additional research is needed to address many of the burning questions about old age and crime (Akers, La Greca, & Sellers, 1988; Fattah & Sacco, 1989; Flynn, 2000). For example, are environmental and situational factors more or less important in the criminality of the elderly than in the criminality by younger people? If the role of alcohol as a related factor more or less pronounced in elderly crime than it is for other age groups? Are the elderly more or less susceptible to some triggering factors (for example, provocation) than other age groups? Does advancing age bring with it greater intolerance, more irritability, and morbid jealousy? Are the elderly more likely to react violently to situational stress than other age groups? Testing theoretical models with the older adult population will be required to further increase our understanding of crime in old age. Theoretical development of elderly crime will help to relate knowledge of elderly crime to the larger body of criminological knowledge and will more accurately guide future policy recommendations.

REFERENCES

Adams, M. E., & Vedder, C. (1961). Age and crime: Medical and sociological characteristics of prisoners over 50. *Journal of Geriatrics, 16,* 177–180.

Aday, R. H. (1994). Golden years behind bars: Programs and facilities for the geriatric inmate. *Federal Probation, 58*(2), 47–54.

Aday, R. H., & Rosefield, H. A. (1992, Winter). Providing for the geriatric inmate: Implications for training. *Journal of Correctional Training, 12,* 14–16, 20.

Agnew, R. (1992). Foundation for a general strain theory of crime and delinquency. *Criminology, 30,* 47–87.

Akers, R. L. (1973). *Deviant behavior: A social learning approach.* Belmont, CA: Wadsworth.

Akers, R. L. (1994). *Criminological theories.* Los Angeles: Roxbury.

Akers, R. L., & Cochran, J. L. (1985). Adolescent marijuana use: A test of three theories of deviant behavior. *Deviant Behavior, 6,* 323–346.

Akers, R. L., La Greca, A. J., & Sellers, C. (1988). Theoretical perspectives on deviant behavior among the elderly. In B. McCarthy & R. Langworthy (Eds.), *Older offenders: Perspectives in criminology and criminal justice* (pp. 51–75). New York: Praeger.

American Psychiatric Association. (1994). *Diagnostic and statistical manual of mental disorders* (4th ed.). Washington, DC.

Atchley, R. C. (1989). A continuity theory of normal aging. *The Gerontologist, 29,* 183–190.

Atchley, R. C. (2000). *Social forces and aging life.* Belmont, CA: Wadsworth.

Balazs, G. J. (2001). The elderly offender. In A. Walsh (Ed.), *Correctional assessment, casework and counseling* (pp. 219–249). Lanham, MD: American Correctional Association.

Barak, Y., Perry, T., & Elizur, A. (1995). Elderly criminals: A study of the first criminal offense in old age. *International Journal of Geriatric Psychiatry, 10,* 511–516.

Barrett, J. H. (1972). *Aging and delinquency.* Springfield, IL: Charles C. Thomas.

Barrow, G. M. (1996). *Aging, the individual, and society.* New York: West.

Beirne, P., & Messerschmidt, J. (1995). *Criminology.* New York: Harcourt Brace.

Blumstein, A., Cohen, J., Roth, J. A., & Visher, C. A. (1986). *Criminal careers and career criminals.* Washington, DC: National Academy Press.

Boritch, H, & Hagan, J. (1990). A century of crime in Toronto: Gender, class and patterns of social control. *Criminology, 28,* 601–26.

Broidy, L., & Agnew, R. (1997). Gender and crime: A general strain theory perspective. *Journal of Research in Crime and Delinquency, 34*, 275–307.

Burnett, C. (1989). Introduction to older offenders. *Journal of Offender Counseling, Services and Rehabilitation, 13*, 1–17.

Burnside, I., & Schmidt, M. G. (1995). *Working with older adults.* Sudbury, MA: Jones and Bartlett.

Burton, V. S., Evans, T. D., Cullen, F. T., Olivares, K. M., & Dunaway, R. G. (1999). Age, self-control, and adults' offending behaviors: A research note assessing a general theory of crime. *Journal of Criminal Justice, 27*, 45–54.

Butler, R. N., Lewis, M., & Sunderland, T. (1998). *Aging and mental health.* New York: Macmillan.

Carlie, M. K. (1970). *The older arrestee: Crime in the later years of life.* Unpublished doctoral dissertation. Washington University, St. Louis.

Chaiklin, H. (1998). The elderly disturbed prisoner. *Clinical Gerontologist, 20*(1), 47–62.

Clark, C., & Mezey, G. (1997). Elderly sex offenders against children: A descriptive study of child sex abusers over the age of 65. *Journal of Forensic Psychiatry, 8*(2), 357–369.

Cupchik, W., & Atcheson, J. D. (1983) Shoplifting: An occasional crime of the moral majority. *American Journal of Psychotherapy, 4*, 593–603.

Dullea, S. (1986, February 10). When the aged start to steal. *The New York Times,* p. B12.

Eliopoulos, C. (1997). *Gerontological nursing.* Philadelphia: Lippincott.

Frazel, S. & Jacoby, R. (2001, September). Health of elderly male prisoners: Worse than the general population, worse than younger prisoners. *Age and Aging, 30*, 198–208.

Fattah, E. A., & Sacco, V. F. (1989). *Crime and victimization of the elderly.* New York: Springer-Verlag.

Feinberg, G. (1984). White haired offenders: An emergent social problem. In W. Wilbanks & P. Kim (Eds.), *Elderly criminals* (pp. 83–188). Lanham, MD: University Press of America.

Flynn, E. E. (2000). Elders as perpetrators. In M. B. Rothman, B. D. Dunlop, & P. Entzel (Eds.), *Elders, crime, and the criminal justice system* (pp. 43–83). New York: Springer.

Gewerth, K. E. (1988). Elderly offenders: A review of previous research. In B. McCarthy & R. Langworthy (Eds.), *Older offenders: Perspectives in criminology and criminal justice* (pp. 14–31). New York: Praeger.

Glick, L. (1995). *Criminology.* Boston: Allyn & Bacon.

Goetting, A. (1992). Patterns of homicide among the elderly. *Violence and Victims, 7*, 203–215.

Goffman, E. (1961). *Asylums: Essays on the social situation of mental patients and other inmates.* Garden City, NY: Doubleday.

Goodwin, J., Cormier, L., & Owen, J. (1983). Grandfather–granddaughter incest: A trigenerational view. *Child Abuse and Neglect, 7*, 163–170.

Gove, W. R. (1985). The effect of age and gender on deviant behavior: A biopsy-chosocial perspective. In A. S. Rossi (Ed.), *Gender and the life course* (pp. 111–144). New York: Aldine.

Greenburg, D. (1985). Age, crime, and social explanation. *American Journal of Sociology, 91*, 1–27.

Hagan, J. (1993). The social embeddedness of crime and unemployment. *Criminology, 31*, 465–491.

Ham, J. N. (1976). *Forgotten minority: An exploration of long-term institutionalized aged and aging male prison inmates*. Unpublished doctoral dissertation, University of Michigan, Ann Arbor.

Heinik, J., Kimhi, R., & Hes, J. P. (1994). Dementia and crime: A forensic psychiatry unit study in Israel. *International Journal of Geriatric Psychiatry, 9*, 491–494.

Henn, P. A., Herjanic, M., & Vanderpearl, R. H. (1976). Forensic psychiatry: Profiles of two types of sex offenders. *American Journal of Psychiatry, 133*, 694–696.

Hirschi, T. (1969). *Causes of delinquency*. Berkeley: University of California Press.

Hirschi, T., & Gottfredson, M. (1983). Age and the explanation of crime. *American Journal of Sociology, 89*, 552–584.

Hirschi, T., & Gottfredson, M. (1995). Control theory and the life course perspective. *Studies on Crime and Crime Prevention, 4*, 132–143.

Hodgins, S., & Cote, G. (1990). The prevalence of mental disorders among penitentiary inmates in Quebec. *Canada's Mental Health, 38*, 1–4.

Hucker, S. J., & Ben-Aron, M. H. (1984). Violent elderly offenders: A comparative study. In W. Wilbanks, & P. K. Kim (Eds.), *Elderly criminals* (pp. 69–82). New York: University Press.

Jemelka, R. P., Rahman, S., & Trupin, E. W. (1993). Prison mental health: An overview. In H. J. Steadman & J. J. Cocozza (Eds.), *Mental illness in America's prisons* (pp. 122–146). Seattle, WA: National Coalition for the Mentally Ill in the Criminal Justice System.

Jennison, M. K. (1984). The violent offender: A research note. *Federal Probation, 50*(3), 60–65.

Jolin, A. (1985). *Growing old and going straight: Examining the role of age in criminal career termination*. Unpublished doctoral dissertation, Portland State University, Portland, OR.

Kercher, K. (1987). The causes and correlations of crime committed by the elderly. *Research on Aging, 9*, 256–280.

Koenig, H. G., Johnson, S., Bellard, J., Denker, M., & Fenlon, R. (1995). Depression and anxiety disorder among older male inmates at a federal correctional facility. *Psychiatric Services, 46*(4), 399–401.

Krajick, K. (1979). Growing old in prison. *Correction Magazine, 5*(1), 32–46.

Kratcoski, P. C. (1990). Circumstances surrounding homicides by older offenders. *Criminal Justice and Behavior, 17*, 420–430.

Kratcoski, P. C., & Pownall, G. A. (1989, June). Federal Bureau of Prisons programming for older inmates. *Federal Probation, 53*(2), 28–35.

Kreuz, L. E., & Rose, R. M. (1972). Assessment of aggressive behavior and plasma testosterone in a young criminal population. *Psychosomatic Medicine, 34,* 321–332.

Long, L. M. (1992). A study of arrests of older offenders: Trends and patterns. *Journal of Crime and Justice, 15,* 157–175.

MacKenzie, D. L. (1987). Age and adjustment to prison: Interactions with attitudes and anxiety. *Criminal Justice and Behavior, 14,* 427–447.

Malinchak, A. A. (1980). *Crime and gerontology.* Englewood Cliffs, NJ: Prentice-Hall.

McNeilly H., & Burke, T., (1998). Stealing lately: A case of late-onset kleptomania. *International Journal of Geriatric Psychiatry, 13*(2) 116–121.

Meyers, A. R. (1984). Drinking, problem drinking, and alcohol-related crime among older people. In E. S. Newman, D. J. Newman, and M. L. Gewirtz (Eds.), *Elder criminals* (pp 51–65). Cambridge, MA: Oelgeschlager, Gunn & Hain.

Miethe, T. D., & McCorkle, R. (1998). *Crime profiles: The anatomy of dangerous persons, places, and situations.* Los Angeles, CA: Roxbury Publishing Company.

Miller, N. S., Belkin, B. M., & Gold, M. S. (1991). Alcohol and drug dependence among the elderly. *Comprehensive Psychiatry, 32,* 153–165.

Moak, G. S., Zimmer, B., & Stein, E. M. (1988). Clinical perspectives on elderly first-offender shoplifters. *Hospital and Community Psychiatry, 39*(6), 648–651.

Moberg, D. (1953). Old age and crime. *Journal of Criminal Law, 43,* 773–782.

Paradis, C., Broner, N., Maher, L., & O'Rourke, T. (2000). Mentally ill elderly jail detainees: Psychiatric, psychosocial and legal factors. *Journal of Offender Rehabilitation, 31*(1/2), 77–86.

Paternoster, R., Dean, C. W., Piquero, A., Mazerolle, P., & Brame, R. (1997). Generality, continuity, and change in offending. *Journal of Quantitative Criminology, 13,* 231–266.

Piquero, A., & Mazerolle, P. (2001). *Life-course criminology.* Belmont, CA: Wadsworth.

Pollock-Byrne, J. M. (1990). *Women, prison, and crime.* Pacific Grove, CA: Brooks/Cole.

Prins, H. (1980). *Offenders, deviants or patients? An introduction to the study of socioforensic problems.* London: Tavistock.

Reckless, W. (1967). *The crime problem.* New York: Appleton.

Richman, J. (1982). Homicidal and assaultive behavior in the elderly. In B. L. Danto (Ed.) *The human side of homicide* (pp. 247–273). New York: Columbia University Press.

Rodstein, M. (1975). Crime and the aged: The criminals. *Journal of the American Medical Association, 234,* 639.

Rosner, R., Wiederlight, M., Harmon, R. B., & Cahan, D. J. (1991). Geriatric offenders examined in a forensic psychiatry clinic. *Journal of Forensic Science, 36,* 1722–1731.

Rowe, A. R., & Tittle, C. R. (1977). Life cycle changes and criminal propensity. *Sociological Quarterly, 18*, 223–236.

Shover, N. (1985). *Aging criminals*. Beverly Hills, CA: Sage Publications.

Shover, N., & Thompson, C. Y. (1992). Age, differential expectations, and crime desistance. *Criminology, 30*, 89–104.

Simon, R. J., & Landis, J. (1991). *The crimes women commit: The punishment they receive*. Boston: Lexington.

Simpson, S, & Ellis, L. (1995). Do gender: Sorting out the caste and crime conundrum. *Criminology, 33*, 47–77.

Small, K. (2000). Female crime in the United States, 1963–1998: An update. *Gender Issues, 18*, 75–90.

Steffensmeier, D. J., & Allan, E. (1996). Gender and crime: Toward a gendered theory of female offending. *Annual Review of Sociology, 22*, 459–488.

Taylor, P. J., & Parrott, J. M. (1988). Elderly offenders: A study of age-related factors among custodially remanded prisoners. *British Journal of Psychiatry, 152*, 340–346.

Uggen, C., & Piliavin, I. (1998). Asymmetrical causation and criminal desistance. *Journal of Criminal Law and Criminology, 88*, 1399–1415.

Villa, V. M., Wallace, S. P., & Markides, K. (1997). Economic diversity and an aging population: The impact of public policy and economic trends. *Generations, 21*, 13–18.

Virkkunen, M. (1986). Insulin secretion during the glucose tolerance test among habitually violence and impulsive offenders. *Aggressive Behaviors, 12*, 303–310.

Whiskin, F. E. (1968). Delinquency in the aged. *Journal of Geriatric Psychiatry, 1*, 242–262.

Winfree, L. T., & Abadinsky, H. (1996). *Understanding crime: Theory and practice*. Chicago: Nelson-Hall.

Wong, M., Lumsden, J., Fenton, G. W., & Fenwick, P. (1995). Elderly offenders in a maximum security mental hospital. *Aggressive Behavior, 21*, 321–324.

Yates, E. (1986). The influence of psychosocial factors on nonsensical shoplifting. *International Journal of Offender Therapy and Comparative Criminology, 30*, 203–211.

Chapter 4

Health Concerns of Aging Inmates

The growing demand for medical services within correctional facilities has become an important issue in prison health care. Research has shown that health-care expenditures have become the most pressing problem facing correctional administrators (Aday, 1994; McDonald, 1995; Shapiro & Shapiro, 1987). The graying of American prisons will only increase the demand for medical services. Research has consistently demonstrated that aging is accompanied by increased disability, more chronic conditions, and the need for accommodation (Falter, 1999; Rosefield, 1993). There is a strong relationship between aging and the need for assistance with activities of daily living (ADLs), which include bathing/showering, dressing, eating, toileting, and transferring in and out of bed, among other things. Aging also brings greater risk of major diseases such as cancer, diabetes, hypertension, and cardiac and renal failure. There is, more often than not, a gradual decline in health as chronic disease complications (e.g., hearing impairment, loss of sight, poor circulation, arthritis, dementia, hypertension) develop.

As medical risks increase, aging offenders have a more frequent need for primary medical care, and treatments may be more extensive. They also have a greater need for specialty clinic services, ancillary services (e.g., labwork, EKGs), and supportive aids such as respiratory support, mobility aids, and sensory aids. They also frequently require costly dental care as teeth and supporting structures deteriorate, optical services, and audiology services. Since older inmates often have multiple chronic illnesses, multiple medications are frequently required.

Prisoners are not a healthy population. High prevalence of tuberculosis, psychiatric disturbances, trauma, and sexually transmitted diseases has been reported (Shapiro & Shapiro, 1987). McDonald (1995) confirms that the demand for health care within the prison is shaped in large part by disorders magnified by drug and alcohol abuse and a lack of adequate access to community health care. As a result, spending for the health care of prisoners has increased rapidly during the last several years.

This chapter will provide an overview of the mental and physical health concerns and issues currently confronting most correctional institutions. Major focuses will be on health policy, health-care utilization, and costs of providing heath care to an aging prison population. Data from a number of states will provide a profile of the health of the older inmate. I will address the importance of race and age in determining a comprehensive health plan as well as a variety of mental health issues. Finally, an assessment of inmate satisfaction with prison health care and the importance of health promotion in prison settings will be included.

PRISON HEALTH MANDATES

The growing demand for medical services within correctional facilities has become an important issue in prisons. The extent to which medical services, social services, and parole planning for inmates should be provided has been debated by policy makers since the early 20th century. There is a growing recognition, however, that inmates should receive service consistent with prevailing community norms. The U.S. Supreme Court in *Estelle v. Gamble* in 1976 decided that having custody of a prisoner's body and controlling his or her access to treatment imposes a duty to provide needed care (Cushing, 1986). Any deliberate indifference to serious medical needs of prisoners may be judged as cruel and unusual punishment. The three basic health-care rights of prisoners are (1) the right of access to care, (2) the right to care that is ordered, and (3) the right to a professional medical judgment (Specter, 1994).

The *Estelle* ruling presented prison and jail health-care providers with a dilemma, for they found themselves caught between the health needs of inmates and the concerns of correctional staff to maintain order and security. There is now scarcely a prison or jail that has remained untouched by the court decision in the medical services it provides for inmates. Prison health administrators are beginning to address the challenges brought about by the medical implications of a rapidly increasing prison population and the increasing number of older inmates. Consequently, prisons now draw much more heavily on health-care resources available in the community at large, including physicians, hospitals, equipment, and supplies (McDonald, 1995).

HEALTH-CARE COSTS

There has been widespread debate over the care and treatment of inmates and the amount of resources that should be allocated to their care. Prison officials are very careful not to leave the impression that they are coddling offenders and are simultaneously very careful to provide medical needs mandated by legal precedent, medical diagnosis, safety considerations, and treatment recommendations. The increases in mandatory and longer sentences have resulted in an increase in correctional health care. McDonald (1995) and a study sponsored by the National Institute of Corrections (1997) have identified several conditions that have forced correctional health care cost to rise:

- The rising costs of health care in society at large
- The increasing number of prisoners in the correctional system
- Implementation of community standards in correctional facilities
- The number of inmates coming into the prison system who need medical services immediately
- The threat of litigation and pressure from federal courts to improve medical services
- The general aging of the prison population
- The improved longevity of inmates as a result of earlier diagnosis and better treatment
- The higher prevalence of infectious diseases among correctional populations

As long as these conditions remain in place, correctional health-care costs will continue to increase dramatically.

The natural process of aging creates complications, especially economic ones (Marquart, Merianos, Herbert, & Carroll, 1997). With prison populations burgeoning, prison health-care costs are now approximately $3.3 billion a year (Appleby, 1997). The cost of long prison terms is high, even without medical expenses. The National Council on Crime and Delinquency has estimated that the cost of housing a prisoner for thirty years, the average time for a life sentence, is more than $1 million, which does not include medical treatment. It has also been suggested that the cost of incarcerating a single inmate for fifty years could exceed $2 million (Pelosi, 1997). More specifically, it has been estimated that it costs, on average, about $70,000 a year to keep an inmate over the age of 60 incarcerated (Beyerlein, 1997). If a 60-year-old inmate lives to 80, this figure would project to a $1.4 million expenditure. In contrast, it costs $22,000 a year to imprison the typical adult inmate (Holman, 1997). For example, the federal prison in Otisville, Iowa, spends $980,000 a year out of its $25 million budget on dialysis for twenty of its inmates, or $49,000 per inmate for just this one health-care expenditure (Henderson, 1998). The average health-care cost per inmate at the SCI–Laurel Highlands facility in Pennsylvania specifically designed for the aged and infirm was $16,362 from 1999 to 2000. The average cost was only $3,000 per inmate in other state correctional facilities (Haberman, 2001). Correctional officials at Laurel Highlands estimate that the total annual cost to house older inmates is $66,000, compared with $27,000 per inmate per year at other Pennsylvania institutions. See Figure 4.1 for a summary of the factors contributing to higher health care expenditures for the aging prison population.

At the McCain Correctional Facility in North Carolina, the state spends close to $200,000 annually to keep just one of many long-term inmates incarcerated. In the past few years, this long-termer has had open-heart bypass surgery, angioplasty, and treatment for a stroke that immobilized him. Medical costs to care for this inmate also included physical therapy to regain his speech and the use of his right leg. There are also daily costs associated with treating his heart disease, diabetes, and hypertension. This inmate is just one of the 185 elderly inmates who are serving time at the McCain Facility, at a cost of $37,000 per inmate per year (Pelosi, 1997).

Of course, national health expenditures have grown rapidly, with double-digit annual rates of increase quite common. As health care in the larger society becomes more expensive, these costs also affect prison systems that purchase goods and services in the health-care market (McDonald, 1995). Between 1980 and 1995 the national health-care expenditures increased by about 15 percent (Cowan, 2001). Although health-care expenditures have slowed with the shift to managed care, general health care costs are expected to continue to increase by 12–15 percent each year (Marquart et al., 1997; McDonald, 1995). Both state and federal prison systems will continue to face significant challenges in financing mandated health care to an aging prison population.

HEALTH OF OLDER INMATES

Health typically refers to the presence or absence of disease as well as the degree of disability in an individual's level of functioning. Understanding the health of the elderly prison population is a perplexing en-

Figure 4.1
Early Aging and Health-Care Expenditures

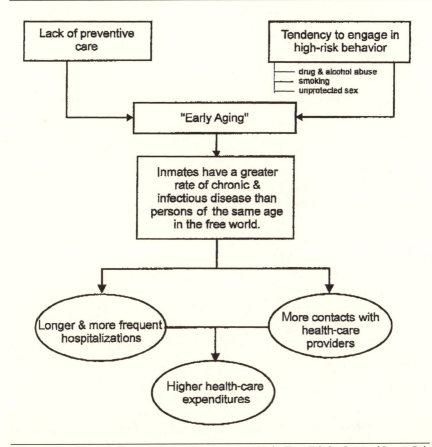

Source: Compiled from *Elder Offenders in Texas Prisons, 1999*, by Tony Fabelo, Criminal Justice Policy Council, Austin, Texas.

deavor. While rather comprehensive in nature, the majority of previous studies are nonrandom in nature. As I mentioned in Chapter 1, another problem that hinders the comparing of prison data is the failure of researchers to agree on an age definition of "older inmate." Common ages used to collect health data on older inmates includes ages 50, 55, 60, and 65. Finally, contributing to the complexity are the vast differences in prison populations and divergent prison settings within which studies have been conducted. For example, Morton (1992) noted that some aging inmates can be extremely healthy and robust at 70 while others will need medical assistance at age 50. Although the majority of older offenders currently reside among the normal prison population, numerous studies have focused only on those inmates assigned to a geriatric or special-needs unit. Such a specialized sample would not be representative of older inmates found among the general prison population.

The Michigan Study

Numerous studies have made valuable contributions to the understanding of the special health needs of the aging inmate. Douglass (1991), in an attempt to develop a profile representative of Michigan's prison population aged 60 or older, conducted personal interviews with 79 inmates housed in 13 correctional facilities. Selected under a systematic, stratified random sample procedure, the group is representative of a population of 440 prisoners aged 60 to 91. The sample represented 14 correctional facilities in the Michigan system. Only 5 percent of the sample rated their health as excellent and 78 percent rated their health as fair or good. When they compared their physical health conditions to what they were two years earlier, 24 percent indicated their health to be worse, 58 percent said it was the same, and 18 percent said it was better. Numerous older inmates were also taking over-the-counter pain medications (31.6 percent), prescription medications for pain (36.7 percent), high–blood-pressure medications (37.8 percent), and nitro tablets for chest pain (24.1 percent). Thirty-five percent reported having been hospitalized during the last year.

The Iowa Study

Colsher, Wallace, Loeffelholz, & Sales (1992) comprehensively studied the health and functional status of older inmates in Iowa state correctional facilities. Their sample of 119 men (81 percent of the target population) aged 50 years and older resided in 7 Iowa state correctional facilities. Although most (65 percent) rated their health as excellent or good, almost half reported that their health had worsened since incarceration. The sample reported a high incidence of chronic illness and many inmates reported limitations in physical functional ability, but most inmates were able to perform routine self-care activities. The physician-diagnosed illnesses reported by older inmates were arthritis (45 percent of the sample), hypertension (39 percent), ulcers (21 percent), prostate problems (20 percent), myocardial infarction (19 percent), emphysema (18 percent), and diabetes (11 percent). Age significantly correlated with chronic illness: Inmates 60 years of age or older reported consistently higher rates of chronic illness than inmates between the ages of 50 to 59.

The Mississippi Study

I conducted a similar analysis of the health of older inmates in Mississippi (Aday, 1995). This group of 102 inmates, with a mean age of 59, reported on average 3.1 chronic illnesses and indicated that they were taking an average of 2.6 medications daily. Although chronic illness was common and many older inmates reported limitations in functional ability, most inmates (75 percent) were able to perform routine self-care activities and engage in other prison activities. Again, hypertension, arthritis, and heart problems were the most common among inmates over the age of 50 in Mississippi. When asked to describe their health compared with others their age, 27 percent of respondents felt that their health was excellent or good. Another 28 percent stated that their health was only fair in comparison, while 45 percent rated it as poor compared with their cohort. In comparison to their own health of two years ago, only 8 percent of the sample felt it was better, 57 percent reported that it was about the same, and 32 percent indicated that it was worse. Only 11 percent of respondents expected their overall health to improve over the next two years. Twenty-eight percent expected no change in their health while 61 percent expected that their health would worsen over the next two years.

The Tennessee Study

With the assistance of Tennessee health services personnel, I conducted a survey of 318 inmates 60 years of age and over (mean age of 66) incarcerated in facilities in the Tennessee Department of Correction (Aday, 2001). The study provided a comprehensive health assessment for inmates in this age group. Eighty-three percent of the population was white, 16 percent African American, and 1 percent Hispanic. Of the 302 males and 16 females, 3.9 percent reported major medical conditions and consumed an average of 4.8 medications daily. As in other studies, hypertension was given as the most frequent health condition, followed by arthritis, heart disease, pulmonary disease, diabetes, and emphysema, respectively. Only about 5 percent required help with ADLs. Although most of the population was functionally independent, 20 percent of them required a cane, walker, crutches, or wheelchair for mobility. One-third were considered to be in an unstable chronic condition at the time the data were collected. Based on the information provided in previous studies (Aday, 2001; Aday, 1995; Douglass, 1991; Colsher et al., 1992), Table 4.1 was created to provide a summary of self-reported chronic illnesses by state. This comparison documents important trends in the health of older inmates. Arthri-

Table 4.1
Comparison of Older Inmate Chronic Illnesses by State

Health Condition	State			
	Iowa (n = 119)	Mich (n = 79)	Miss (n = 102)	Tenn (n = 318)
Arthritis	45.4	42.8	36.2	15.3
Hypertension	39.7	28.8	42.1	49.6
Venereal disease	21.6	7.6	****	****
Stomach ulcers	21.6	13.8	19.5	11.9
Prostate problems	21.0	21.1	16.4	3.1
Myocardial infarction	19.0	29.1	27.4	33.9
Pulmonary disease	****	****	****	25.4
Emphysema	20.2	22.5	15.5	15.0
Unitary track problems	****	16.5	11.7	14.0
Ulcers	****	13.8	17.6	11.8
Diabetes	11.2	5.1	15.6	16.6
Asthma	9.2	12.4	****	****
Stroke	7.8	6.3	10.1	****
Cancer	6.9	****	10.7	4.4
Cimhosis or liver disease	4.2	2.3	3.3	3.5

****Not reported.

From "Health Status of Older Male Prisoners: A Comprehensive Survey." (1992) by P. L. Colsher, R.B. Wallace, P.L. Loeffelholz, & M. Sales. *American Journal of Public Health*, 82, 881–884. "Oldtimers: Michigan's elderly population," by R.L. Douglass (1992), Unpublished report. (1999). Michigan Department of Corrections. From "A Preliminary Report on Mississippi's Elderly Prison Population," by R. Aday (1995), Parchman, MS: Mississippi Department of Corrections. "A Comprehensive Health Assessment of Aged and Infirm Inmates," by R. Aday, 2001, Tennessee Department of Corrections.

tis and hypertension are the two leading chronic illnesses for aging inmates. Of the 618 total inmates in the four samples, almost 40 percent reported various forms of arthritis and 39 percent reported high blood pressure to be a problem. In addition, heart problems, emphysema, stomach ulcers, and prostate problems each reportedly affect approximately 20 percent of the older inmates in these four samples. Urinary tract problems, diabetes, and asthma are present in 9–17 percent of the respondents who participated in the four separate studies.

Functional Health Status

The activities that older people can engage in, or think that they can engage in, are important indicators of both how healthy they are and what services and environmental changes they need in order to cope with their impairments. While the majority of aged individuals are able to function within the physical limitations of their body and continue to live to a healthy older age, severely disabled persons are often unable to carry on normal activities without assistance. The extent of disability and need for personal care increase with age. The most commonly used measure of functional health is the ADL. This instrument summarizes an individual's performance in personal care tasks such as taking a shower, dressing, using the toilet, eating, and getting in or out of bed or a chair. Other functional measures or Instrumental Activities of Daily Living (IADL) are taking medications, performing light work, keeping room or cell clean, taking care of one's own appearance, handling own money, walking to meals, and making phone calls.

In determining the functional status of inmates over age 60, Douglass (1991) conducted a functional assessment using a modified version of the ADL. Respondents were asked to place each routine activity into one of three categories: (1) able to do without help, (2) able to do with some help, or (3) completely unable to do. Almost all (98.7 percent) of the 79 older inmates needed some help with at least one category. The remaining respondent needed some help with five of Douglass's modified ADL activities. In the Tennessee sample, however, I found a higher level of functioning. Of the 318 inmates over the age of 60, only 17.6 percent reported needing help with at least one ADL (dressing, eating, bathing, and maintaining personal hygiene).

Table 4.2 provides detail on functional health in the Iowa and Michigan samples. While many of the items listed are not typically found in the most commonly used functional assessment tools, they are important indicators of self-care and coping ability.

Over one-third of older inmates in the Iowa sample report gross functional disabilities and more than two-thirds have impaired movement (Colsher et al., 1992). Chest pain, breathing problems, missing teeth, and difficulty in walking were frequently reported by both samples. Missing teeth, chewing problems, and swallowing problems 46.8 percent were contributing factors in the Michigan sample of respondents who regularly leave significant portions of their food uneaten. Douglass (1991) reported that these factors have resulted in a significant weight loss for 16.7 percent of these inmates.

Age, Race, and Health

The extent of disabilities and need for assistance in personal care activities increase with age. Typically, males are less likely to have ADL limitations and experience a smaller increase in disability with age than females (National Center for Health Statistics, 1995). In 1995 approximately

Table 4.2
Self-Reported Health and Functional Status, by State

Functional Status	% Reporting
Iowa Sample	**(n = 119)**
Chest pain	61.2
Low back pain	30.2
Any incontinence	21.6
Missing all teeth	38.7
Missing some teeth	58.7
Trouble hearing	16.8
Dependency with IADL's	20.7
Hearing aid	9.5
Gross functional disability	36.6
Routine self-care dependency	11.2
Isolated movement hindered	73.2
Michigan Sample	**(n = 79)**
Missing teeth	54.4
Shortness of breath	48.1
Regularly leave food uneaten	46.8
Chest pain	41.3
Breathing problems	39.2
Recent change in vision	39.0
Difficulty walking	30.4
Chewing problems	25.3
Constipation	24.1
Edema (hand/foot swelling) 21.5	
Urinary tract infection	16.7
Weight loss	16.7
Partial/total loss of arms/legs	13.9
Swollen, bleeding gums	13.9
Loss of arm/leg movement	13.9
Swallowing problems	6.3

From "Health Status of Older Male Prisoners: A Comprehensive Survey." (1992) by P.L. Colsher, R.B. Wallace, P.L. Loeffelholz, & M. Sales. *American Journal of Public Health*, 82, 881–884. "Oldtimers: Michigan's elderly population," by R.L. Douglass (1992), Unpublished report. (1999) Michigan Department of Corrections.

7.1 million persons 65 years or older needed some assistance in order to live independently in the community (including 10.5 percent of those age 65–79 and 51 percent of those over age 85). Those age 85 and older are four times as likely to require help as those 65 to 75 years of age (Hooyman & Kiyak, 1999).

McCarthy (1983) illustrates the gradual decline in health with advancing age. When inmates were asked to rate their recent health, 33 percent of the inmates between 55 and 64 years old rated themselves in poor health compared with 36.4 percent of those ages 70 to 74. For inmates 75 years and older, 44.4 percent rated their health as poor. The older the inmate, the more likely the self-perception of "going downhill." The results point to a gradual decline in health with advancing age. My own data support the view that increased age leads to a gradual decline in health and functional capabilities (Aday, 2001). When comparing inmates age 60–64 with those over the age of 65, I found that those in the latter category were more likely to have difficulties with mobility. They were viewed by staff as being frail, brittle, unstable, and weak, with a higher risk for victimization. This older group was also more likely to participate in special health needs consultations and was generally housed in close access to health services. While there were no differences in the number of major medical conditions, the oldest group required significantly more medication.

Initial analyses reported in the Iowa sample examined the differences in functional health status according to two age groups (50 to 59 years, 60 years and older). Table 4.3 provides a comparison of the age groups. Health problems were typically higher among inmates aged 60 years and older in the Iowa sample. Almost every health category showed a marked increase. This was not the case in the Mississippi sample (not shown) in which those over the age of 60 tended to be in better health and only a few health conditions showed an increase with age.

Few studies have addressed the variable of race when developing a profile of the aging prisoner. Falter (1999), when controlling for race, failed to find the variable as a significant indicator of health care utilization in the over-50-year-old population. In contrast, I found numerous measurable associations between race and health variables (Aday, 1995). Older Caucasian inmates did report significantly more chronic illnesses (mean = 3.9) than African Americans did (mean = 2.6). Caucasians also indicated that they were taking more medications (mean = 3.2) than the African American sample were (mean = 2.2). As Table 4.4 illustrates, with the exception of hypertension and diabetes, African Americans also reported fewer chronic health conditions than their Caucasian counterparts.

Infectious Diseases

Health problems are common among geriatric inmates, and added factors such as chronic medical illness or a history of drug or alcohol use play an important role in the infectious manifestations in this inmate group (Glaser, Warchol, D'Angelo, & Guterman, 1990). Various factors may predispose the elderly to such threats. The elderly are particularly susceptible to a variety of diseases that are spread within institutions. Numerous outbreaks of tu-

Table 4.3
Percentage of Male Inmates with History of Self-Reported Chronic Illnesses by Age (Iowa Sample)

Health Condition	Age 50-59 (n = 82)	> than 59 (n = 37)	Overall (n = 119)
Arthritis	40.2	56.8	45.4
Hypertension	36.7	45.9	39.7
Venereal disease	21.5	21.6	21.6
Stomach ulcers	18.3	27.0	21.6
Prostate problems	17.1	27.0	21.0
Myocrdial infarction	17.7	21.6	19.0
Emphysema	14.6	27.0	20.2
Diabetes	10.1	13.5	11.2
Asthma	8.5	10.8	9.2
Stroke	3.8	16.2	7.8
Cancer	6.3	8.1	6.9
Cimhosis or liver disease	4.9	2.7	4.2

From "Health Status of Older Male Prisoners: A Comprehensive Survey" (1992) by P.L. Colsher, R.B. Wallace, P.L. Loeffelholz, & M. Sales. *American Journal of Public Health*, 82, 881–884.

berculosis have occurred within jails and prisons (Braithwaite, Braithwaite, & Poulson, 1998). The risk of the spread of mycobacterium tuberculosis within the prison setting has increased significantly because of its relationship to the HIV infection (Snider & Hutton, 1989). Although younger inmates are more vulnerable to these diseases, primary cases of tuberculosis among the institutionalized elderly are not uncommon (Braithwaite, et al., 1998; Stead, 1981). The potential for intraprison spread of tuberculosis between HIV-infected and elderly prison inmates typically depends on the segregation policies in the institution. Currently, most fully functioning elderly inmates are integrated into the general prison population.

Various other viruses and infections contribute to the health threat among geriatric inmates. Airborne viruses such as influenza and respiratory viruses are common in this age group. Gastrointestinal infections have been frequently identified among the elderly (Falter, 1999). Food-borne gastroenteritis outbreaks may also occur when people are housed in close quarters. Hepatitis and pneumonia are other infections that can quickly strike the elderly. Elderly inmates with chronic diseases such as congestive heart failure, chronic lung disease, renal failure, cirrhosis, and diabetes are particularly vulnerable to infection and should receive appropriate vaccines. Elderly inmates are also at risk for tetanus, which can be caused by injury or breakdown of the skin among the elderly (Glaser et al., 1990).

Table 4.4
Percentage of Older Male Inmates with a Self-Reported History of Illnesses
by Race (Mississippi Sample)

Health Condition	Race Black (n=58)	White (n=44)	Overall (n=102)
Hypertension	46.7	35.0	42.1
Arthritis	29.0	47.5	36.2
Myocardial infarction	25.8	30.1	27.4
Emotional problems	14.5	27.5	19.5
Stomach/intestinal ulcers	12.9	25.0	17.6
Emphysema/Asthma	14.5	17.5	15.6
Diabetes	16.1	15.2	15.6
Injury requiring treatment	11.8	15.7	13.7
Hernia	11.2	15.0	12.8
Kidney disease	11.2	15.0	12.6
Urinary problems	8.0	17.5	11.7
Cataracts	9.6	15.0	11.4
Skin problems	6.5	17.5	10.7
Cancer	8.0	15.0	10.7
Stroke	8.5	12.5	10.1

From "A Preliminary Report on Mississippi's Elderly Prison Population," by R. Aday (1995), Parchman, MS: Mississippi Department of Corrections.

Older individuals are also more susceptible to urinary tract infections and prostate problems (Hooyman & Kiyak, 1999). Poor oral hygiene and frequency of cigarette smoking among inmates contribute to life-threatening diseases, particularly pulmonary infections (Ebersole & Hess, 1998). Infections are also common among inmates who require maintenance dialysis for end-stage renal failure. Glaser et al. (1990) found that inmates over the age of 50 receiving dialysis experienced complicating infections such as pneumonia, sepsis, and recurrent catheter-associated peritonitis. Sixty percent of these inmates required one or more hospitalizations from infectious side effects from dialysis.

HEALTH-CARE UTILIZATION

It has been reported that older prisoners are disproportionately heavy consumers of health-care services putting added pressure on correction officials. (McDonald, 1995; Smyer, Gragert, & LaMere, 1997). Inmates serving long sentences will have a major impact on institutional health programming, personnel, and budgets throughout their confinement (Marquart et al., 1997). The poor health condition of prisoners incarcerated late in life will only increase the demands for health care services over time and with age.

Falter (1999) investigated the health-care needs of inmates over 50 years of age in the federal correctional system. He reported that a random sample of 1,051 inmates with a mean age of 57, predominately male (93 percent), and mostly white (78 percent) showed frequent health care utilization because of hypertension, arteriosclerotic heart disease, diabetes, chronic obstructors pulmonary disease, and other chronic health conditions. Greater health-care utilization was also associated with greater age. Race and gender were not significant indicators of health-care utilization in federal inmates over 50 years old.

Contrary to these findings, I found that only 16 percent of the respondents in my study indicated that they go to sick call as frequently as once a week, 25 percent once or twice a month, 43 percent once every few months, and another 16 percent hardly ever (Aday, 1995). In my sample of 102 older inmates 50 years of age or older, Caucasians reported visiting a health clinic or doctor an average of 3.2 times each month compared with 2.2 times for their African American counterparts, a difference that proved to be statistically significant.

Douglass (1991) also discovered that a majority (53.2 percent) of a sample of older inmates in Michigan reported visiting a doctor in the previous three months. Almost 20 percent of this subgroup had seen a doctor from three to five times during that same period. About half of the total sample (49.4 percent) indicated that a health provider had assessed their physical and mental health. Among 318 inmates age 60 and above in Tennessee, I also found frequent utilization of health services (Aday, 2001). Of this group, 26 percent made frequent sick calls. A significant number of older inmates in this age category also required close access to other health resources. For example, 30 percent required consultations with specialists at the special needs comprehensive health facility, 20 percent had visited local emergency medical resources, and 11 percent had been admitted frequently to local community hospitals..

Contributors to greater demands for health-care services include socioeconomic status, race and ethnicity, education, lifestyle, and education. In particular, when coupled with age, these factors are known to affect the incidence and prevalence of morbidity and mortality. For example, House (1990) reported that the lowest socioeconomic stratum manifests a prevalence of chronic conditions at ages 35–44 that is not usually seen in the highest socioeconomic stratum until after age 75. In particular, the lowest socioeconomic groups manifest the greatest frequency of chronic conditions and accompanying limitations of functional capacity. Older inmates have typically been placed in the at-risk health category because they are frequently uneducated and underemployed and lead high-risk lifestyles, often involving excessive use of alcohol, tobacco products, and illicit drugs (Marquart et al., 1997). Many late offenders have had little systematic access to health care prior to incarceration. In partial corroboration, Black (1989) attributed poorer health among older inmates to the stress of prison life and the disadvantaged backgrounds of most inmates.

MENTAL HEALTH ISSUES

Mental disorders in later life are significant in number and have pervasive effects on older persons and those who are close to them. It is clear from examining the literature on the prevalence and distribution of mental disorders that much remains to be learned about risk factors, predictors of treatment response, and the general burdens of disability and dysfunction among older adults. While mental illness does not occur disproportionately often in later life, among certain subgroups mental disorders are more common.

Unfortunately, a significant number of the general population suffering from mental disorders is increasingly entering into the prison system. Correctional facilities in the United States currently house more mentally ill individuals than hospitals and mental institutions, and approximately 300,000 persons housed in state and federal prison facilities either have been found to suffer from a current mental condition or have stayed overnight in a mental hospital, medical unit, or treatment program (Ditton, 1999). It has also been further estimated that approximately 210,000 of those 300,000 individuals have severe mental illnesses (Vitucci, 1999). This number constitutes approximately 15 percent of state and federal prisoners identified as mentally ill.

Many of the aged suffer from mental or emotional disorders of one kind or another. The prevalence of psychiatric disorders among older persons who are living in the community is estimated at anywhere from 15 percent to 25 percent, the figure depending on the population and categories of disorders examined (Hooyman & Kiyak, 1999). People aged 65 and over currently account for about 15 percent of all residents in inpatient psychiatric facilities in the United States (Cockerham, 2000). Substance abuse problems (drugs and alcohol), anxiety disorders, and schizophrenia increase significantly in middle age. In old age, dementia becomes more prevalent. Of all resident patients in state and county mental hospitals, 26 percent have dementia as a primary diagnosis (National Institute of Mental Health, 1995).

In a national survey, Ditton (1999) discovered that offenders between the ages of 45 and 54 were the most likely age group to be classified as mentally ill. About 20 percent of state prisoners, 10 percent of federal prisoners, 23 percent of jail inmates, and 21 percent of probationers in Ditton's survey between the ages of 45 and 54 reported at least one mental illness. Rates were significantly lower for inmates under the age of 24. Inmates age 55 and older also exhibited frequent symptoms of mental illness. In this group, a little over 15 percent of state prisoners, 9 percent of federal prisoners, 20 percent of jail inmates, and 16 percent of probationers were identified as mentally ill. The highest rates of mental illness were among white females in state prisons. An estimated 29 percent of white females, 20 percent of black females, and 22 percent of Hispanic females in state prison were identified as mentally ill.

Koenig, Johnson, Bellard, Denker, & Fenlon (1995) found that depression, anxiety, and psychiatric disorders were much more common in a group of 95 male inmates over the age of 50 than among men in a similar community sample. The one-month prevalence of major depression was fifty times that in the community. Anxiety disorders such as generalized anxiety and simple phobia were also prevalent. Overall, 54 percent of the older inmates fit criteria for an active psychiatric disorder. Interestingly, most inmates with a greater prevalence of psychiatric disorders had been sentenced under the new determinate-sentencing law that eliminated any chance of parole. Inmates with a previous history of alcohol or drug abuse were also at greater risk of having a current psychiatric disorder.

Other studies have reported the presence of senile dementia in a substantial number of older inmates who were incarcerated late in life. One such study (Rosner, Wiederlight, Harmon, & Chan, 1991) was conducted on fifty-two defendants between the ages of 62 and 88 who were referred for assessment of their competence to stand trial. Thirty-two were 64 and under and 20 were age 65 and older. Eighty-three percent of the defendants were facing charges related to violent criminal offenses. The overwhelming majority were male, 21 were African American, 16 white, and 12 Hispanic. Three respondents classified themselves as Native American. Ten out of the 52 defendants, about 19 percent, were diagnosed with severe senile and arteriosclerotic dementia. Another 20 percent were also diagnosed with schizophrenic disorders. The remainder of the sample showed other disorders, such as atypical psychosis, adjustment disorders, and personality disorders. It should be pointed out that this study does have certain limitations. Not all geriatric offenders are caught, some are never arraigned, and not all those who are arraigned are referred for psychiatric evaluation. Therefore, the findings should be generalized with caution to the overall population of geriatric offenders. About half the elderly offenders in a similar study, conducted by Barak, Perry, and Elizur (1995), were diagnosed as suffering from a psychiatric disease or disorder.

Research has also suggested that life in correctional settings can be profoundly stressful (Faiver, 1998). Older inmates in particular have more stressors to contend with than younger inmates who have not experienced ill health or major changes in strength, vitality, and endurance (Booth, 1989). Vega and Silverman (1988) confirm the numerous health concerns and problems of older inmates as significant stressors. The noisy, physically strenuous environment of jail and prison, with frequent threats from younger inmates in addition, creates an ominous situation

Bachand (1984) has described the health of elderly inmates as compounded by excessive mental worry. This view is supported by McCarthy (1983), who described about half of a sample of 248 elderly offenders in Florida as "worriers." She reported that in her sample some inmates were concerned about their health or family members, while others worried about their safety or other issues related to incarceration. Worrying can aggravate the health of the incarcerated elderly frailties. According to McCarthy, depression and anxiety symptoms are common, but psychotic symptoms were less frequently reported and she found little evidence of cognitive impairment.

Other studies have explored the general mental outlook of older inmates in Mississippi and Michigan (Aday, 1995; Douglass, 1991). Inmates in these two samples were found to exhibit numerous indicators of depression. I found in my sample that over 75 percent of the older inmates indicated that they were sometimes or often restless, anxious about the future, helpless, bored with life, lonely, depressed, and unhappy. While Douglass's sample had a more positive outlook overall, 70 percent did indicate they sometimes or often experienced feelings of depression and unhappiness. An important contributor to this low satisfaction with life was poor health.

SATISFACTION WITH HEALTH CARE

The increasing number of aging inmates has put health-care providers in a dilemma, caught between the needs of the prisoners and the concerns of correctional staff to curb spending and maintain security. Responses to prison inmates vary from state to state and from prison to prison. The response of prisons to overburdened health-care resources is no different from that of nursing homes; some simply provide more comprehensive care than others. For the aging inmate, appropriate health care may be influenced heavily by early detection of illnesses, financial considerations, demands of overcrowding, adequately trained medical staff and personnel, patient's wishes, and public opinion. We have already discussed the fact that many inmates come to prison in poor health, which challenges the prison health-care system's medical resources. Many elderly offenders incarcerated for the first time bring unrealistic expectations from the free world. For example, they may expect to receive the same quality of health care in prison as they received on the outside. It can be a shock to see a different doctor each time they make a sick call.

A review of the literature on satisfaction with prison health care, sparse though it is, provides us with some useful information. A significant number of older inmates are very unhappy with the current medical care they receive (Schaefer, 1998). Over one-third of the respondents in the Michigan sample (Douglass, 1991) felt that they needed more medical care and treatment than they currently receive. About one in five reported physical problems or illnesses that tended to hinder their self-care. In McCarthy's (1983) Florida sample, dissatisfaction was even greater. Over half this sample (54 percent) believed that their health needs were not being adequately met. Almost half (48 percent) indicated that they needed more medical care than they were receiving at the time.

When conducting research in Mississippi, I asked prisoners to voice their opinion on whether they felt that the prison facility provided adequate health care (Aday, 1995). Thirty-six percent of the 102 respondents alleged that the correctional facility did not provide them with adequate health care. These responses were divided into five categories. Slightly over one-third (35 percent) wanted medical services to be more responsive at the time services were needed. Medication problems were the basis of 33 percent of the complaints and suggestions. Another 13 percent voiced complaints about food service in reference to inconsistency in time of arrival, lack of adequate nutrition, or general poor quality. More respect and consideration from the medical staff was a change suggested by 10 percent of respondents, and the need for more physical and other rehabilitative therapies was voiced by another 10 percent.

Other research has also presented older inmate concerns with prison health care (Aday & Nation, 2001; Schaefer, 1998). In one women's institution, 85 percent of older females voiced numerous complaints about prison health care. Major concerns included inadequate response to chronic health needs as well as a perception that reactions to emergencies were slow and uncaring. As a whole, this population seemed to distrust or lack confidence in the prison doctors administering health care. In some cases, they felt a second opinion from an outside doctor was warranted. Many felt that the doctors did not understand the special mental and physical health concerns of older females. More frequent exams and tests were also expressed as needs.

Other inmates' complaints were not getting their medication on time or being prescribed the wrong medication. Inmates also frequently complain about the ineffectiveness of generic medication and the frequency with which doctors prescribe Motrin, the inadequate response to diabetic inmates, and difficulty in getting eye exams and glasses (Aday & Nation, 2001; Schaefer, 1998). As a whole, aging inmates are cognizant of the need to maintain health-care costs in society in general. They feel the inadequate health care is, in part, a result of the prison's effort to curb health-care costs. The use of managed care in prison settings and the introduction of co-payments for visits to the infirmary are telling reminders.

HEALTH-CARE INTERVENTION

The special health concerns of aging inmates will require providers of health care in correctional facilities to refine their clinical skills in the diagnosis of infectious conditions. Health conditions in the incarcerated elderly may be difficult to detect and manage. Older inmates frequently respond to diseases differently from their younger counterparts. Pain, elevated temperature, redness, and swelling, which are classical signs and symptoms of infection in younger persons, do not necessarily present themselves with the same intensity in the elderly (Booth, 1989). For example, elderly inmates with pneumonia may present only a minimal cough, and physical examination rarely shows signs of consolidation (Bentley, 1984). Chest X-rays may not demonstrate typical findings in elderly patients with common bacterial pneumonia. Certain common chronic diseases may obscure the correct diagnosis of an acute infection.

The elderly are often underrepresented among the patients of mental health clinics. It has also been documented that there are few services for mentally ill offenders, and those that do exist are primarily on paper (McDonald & Teitelbaum, 1994). The inadequate psychological service to the elderly offender is incommensurate with the rise in psychological distress and disorders in that population. A number of barriers currently prohibit adequate clinical responses: Scarce resources and organizational constraints in the correctional setting make it difficult to conduct therapy. Treatment is often carried out in cramped conditions with little privacy. There is a general lack of understanding about how to organize, develop, and implement mental health services for elderly prisoners (Morris, Steadman, & Versey, 1997). Stereotypes of age from society at large impede doctor-

patient communication. Conflicts and ambivalence in the psychothera-
pists themselves about their own aging, parental figures, disease, and death
can compromise professionalism (Poggi & Berland, 1985).

Many correctional therapists work under conditions that make mental
disorders difficult to identify. A lower than acceptable detection rate is likely
even with severe mental illness (Teplin, 1990). Accurate diagnosis can be
complicated by a number of factors. First, counselors may have difficulty
differentiating normal aging effects from symptoms of depression or mild
dementia. Apathy, forgetfulness, and disinterest may be seen as signs of advancing age. A second factor that complicates diagnosis is differentiating
symptoms of a physical disorder from those of a functional mental disorder
(Ebersole & Hess, 1998). The scope of this problem is highlighted by the
fact that the majority of older offenders have, on average, three chronic diseases and most take three or more medications on a daily basis (Aday, 2001).

A third complicating factor is the age-related differences in the manifestation of psychopathology (Rubin, Kinscherf, & Morris, 1993). For example, one problem with detecting depression in older people is that they
may be more successful than younger people at masking or hiding symptoms. Numerous cases of depression in older persons are not diagnosed because the individual either does not express mood changes or denies them
in the clinical interview. This has often been the case with aging prisoners, who frequently insist that they are highly satisfied with life (Chaiklin,
1998). What the inmate may very well complain of, however, are health
problems, sleep disturbance, apathy, and withdrawal from others. These
are common responses in older people when open expression of feelings
are not socially acceptable (Hooyman & Kiyak, 1999).

Ineffective communication between the elderly inmate and health-care
providers can contribute to inadequate physical and mental health care.
Geriatric inmates may underreport illness or fail to seek medical evaluation for acute affections. Older inmates may not be fully educated about
their symptoms or may be fearful of diagnostic outcomes. Some elderly inmates may be disoriented from illness, such as acute pneumonia or dementia. Booth (1989) has also pointed out that when incarcerated elderly
feign illness regularly they are at a greater risk of receiving an inadequate
medical response because of their reputations as malingerers. A delay in
diagnosis for numerous diseases can very well contribute to greater morbidity within the geriatric prison population. Health-care providers in correctional facilities must improve their assessment, diagnostic abilities, and
communication skills when working with older offenders.

The quality of interaction is essential in determining inmate satisfaction
and performance. However, no matter how well trained or prepared the cli-

nician is, some "toxic agers" can be almost impossible to work with (Davenport, 1999). About 10 percent of the older population are both "old and ornery" (McShane & Williams, 1990). Davenport (p. 39) describes toxic people as "those who do not take responsibility for their lives. They manipulate others. And the more self-control they relinquish, the more they become blaming, vindictive, suspicious, hostile, and critical. Toxics are more than difficult; they will destroy a group, program or plan in seconds."

A final challenge to overcome in responding effectively to older inmates is what to do when disturbed older offenders refuse treatment (Chaiklin, 1998). Older adults are generally unwilling to interpret their problems as psychological, preferring to attribute them to physical or social conditions (Hooyman & Kiyak, 1999). The current cohort of older persons may be less oriented to using mental health services because of societal stigmas, limited knowledge about mental disorders, and a lack of confidence in mental health workers. Older inmates may frequently refuse to take the medication necessary to alter their behavior. Although the courts currently support involuntary treatment, La Fond (1994) has suggested that we should prohibit the use of involuntary treatment for punishment. It is important to define whether the patient is dangerous to self or others.

HEALTH PROMOTION

With a social climate that is deeply concerned with the high cost of prison health care, the need for programs that deal with health promotion and wellness is evident (Glaser, et al., 1990; McDonald, 1995; Merianos, Marquart, Damphousse, & Hebert, 1997). Fitzgerald, D'Atri, Kasi, & Ostfeld (1984) have documented that although the yearly rate of visits to a health clinic for prison inmates is five times as great as the rate for patients of similar age in the general population, inmates make only 30 percent as many visits for diagnostic, screening, and preventive services. Hooyman and Kiyak (1999) further estimate that only 6 percent of the national health-care dollar as a whole is spent on prevention and early detection. It has been noted that the trend is similar in prison settings with the bulk of the health care dollars going for accute and chronic health care treatments (Aday, 1994; McDonald, 1995).

As an increasing number of inmates serve longer sentences, preventive care programs are being developed by some correctional systems. According to the National Institute of Corrections (1997), chronic care clinics are becoming increasingly popular for prison health care planners. Older male and females with chronic disease or disorders frequently receive continuity of care through systemwide programs that provide appropriate care, monitoring of complications, and follow-up. Chronic care clinics treat cardio-vascular disease, hypertension, diabetes, infectious disease, seizure disorders, and asthma and respiratory problems, to mention a few. Educational programs that stress to prisoners the importance of smoking cessation, keeping one's weight near the ideal, getting adequate rest, and maintaining moderate levels of aerobic exercise have been introduced in several states. Ohio, in particular, has been instrumental in developing health education classes and other health promotion activities (see Chapter 6). The frequency of conducting chronic care clinics varies by penal system; programs are conducted weekly or monthly, bimonthly, or less, the frequency depending on the nature of the illness. The clinics provide patient education and counseling on self-care. These programs of preventive care are far less costly and less time consuming and can prevent painful illness rather than having to treat it.

Increasing the emphasis on self-care is one initiative that has been projected as a possible solution to the ever-growing threats on the health of older adults and the increasing cost of medical care. Correctional officials are beginning to recognize that encouraging older adults to make knowledgeable choices about medical services and individual health practices can reduce unnecessary and expensive medical care in prison. Older inmates practicing more self-care can bridge the gap between health-care needs of elders and the present expensive health-care system.

SUMMARY

The mission of the prison health-care system is clear and concise. The law mandates reasonable accommodations and program accessibility for persons with disabilities and other chronic health conditions. The basic premise of this system of health care is that prisons are comprehensive communities. Like most communities, prisons include persons with serious illnesses who have both ongoing and emergency needs for health services. It is important to reduce the unnecessary extremes of human suffering caused by mental and physical health symptoms. To be most effective, health services should be individualized, with treatment plans or a case management approach for every recipient. Health promotional programs and screening services in community-based settings have led to fewer disabling chronic conditions and the accompanying dependency, and such programs should have a similar outcome in a prison setting.

In spite of wellness programs, older inmates continue to be disproportionately heavy consumers of health-care services. Accommodating offenders with special needs requires a wide variety of services, medical equipment, staff, and protected environments. Increasingly, inmates coming into prison need immediate medical services. Like inmates in general, aging prisoners have not had proper access to health care on the outside. They come into the prison system with numerous chronic illnesses and consume multiple medications. As the number of older inmates increases, correctional systems will be even more challenged to provide adequate physical and mental health services.

REFERENCES

Aday, R.H. (1994). Golden years behind bars: Programs and facilities for the geriatric inmate. *Federal Probation, 58*(2), 47–54.

Aday, R.H. (1995). *A preliminary report on Mississippi's elderly prison population.* Parchment, MS: Mississippi Department of Corrections.

Aday, R.H. (2001). *A comprehensive health assessment of aged and infirm inmates.* Nashville, TN: Tennessee Department of Correction.

Aday, R.H., & Nation, P. (2001). *A case study of older women in prison.* Nashville: Tennessee Department of Correction.

Alligood, L. (1988, August 10). On older inmates' aches, pains: A challenge for health officials. *The Nashville Banner,* p. 6.

Anderson, J.C., & Morton, J.B. (1989). Graying of the nation's prisons presents new challenges. *Aging Connection, 10,* 6–7.

Appleby, C. (1997). Going private to capture prison health care savings. *Hospitals and Health Networks, 71*(10), 70–72.

Bachand, D.J. (1984). *The elderly offender: An exploratory study with implications for continuing education of law enforcement personnel.* Unpublished doctoral dissertation, University of Michigan, Ann Arbor.

Barak, Y., Perry, T., & Elizur, A. (1995). Elderly criminals: A study of the first criminal offense in old age. *International Journal of Geriatric Psychiatry, 10,* 511–516.

Bentley, D. (1984). Bacterial pneumonia in the elderly: Clinical features, diagnosis, etiology and treatment. *Journal of Gerontology, 30,* 297–307.

Beyerlein, T. (1997, April 27). Prison grays. *Dayton Daily News,* p. 1A, 4A.

Black, C. (1989, June 12). Aging behind bars: Effects of the graying of America's prisons. *The Boston Globe,* p. 5B-8B.

Booth, D. (1989). Health status of the incarcerated elderly: Issues and concerns. *Journal of Offender Counseling, Services and Rehabilitation, 13,* 193–214.

Braithwaite, R.L., Braithwaite, K., & Poulson, R. (1998). HIV and TB in prison. *Corrections Today, 60*(2), 108–112.

Caniglia, J. (1996, October 13). Old outlaws: When bad boys get old, the cost of caring for them in prison. *Elyria, Ohio, Chronicle-Telegram,* 1A, 3A.

Chaiklin, H. (1998). The elderly disturbed prisoner. *Clinical Gerontologist, 20*(1), 47–62.

Cockerham, W.C. (2000). *This aging society.* Upper Saddle River, NJ: Prentice-Hall.

Colsher, P.L., Wallace, R.B., Loeffelholz, P.L., & Sales, M. (1992). Health status of older male prisoners: A comprehensive survey. *American Journal of Public Health, 82,* 881–884.

Cowan, C.A. (2001, Summer). National health expenditures, 1999. *Health Care Financing Review, 22,* 77–301.

Cushing, M. (1986, December). Who says prisoners have a right to health care? *American Journal of Nursing, 86,* 1333–1334.

Davenport, G.M. (1999). *Working with toxic older adults.* New York: Springer.

Ditton, P.M. (1999). *Mental health and treatment of inmates and probationers.* Washington, DC: Bureau of Justice Statistics.

Douglass, R.L. (1991). *Oldtimers: Michigan's elderly prisoners.* Lansing: Michigan Department of Corrections.

Ebersole, P., & Hess, P. (1998). *Toward healthy aging.* St. Louis: Mosby.

Faiver, K.L. (1998). Special issues of aging. In K.L. Faiver (Ed.), *Health care management issues in corrections* (pp. 123–132). Lanham, MD: American Correctional Association.

Falter, R.G. (1999). Selected predictors of health service needs of inmates over age 50. *Journal of Correctional Health Care, 6,* 149–175.

Fitzerald, E.F., D'Atri, D.A., Kasi, S.V., & Ostfeld, A.M. (1984). Health problems in a cohort of male prisoners at intake and during incarceration. *Journal of Prison and Jail Health, 4,* 61–76.

Gallagher, E.M. (1990). Emotional, social, and physical health characteristics of older men in prison. *International Journal of Aging and Human Development, 31,* 251–266.

Glaser, J.B., Warchol, A., D'Angelo, D., & Guterman, H. (1990). Infectious diseases of geriatric inmates. *Reviews of Infectious Diseases, 12,* 683–692.

Haberman, E.L. (2001, August). Mission seemingly impossible: Community place of chronic inmates. *Corrections Today, 63,* 115–118.

Henderson, C.W. (1998, November). Prison inmates wants kidney transplant. *Transplant Weekly, 8,* 1–2.

Holman, J.R. (1997, March–April). Prison care: Our penitentiaries are turning into nursing homes. Can we afford it? *Modern Maturity, 40,* 30–36.

Hooyman, N., & Kiyak, H.A. (1999). *Social gerontology.* Boston: Allyn & Bacon.

House, J. (1990). Age, socioeconomic status, and health. *The Milbank Quarterly, 68,* 383–411.

King, L. (1981). Morbidity and mortality among prisoners: An epidemiologic review. *Journal of Prison Health, 1,* 7–29.

Koenig, H.G., Johnson, S., Bellard, J., Denker, M., & Fenlon, R. (1995). Depression and anxiety disorder among older male inmates at a federal correctional facility. *Psychiatric Services, 46*(4), 399–401.

La Fond, J.Q. (1994, April). Law and the delivery of involuntary mental health services. *American Journal of Orthopsychiatry, 64,* 209–223.

Marquart, J. W., Merianos, D. E., Herbert, J. L., Carroll, L. (1997). Health condition and prisoners: A review of research and emerging areas of inquiry. *Prison Journal, 77*, 184–208.

McCarthy, M. (1983, February). The health status of elderly inmates. *Corrections Today, 45*, 64, 65, 74.

McDonald, D.C. (1995). *Managing prison health care and costs*. Washington, DC: National Institute of Justice, U.S. Department of Justice.

McDonald, D.C., & Teitelbaum, M. (1994). *Managing mentally ill offenders in the community: Milwaukee's community support program*. Washington, DC: U.S. Department of Justice.

McShane, M. D., & Williams, F. P., III. (1990). Old and ornery: The disciplinary experiences of elderly prisoners. *International Journal of Offender Therapy and Comparative Criminology, 34*(3), 197–212.

Merianos, D. E., Marquart, J. W., Damphousse, K. & Hebert, J. L. (1997). From the outside in: Using public health data to make inferences about older inmates. *Crime and Delinquency, 43*, 298–313.

Morton, J. B. (1992). *An administrative overview of the older inmate*. Washington, DC: U.S. Department of Justice.

National Center for Health Statistics. (1995). Current estimates from the National Health Interview Survey: U.S. 1994. *Vital and Health Statistics*, series 10. Washington, DC: National Center for Health Statistics.

National Institute of Corrections. (1997). *Prison medical care: Special needs populations and cost control*. Washington, D.C.: U.S. Department of Justice.

Novick, L. (1987). Health services in prison. *Journal of Community Health, 12*(1), 1–3.

Pelosi, A. (1997). Age of innocence: A glut of geriatric jailbirds. *New Republic, 216*(18), 15–18.

Poggi, R. G., & Berland, D. I. (1985). The therapists' reactions to the elderly. *Gerontologist, 25*, 508–513.

Rosefield, H. A. (1993). "The older inmate: Where do we go from here?" *Journal of Prison and Jail Health, 12*, 51–58.

Rosner, R., Wiederlight, M., Harmon, R. B., & Cahan, D. J. (1991). Geriatric offenders examined at a forensic psychiatry clinic. *Journal of Forensic Sciences, 36*, 1722–1731.

Rubin, E. H., Kinscherf, D. A., & Morris, J. C. (1993). Psychopathology in younger versus older persons with very mild and mild dementia of the Alzheimer type. *American Journal of Psychiatry, 140*, 639–642.

Schaefer, M. S. (1998). *Older inmates: Caring for this growing population*. Unpublished master's thesis. New Mexico State University, Las Cruces.

Shapiro, S., & Shapiro, M. (1987). Identification of health care problems in a county jail. *Journal of Community Health, 12*(1), 23–30.

Smith, P. W. (1984). Epidemic investigation. In P. W. Smith (Ed.), *Infection control in long-term care facilities* (pp. 169–203). New York: Wiley.

Smyer, T., Gragert, M. D., & LaMere, S. H. (1997). Stay safe! Stay healthy! Surviving old age in prison. *Journal of Psychosocial Nursing, 35*(9), 10–17.

Snider, D. E., & Hutton, M. D. (1989). Tuberculosis in correctional institutions. *Journal of the American Medical Association, 261*, 436–437.

Specter, D. (1994). Cruel and unusual punishment of the mentally ill in California prisons: A case study of a class action suit. *Social Justice, 21*, 109–118.

Stead, W. W. (1981). Infections in nursing homes. *New England Journal of Medicine, 324*, 302–306.

Teplin, L. A. (1990). Detecting disorder: The treatment of mental illness among jail detainees. *Journal of Consulting and Clinical Psychology, 58*, 233–236.

Tofig, D. (1997, February 18). Aging behind bars: Connecticut's prisons house an increasing number of over-50 inmates. *The Hartford Courant*, p. A1, A-10.

Vega, M., & Silverman, M. (1988). Stress and the elderly convict. *International Journal of Offender Therapy and Comparative Criminology, 32*, 153–162.

Vitucci, J. (1999). Inmates with severe mental health increasing in jails and prisons. *CorrectCare, 13*, 1, 4.

Weinstein, H. C. (1990, January–February). Psychiatric services in jails and prisons: Who Cares? *CorrectCare, 4*, 1, 7.

Chapter 5

Adjustment to Prison Life

Most inmates come to prison with few coping skills. They have shown poor judgment in dealing with choices or in structuring their lives on the outside. Many older prisoners have little formal education, are in poor health, have little family support, and have frequently abused drugs and alcohol. Unfortunately, prison does not necessarily enhance one's ability to cope. In fact, prison frequently magnifies the problems that bring people to prison in the first place. Zamble and Porporino (1988) have suggested that inmates without previous prison experience cope better on the inside than those with prior experience. Moore (1989) further suggests that while the needs of elderly inmates are the same as those of any other prison population, they are more critical. Aging inmates have less ability to cope, and trying to accommodate those specialized needs in the typical prison setting adds complexity to the problem. Little research has been conducted on coping strategies of aging prisoners.

A greater understanding of this "forgotten inmate" is important for developing policies that are cost-effective. Up to this point, correctional agencies have neither anticipated nor responded to the challenge of the increase in long-term inmate populations (Flanagan, 1992) nor to the increase in those entering prison for the first time late in life (Yates & Gillespie, 2000). A number of researchers have suggested that the diversity of the older offender must be recognized and incorporated into our rehabilitative programs (Kratcoski, 2000; Smyer, Gragert, & LaMere, 1997; Vito & Wilson, 1985). For example, some older inmates who are ideal candidates to return to society will need programs that assist in making this transition a successful one. Other aging inmates will simply need a protective prison environment conducive to their growing old and dying in prison. In this case, health and wellness programs targeted for this group could, in the long run, reduce the demand for chronic health care.

This chapter will provide a general profile of the aging prisoner as well as the distinguishing differences in the older offender types. Addressed here will be the transitional issues that face elderly offenders as they enter prison for the first time in old age as well as the consequences of long-term imprisonment and how this subgroup copes with extended confinement. This discussion will involve the various losses encountered in the prison setting, including the loss of outside relationships, declining health, and issues related to dying in prison. The final section will focus on building a life in prison and the importance of various prison activities that serve to provide aging prisoners with "a home away from home." The importance of prison friendships, religious activities, and work are introduced as important indicators of successful adjustment to prison life.

NEW ELDERLY OFFENDERS

Regardless of the type of crime committed and the criminal history of the older offender, being in prison and being elderly is not easy. Simply coping with the aging process itself can be difficult for many older adults. Previous research that has focused on the effects of institutional and personal factors on the adjustment of older inmates to incarceration seems to support the notion that older inmates and certain subgroups of them exhibit different adjustment patterns. Although sparse, research has addressed the unique problems facing the various older offender types, including new elder offenders. To explore the transition to prison life, I conducted a case study of twenty-five new elderly offenders with a mean age of 68 serving time in a southeastern prison (Aday, 1994). My research found for the "new elderly" offender a number of stressors associated with entering a maximum-security prison for the first time late in life. Older inmates frequently indicated that they experience a type of culture shock. As one older inmate noted, "I was in a state of mind when I first came in that I couldn't even think. . . . When I first came into prison, I was more like a vegetable. . . . I was a complete stranger to myself" (Aday, p. 84). Similarly, Santos (1995, p. 39) noted that "prison is where you meet shock, hopelessness, helplessness, fear, depression, hate, extreme sadness, coldness, and loneliness all at once. It all hits like a freight train, and no one can help." Most inmates describe this transition to prison as "doing hard time."

Other elderly new offenders reported that one of the first tasks is overcoming a variety of stigmas associated with late-life incarceration. Having lived the majority of their lives as model citizens with no prior arrests, overcoming the shame of engaging in criminal activity can prove challenging. Since most new elderly offenders are incarcerated for violent crimes such as murder or sexual crimes, societal reactions can be harsh. For example, when sexual crimes are committed against young family members, conflicts with the family are typical. Indicators of guilt, depression, and shame are frequently evident in first offenders. As one new elderly offender mentioned during our conversation "Living the lie that got me here.... What people will think about me that know me is the most difficult problem I've had to overcome" (Aday, 1994, p. 84). Numerous inmates discussed their thoughts about suicide, and one inmate refused to eat and was confined to a wheelchair during his first month in prison. A frequent pattern for some older inmates is simply to withdraw in a depressive state and to hide from their pain.

Old, frail, and vulnerable, these offenders usually come into the prison system fearful of victimization. First-timers may be particularly vulnerable to intimidation by other younger and stronger inmates. Going into prison for this group of aging offenders is like moving to a foreign country. Prison offers a new subculture; a new set of rules, and language that can be most overwhelming for mentally fragile inmates who may not fully grasp why they are incarcerated. For the first time in their lives, older individuals are now in a system in which they must submit to orderly routine and uncreative occupation and in which they exercise very little self-determination. Prior to imprisonment, elderly prisoners typically had established lifelong routines and familiar patterns for coping. They are accustomed to living, working, and playing with separate groups of people. Prison life does not permit a separation of these facets of life. Isolated from free society late in life, many older inmates are aware of their social rejection, experiencing frustration and loss of hope.

I also found that whether the prisoner maintains close relationships with family members on the outside depends on a variety of factors, including crime history. Some new elderly offenders report being divorced by their wives after having committed sexual crimes or other violent crimes against family members. One sexual offender who has a 12-year-old son with his wife indicated that he would not return to his family because of the charges filed by his stepdaughter. New offenders frequently express feelings of having let their families down and are shameful to be in such a "fix" at their age. Generally, these feelings are associated with classic depressive symptoms, and inmates report frequent episodes of crying and feelings of restlessness and emptiness. Inmates in this psychological state frequently engage in excessive sleep patterns and remain highly passive. Others may experience episodes of anxiety and may have difficulty remaining calm and under control. The result can be toxic behavior aimed at the staff or other inmates in close proximity.

Of course, not everyone reacts in exactly the same way to the dehumanizing effects of institutionalization. For example, some elderly people make smooth transitions to nursing home life while others react quite negatively to it. Likewise, not all correctional institutions exert the same impact (Stinchcomb & Fox, 1999). It should also be mentioned that some inmates simply have better coping skills than others. Older inmates who have accepted the fact that they should receive some punishment for the crime committed may adjust better. As one female in her 60s stated, "I committed a horrible crime....I had a nervous breakdown and killed my mother-in-law. I must be punished for my crime and have accepted that I will die here. Other inmates complain about the health care here, but it's not all that bad" (Aday & Nation, 2001, p. 15). Another older inmate compared prison life with the starting of a new job. In other words, you become integrated into a new social structure and through a process of socialization you adjust to your new position in life. Some inmates look for the advantages of imprisonment late in life. As one older inmate indicated, "There is no rent here and no food bills" (Williams, 1989, p. 42). Another aging inmate also painted a positive picture of prison when he stated, "I have a sister in a nursing home and it is costing her over $2000 a month. ...Look at that and look at how I am. What I got is hard to beat and it don't cost me nothing" (Williams, p. 43).

For some, then, prison may serve as a haven or a place of safety from the dangerous elements of life in the "free" world. Despite criticisms of prison life, I found the majority of new elderly offenders making a successful transition to prison life (Aday, 1994, p. 88). Contributing to this satisfaction was the favorable reaction to being grouped with similar inmates for safety and support. As one inmate stated, "I'm just happy to be here and alive." This inmate was generally happy with his life even though he felt he would continue to be imprisoned five years from now. Another felt relief that he was incarcerated. "If I was on the outside, I would probably be dead by now." Finally, an older sex offender serving a ten-year sentence summed up the notion of prison becoming a home away from home (Aday, 1994):

Not long ago I sat down and analyzed my situation. Heck, I couldn't work outside, and I certainly wouldn't like having nothing to do. I'm better off here than I would be anywhere else ... I have friends in here, and I get along with most everybody....My medications and everything are there when I need them. . . . I can't complain about the price either. . . . If they'd let me take off a week and spend it with my family, I'd come back happy as a lark. (p. 89)

In this way, prison for some new elderly offenders may present an alternative as good as or better than life on the outside. Rapidly declining health would force many to trade the prison environment for a nursing home bed, and most would probably choose a prison setting over the nursing home if the prison environment is sheltered. Coming from a lifestyle filled with poverty and lacking access to health care, older inmates are frequently unaccustomed to the regular food, medicine, housing, and clothing now readily available. For many, prison life can actually be a significant improvement in their standard of living.

LONG-TERM INMATES

Previous studies have noted that long-term inmates frequently constitute a one-dimensional group whose reactions to incarceration would form a consistent pattern of adjustment (Richards, 1978; Sapsford, 1978). Other researchers have stressed the importance of considering personal characteristics that might lead to differences in adjustment patterns (Cohen & Taylor, 1972; Flanagan, 1982; Wikberg & Foster, 1990). For example, many older chronic offenders enter prison with previous knowledge of the prison milieu. They may have already spent a significant portion of their adult life behind bars. As discussed in the previous section, first-time offenders imprisoned for the first time late in life may react very differently to the process of incarceration. Of course, current sentencing laws, will cause these inmates, in time, to become long-termers, and many will eventually die in prison.

Flanagan (1982) makes the argument that long-termers include various subgroups of offenders with diverse backgrounds and presumably different needs:

Data on the criminal histories of long-term prisoners indicate that diversity is a hallmark of this group. It includes career criminal robbers in whose lives before imprisonment crime was a daily activity and who adapt to incarceration by continuing careers of deceit and violence. In contrast, other long-term prisoners are essentially noncriminal individuals, whose act of violence was unprecedented and is unlikely to be repeated, and whose interest and perspectives within the prison coincide more closely with those of the officers than those of fellow inmates. Although murderers make up a large percentage of long-term prisoners, the motives, justifications, and behaviors that are incorporated under the "homicide" label are themselves of broad scope. (p. 82–83)

Figure 5.1
State Prison #4017

Source: Cartoon courtesy Sandy Campbell, *The Tennessean*, April 10, 1994.

It is important to recognize the existence of long-term offenders who by virtue of their personal characteristics will have different social needs and orientations to prison life. This perspective is emphasized by recent sentencing reforms that have led to significantly longer sentences in many states (Anderson, 1997). While the inmate who has served a complete life sentence for one crime is relatively rare, every prison system has its share of long-termers, which account for about half the prison population over the age of 55 (Beck, 1997). Somehow these old inmates have slipped through the cracks and stayed in prison while most of their partners in crime were released and resumed their lives in the free world. Referred to as the forgotten minority or the long-termers, they have spent a significant portion of their lives behind bars. More often than not, these inmates are model inmates with excellent patterns of behavior in prison.

Dugger (1990) has proposed that long-term inmates can be grouped into five categories: (1) younger inmates with long sentences, (2) middle-aged inmates, frequently career criminals, with long sentences, (3) inmates who have grown old in prison, (4) inmates who were old when sentenced, usually for either murder or sexual crimes, and (5) female offenders with long sentences. Wikberg and Foster (1989) profiled twenty-five long-termers whose terms exceeded twenty-five years and pointed to numerous examples of other inmates convicted of similar crimes who were freed years before. The authors found that one or a combination of four factors set the inmates apart from others convicted of similar crimes but released long before: (1) A record of frequent, serious prison misconduct, (2) strong opposition to release by the victim of the crime, (3) a lack of outside assistance for the prisoner upon release, or (4) a lack of serious effort by the inmate to win release.

An aging long-termer imprisoned today typically is someone who entered prison as a poor young male, is usually black, and committed a violent crime such as murder or rape. Legally ignorant and undereducated, the defendant is often poorly served by an appointed counsel. At trial, the defendant generally pleaded guilty, was convicted, and was given a life sentence. For years the inmate may have made only a minimal effort to be released. The inmate did his time, worked, and settled into the prison routine. His family now has forgotten him or is unable to help. The only ones who remember are his victims and legal system officials (Flanagan, 1985).

CONSEQUENCES OF IMPRISONMENT

Because an increasing number of prisoners will spend most of their adult lives in prison, it is important to examine some of the models that attempt to explain the consequences associated with institutional confinement. To better determine the impact of social structures on the institutional adjustment of this population, it is important to keep in mind the diversity in the prison population as well as the diversity in prison environments. Prisons' "geriatric facilities" that provide a wide range of special programming for aging inmates could have fewer detrimental effects. The variations in the degree of security may influence the special needs and eventual adjustment of older inmates (Walsh, 1990).

The Concept of Prisonization

One of the most serious attempts to understand the effects of incarceration has been provided by Donald Clemmer in his work *The Prison Community* (1958). Clemmer described the culture and social organization of the prison and coined the concept of prisonization to summarize the consequences of exposure to inmate society. He formally defined prisonization as "the taking on, in greater or lesser degree, of the folkways, mores, customs and general culture of the penitentiary" (p. 287). Clemmer saw prisonization as a specific illustration of more general processes of assimilation occurring wherever persons are introduced to an unfamiliar culture. He believed that every individual is subject to certain influences, which he referred to as the "universal factors" of prisonization. Clemmer devoted a good deal of attention to variables that he thought influenced both the speed and the degree of prisonization. The feature that Clemmer thought most important in determining the degree of prisonization was simply the degree of close interpersonal contact with other inmates in the prison environment.

Although Clemmer concentrated on the process of induction into the prison community, he failed to address changes that might occur as inmates neared the time for release. Clemmer's investigation did examine the length of time served and the socialization processes within the prison environment and, particularly, the relationship between what an inmate experiences within the prison and his attachment to the outside world. Neither did his construct deal specifically with phases of institutional career important to the study of old prisoners. For example, although he indicates that age and criminality are important determinants of prisonization, he neglects to explicitly integrate them into his models. Clemmer's study failed to consider the unique characteristics of the older prisoner and his relationship to the later stages of the life cycle.

Other researchers have shared Clemmer's view, focusing on the inmate subculture that developed around shared "pains of imprisonment" (Sykes, 1958). This portrayal of prison life has been described as the "deprivation" model and has received mixed empirical support (Hemmens & Marquart, 2000). Other researchers have attributed the process of prison assimilation to the attributes and experiences that inmates brought with them to prison. For example, Wright (1988) has taken the position that it is not simply the prison structure itself that matters most, but rather the subtle ways each prisoner uses to socially construct a meaningful life in prison. Other researchers have examined a variety of factors external to prison, including age, race, socioeconomic class, and criminal history. For this approach, referred to as the importation model, there is considerable empirical support (Lawson, Segrin, & Ward, 1996). It is recommended that an integration of theories might be better suited to explain the consequences of prison rather than utilize a single mode such as "prisonization."

Process of Depersonalization

A review of the literature reveals numerous references to the potentially detrimental impact of long-term confinement (Mackenzie & Goodstein, 1985). The concept of "institutional dependency" has been used to describe the psychosocial effects of long-term incarceration. Correctional staff and prisoners frequently use this concept to describe a process involving such reactions as losing interest in the outside world, losing touch with family and friends on the outside, losing the ability to make independent decisions, relying on the institution for health care and other social support needs, viewing the prison as home, and, in general, viewing oneself totally within the institutional context (Aday, 1995; Ham, 1980; Krebs, 2000). This point is illustrated by excerpts from a letter written by William Heirens, a convicted murderer, who has been confined to Illinois prisons since age 17. Heirens was imprisoned in 1946. World War II had just ended and GIs were returning home.

> The most debilitating thing about spending a long time in prison is becoming institutionalized and that happens when you cut yourself off from the outside so that your thoughts are all about your life in prison. In other words, you learn to cope with the prison environment but can no longer cope with life outside prison.... I have seen this happen many times with prisoners who have been kept incarcerated too long.... These people were institutionalized; their family were the fellow prisoners left behind.... The hardest time in coming to prison is the first couple of years as that is the period in which one learns to cope and the same can be said on leaving prison—it takes a couple of years to learn to cope in a free society. (Kline, 1999)

Another long-term inmate who has served 41 years in a West Virginia prison provides a similar illustration of the process of institutionalization (Kline, 1999): "I don't think I deserve to be out, the kind of crime I committed. I don't think I could make it out there by myself. I've got high blood pressure and arthritis. I couldn't do much. I wouldn't want to be a burden upon anybody."

A variety of terms, usually negative in connotation, have been used to describe the sociopsychological effects of living in such institutions, some of which are "mortification and curtailment of the self" (Goffman, 1961), "depersonalization" (Townsend, 1962), and "institutional neurosis" (Ham, 1980). In prison people live communally with a minimum of privacy and yet their relationships with one another may be distant. Many inmates subsist in a kind of defensive shell of isolation. Their mobility is restricted and they have little access to a general society. Typically, social experiences are limited, and the staff leads a rather separate existence from them. The result for the individual seems fairly often to be a gradual process of depersonalization.

According to Santos (1995), one of the major consequences of long prison terms is a loss of the prisoners' sense of their own efficacy. Once incarcerated, prisoners are told where to live, what to wear; an indifferent prison system prepares their food and forces them to work in jobs unrelated to their skills. Coe (1962), using a model assessing institutional structure, found some association between the degree of depersonalization on environment and the effects of self-image. Coe further suggested that the more total the institution (based on such characteristics as orientation on activities, scheduling of activities, provisions for dissemination of rules and standards of conduct, provision for the allocation of staff time, type of sanction system, how personal property is dealt with, decision making about the use of private property), the greater its depersonalizing effects. As a result, time fills the long-term prisoners with boredom and resentment. "They lie on their beds, staring at the bunks about them and the walls surrounding them. The prison system has taken their identities; it has removed their abilities to distinguish themselves" (Santos, 1995). It is difficult to accept that release from prison will come for several decades and, for some, it will never come.

To be locked up for decades is to know sensory deprivation and mind-numbing isolation. As you reach the age category of the oldest old, knowing you'll never leave prison can suck the last bit of hope from a prisoner's soul. As an 85-year-old convicted murderer stated, "It seems to me there's no outside world. It's dead. Everything is dead. Although you're living, you feel like you're dead. You get numb. That's what makes you do your time" (Aday, 1995, p. 20). As time passes, fewer visitors are received and eventually the last family member on the outside may die, leaving the aging inmate resigned to spend his or her final months or years behind bars without any hopes for parole or family visits.

In general, the evidence accumulated over the past several decades leaves very little doubt that institutionalized populations exhibit significant differences from noninstitutional populations. According to Rieske and Holstege (1996, p. 266), "No matter what the particular characteristics of the population or the unique qualities of the total institution, the general thrust of empirical evidence emerging from many studies suggests that living in an institutional environment has noxious, physical, and psychological effects upon the individual, whether young or old."

Relationship Deterioration

The influence of important reference groups on the lives of inmates who are serving lengthy sentences is another possible frame of reference within which to describe and interpret institutional adjustment patterns. Clemmer (1958) stressed that the most important feature in determining the degree of prisonization was the degree of primary group affiliation inmates had with other inmates within the institution. Atchley (2000) also concluded that while the social groups we belong to may vary, the most important element for most people is those groups within which they participate directly and frequently.

More specifically, Adams and Vedder (1961) addressed certain implications of institutional dependency during the final stages of imprisonment encountered by many older prisoners:

> A long sentence may persist despite good prison conduct and parole may be denied reasonably because the prisoner has no family to whom he could go. Long confinement results in physical, intellectual, and emotional deterioration.... If society has little place for the older man in general, it has even less place for the elderly prisoner or exconvict. (p. 179)

Other research has also suggested that those who had lived in institutions for long periods indicated more concern about reentry into the community and less willingness to attempt it (Aday, 1995; Walker, 1993). In a more general fashion, Santos (1995) supports this viewpoint when he indicates that links with persons in the free community weaken as the years pass. Many gradually lose interest in the world outside and focus only on their time inside the prison walls. In particular, for many inmates, the prison environment helps to destroy relationships with those who, at one time, might have been significant others. If the social attachments outside the prison decrease, this broken relationship may serve to make the older prisoner more dependent on the institution, especially if he has no immediate family or friends on the outside to which to return. The length of imprisonment as well as old age itself may serve to decrease the number of family and friends on the outside.

The loss of contact with family and friends outside the prison is a major concern for any prisoner, but for long-term prisoners the fear that these relationships will be irrevocably lost creates a unique set of concerns (Johnson & Toch, 1982). Most realize that the prospects for maintaining these relationships over a long time are dim, and decisions must be made to construct a new sense of reality so that life can proceed. Most recognize that ties to their families and communities will be a separate entity. Relatives will enter into their family systems through birth and marriage and some will exit through death. These events will occur without the prisoner's participation and, in some cases, knowledge (Santos, 1995). As a coping mechanism, prisoners often seek to "freeze" a picture of life on the outside as a means of protecting the ego, for it is difficult to accept the fact that your family or friends have deserted you. This often creates a condition of ambivalence for the long-term inmate. Seeking to keep relationships with the outside world salient may, in effect, add to the stress of confinement by doing so. Cohen and Taylor (1972) suggest that very few long-termers are able to maintain high levels of outside contact over a long sentence, and most end up in a reduced level of contact with the outside world.

For many aging prisoners, maintaining contact with family or friends on the outside may be a function of health. For example, aging prisoners often lose touch with the outside world, outliving many relatives and friends. In addition, older family members may be in poor health and unable to make the trip to prison for visitation. A significant number of older inmates may not be able to read or write, which often reduces the activity of letter writing. The break in the link with the free community can be a traumatic experience for the older offender already attempting to adjust to certain physical and emotional changes associated with aging itself. If the social attachments outside the prison decrease, this broken relationship may serve to make the older prisoner more dependent on the institution, especially if he has no immediate family or friends on the outside. When accompanied by a shrinking social environment, the length of institutionalization, as old age itself, may serve to decrease the number of significant others on the outside.

For example, Wikberg and Foster (1989) reported in their sample of thirty-one long-termers at Angola Prison in Louisiana that most have had few visitors over the years. Their parents have grown old and died, their brothers and sisters are getting up in years and have stopped visiting, and if they were married their wives have divorced them. Other research further illustrates the decline in family relationships for older inmates. Wilson and Vito (1986) discovered that many aging inmates complained of not receiving regular visits from family and friends. Aday and Webster (1979) concluded that chronic offenders who had spent a significant amount of their lives incarcerated were less likely to be married and more likely to exhibit a dependency on the institution.

A study of male inmates by Sabath and Cowles (1988) concluded that family contacts, education, and health had the greatest effects on positive institutional adjustment. Older inmates who were able to maintain regular family contacts were better adjusted than those who could not. However, aging prisoners often lose touch with the outside world, outliving many relatives and friends (Aday & Rosefield, 1992). Older offenders who have committed sexual crimes or other violent acts against family members develop conflictive relationships (Aday, 1994; Williams, 1989). The lack of a supportive social network can adversely affect the incarcerated elderly because social support from family and friends is one of the key factors that can serve to buffer the effects of continuous stress. Gallagher

(1990) found in her comparison of older and younger inmates in three medium-security federal prisons in Canada that older men reported more personal visits than their younger counterparts. The older inmates, ranging in age from 45 to 87, also had significantly more friends in prison and were more likely to have a confidant inside the prison.

I also gathered other specific information about family interaction from 102 older inmates incarcerated at Parchman, Mississippi (Aday, 1995). Only about one-third of this group of older inmates was married. Seventy percent of respondents' parents were deceased. Over two-thirds had living siblings, 72 percent had living children, and 53 percent had living grandchildren. Twenty-four percent of respondents in this sample "often" or "fairly often" received visits from their family but were more often (38 percent) likely to have contact with family members through telephone calls and letters sent and received. Thirty-five percent were "occasionally" visited by family members and just slightly (36 percent) more likely to exchange letters or telephone calls. Forty-one percent of the sample claimed family "never" visited them. Approximately one-fourth claimed that their family lives were "poor" or they were "not close." The remaining 10 percent offered miscellaneous answers such as "O.K.," "they do the best they can," or their family was "ashamed" of them. Interaction with friends was less likely overall. Seventy-seven percent claimed to "never" receive visits from friends and 67 percent "never" exchanged letters or telephoned. This research supports similar findings from other state samples (Douglass, 1991).

These accounts suggest that long-termers often become estranged from the outside world and they come to think of prison as their natural home. In short, imprisonment automatically disrupts and curtails previously established family roles, since the inmates' separation from the outside world is continuous and may exist through several stages of the life cycle (Goffman, 1961). The longer the normal roles (parent, child, grandparent) are disrupted, the more painful or difficult it will be to reestablish specific roles. For instance, it may not be possible for the older prisoner to make up at a later phase of the life cycle the time missed in education or job advancement, in marriage, or in being a father to one's children. The long-term inmate then finds certain roles are forever lost by virtue of the barrier that separates him from the outside world.

Deterioration of Health

As with any aging group, the incidence of chronic illness increases, especially for ailments such as arthritis, heart disease, emphysema, cancer, and stroke. On average, elderly prisoners suffer from three or more chronic illnesses (Douglass, 1991; Krebs, 2000). Chronic illness has been reported to negatively affect a person's body image, psychological well-being, and social identity (Royer, 1995). At a minimum, for many persons, the diagnosis of a chronic illness forces an awareness of a permanent defect, however slight, that can reduce the accustomed level of functioning. As they experience a restricted life, chronically ill persons become cognizant of the fact that they cannot engage in many of the activities they valued and enjoyed in the past. If they are able to participate on some level, that level is much diminished from that of the past.

Loss issues appear to be a significant factor for older inmates coping with chronic illness. Zemzars (1984, p. 44) indicated that the one characteristic common to all chronic illnesses is that the person "can never fully return to his or her former state of health. Thus the experience of a loss ensues." The loss of independence can be most devastating. The restrictions the disease imposes on normal daily activities make the individual feel controlled by the disease. For some, this change in lifestyle is overwhelming. Barnard (1984, p. 341) stated that illness is an "encounter with limitation and finitude. In particular, chronic incurable conditions require major adjustment in personal identity." Aging inmates must assimilate the fact that impairment and constraint will be a permanent condition. In this regard, most aging inmates see their health as becoming worse over time.

Royer (1995) reports that uncertainty about the duration of an illness or its outcome is the greatest single psychological stressor for people with life-threatening chronic illness. Lack of confidence and trust in the physician also leads to high degrees of uncertainty (Mishel, 1988). Entry into and immersion in the prison medical world can be strange and frightening for older inmates, who complain of the lack of consistency in case management practices. Seldom do they see the same doctor twice in a row, and it is most difficult to develop a sense of trust with those providing care. These feelings can lead to more uncertainty, not least because prison health care is very structured with its own rules, schedules, and system of interaction that differ from those of the general prison environment. Some older inmates are not prepared for these drastic changes.

Concern with deterioration and accelerated aging is another real concern for prisoners facing long sentences. Cohen and Taylor (1972) reported that many long-term inmates are obsessively concerned and highly self-conscious about outward signs of deterioration. The features of prison that provoke these concerns include the fact that prisoners frequently receive unfavorable labels. Also, with an abundance of time to fill and few opportunities to fill it, inmates often become preoccupied with physical aging and their increasing health problems. For many aging prisoners, the most important "role loss" influencing institutional adjustment is that of health. Concern with deterioration is a major source of stress often identified by lifers and long-term inmates.

With some chronic illnesses, older adults first confront their own mortality, which may lead to greater uncertainty and profound fear. Inmates housed in correctional facilities at some institutions in remote areas may fear having a heart attack or some other sudden life-threatening medical event and the response time of getting them to a medical facility where they could receive proper treatment. Having a chronic illness can create a sense of vulnerability among aging inmates who frequently have to rely on an unfamiliar or untrusting medical system for critical care. Of course, chronic conditions also leave the aging inmate more vulnerable to victimization.

Coping with Death

Another stressor of long-term confinement is the probability of dying while in prison. Increasingly, older offenders are receiving sentences that will keep them imprisoned for the remainder of their lives. Dying in prison is a fear that haunts the existence of almost every prisoner. As an older inmate serving life for second-degree murder proclaimed (Sheppard, Demont, Jenish, Nicol, and Macqueen, 2001),

> I've seen a number of people who've come into prison after me and are dead today.... Some are dead from AIDS, some from hanging themselves. Some are just dead from a broken heart. They just gave up. If you go down to the hospital here, at the back part, you'll see six to eight inmates lying there, waiting to die. There's something wrong with that picture. To keep a man in prison when you know he's going to die, when his chances of being a threat to society are long passed.... I'm scared to death of that. (p. 31)

Williams (1989) also found that aging prisoners experienced some of the common "pains of imprisonment" such as physical deterioration, fear of dying, thoughts of suicide, and the realization that the rest of their life will be spent in prison.

Death for some long-term inmates who are living with their only friends in the world may find death in prison to be a suitable eventuality. Anderson and Morton (1989) described an inmate who was dying of cancer in the prison hospital. The inmate had begun serving a life sentence for a variety of crimes in 1937. At 82 years of age, he refused parole because the only people he knew were in prison. When death finally came, his friends served as pallbearers and he was buried in the newly created state prison system cemetery.

However, dying in prison generally means dying alone, and more often than not, a prisoner's final hours are spent with people who treat him with indifference. As Wilbert Rideau, a noted murderer sentenced to life for killing a bank teller in 1961, stated, "Dying in prison is the most dreaded nightmare of prisoners—perhaps because they spend all their lives scratching at the walls to get out" (Krane, 1999, p. 2). For many aging prisoners, a stigma seems to be associated with dying in prison. As a 65-year-old serving life in a Tennessee prison stated, "Dying in prison would have a negative impact on my children....I would rather die a free man." Other long-term inmates have expressed fears relating to how prison staff treat a dead person. "I've seen a few die here and I wouldn't want to.... This idea of handcuffing the corpse when they take them out of here is not for me" (Williams, 1989, p. 72–73).

Some lifers must also cope with the death of friends or family members on the outside. When combined with their own personal fears of dying and declining health, such losses can be devastating. One aging inmate I interviewed recalled, "I have lost a brother and sister since I've been here. I have another brother dying of cancer now. I've just about lost everybody" (Aday, 1995, p. 16). Being able to pay one's final respects may also pose a problem for a significant number of aging prisoners. Some are in poor health and are unable to attend funerals on the outside. For others, requesting permission to go to a funeral of a loved one may be out of the question. Some states have policies that regulate outside visitation. For example, in Tennessee inmates have a choice of either visiting their loved one prior to death or attending the funeral. Most inmates seem to prefer the former option. For most, attending a funeral in chains with everyone watching is a difficult stigma to overcome. As one long-term inmate suggested, "They keep you chained down like some animal in church. You have all those people watching you" (Aday, p. 16).

Like the elderly in the free world, older inmates in poor health are more likely to think frequently about death (Aday, 1995). Poor health tends to create a feeling of greater vulnerability among older inmates leading to heightened fear of death. I also discovered, when researching a group of 102 older male inmates, that those in poor health exhibited a number of other fears. A majority of older inmates who characterized their health as poor expressed a fear of getting sick, getting cancer, or having a heart attack and expressed a marked fear of dying a painful death in prison. Younger inmates (50–59) reported a significantly higher level of death anxiety than inmates over the age of 60, which was attributed to the poor health of the younger group.

An open-ended question asked respondents, "Generally, how do you cope with these thoughts of dying in prison?" While 64 percent indicated that they frequently thought about dying in prison, a substantial number of older inmates reported deliberately avoiding thinking about death. Others reported that they used religious beliefs for strength in coping with the thoughts of dying in prison. Some older inmates revealed that death was inevitable anyway, regardless of where you are, and others simply "kept busy" or tried to take life one day at a time. Fearlessly or gladly anticipating death was voiced by a few of the respondents. Some inmates viewed death more like a friend that would take them away from their horrible life in prison.

MAKING A LIFE IN PRISON

Many things are important for understanding how individuals cope with the prison experience. Chronic offenders know what to expect in prison, because they have served time before. Other older offenders, the ones imprisoned for a serious crime late in life but without a criminal background, are ill prepared to successfully adjust to prison life. The social patterns that develop in a prison result from the interactions between the prison's environmental characteristics and the adaptation prisoners must make to the dehumanizing conditions and deprivations of a prison life. The availability of prison programs may spell the difference in whether the inmate suffers disorganization and withdrawal or manages to cope with a minimum of damage to self (Wright, 1993). As inmates "age in place," correctional facilities are becoming increasingly aware of the need to tailor the various service provisions and levels of activity criteria to meet inmates' changing needs.

Prison Work

Prison work for inmates consists of two types of jobs. One type of jobs consists of those that maintain the institution, such as preparing meals and cleaning the dormitories. Other jobs can be called industrial or productive in nature. Work in prison serves several functions: It keeps the prison running smoothly, gives inmates something to do, creates a positive identity, produces goods and services, and teaches useful skills. In the long run, prison work saves the state and federal government money by employing inmate labor. These functions make prison work a necessary part of any prison's program (Silverman & Vega, 1996).

For the aging inmate, work is a very important activity. Many inmates have grown old while incarcerated and, for them, prison labor actually takes the place of a work career. As a result, inmates value their prison jobs and any program involvement they have, for keeping themselves occupied and having a sense of worth is important. As one 61-year-old laundry worker stated (Marquart, Merianos, & Doucet, 2000),

> I got to work or else I'll go crazy. I mean, I've worked since I was a kid and working keeps me busy and it makes my time go by faster. You know, a routine like getting up every day just like out there forces me to be somewhere and to be involved no matter what I think about the job, I got something to look forward to. When you do time, and I been doing time all my life, you got to stay busy. (p. 88–89)

This inmate illustrates the important function that work serves in making prison life more bearable. Of course, the big challenge is finding suitable work opportunities for all those who desire them. Older inmates housed in the general prison population generally have much greater opportunity for prison employment than those in sheltered environments. A recent study reported that 75 percent of older inmates mainstreamed in the general population were active in a variety of daily work assignments. While a few worked a few hours each day, a significant number worked up to nine hours each day, six or seven days a week (Marquart et al., 2000).

Work provides a variety of latent functions in the prison setting. Not only does work give inmates a sense of identity and purpose, it is also important for aging inmates' mental and physical health. When large segments of the day are filled with work, less time is left for inmates to contemplate their situation or engage in self-pity or for boredom to take over. Participating in work enables older inmates to stay in routines similar to those of younger inmates. Work encourages inmates to remain engaged and physically active. In this regard, work can be considered a "wellness" activity, since older inmates have to walk to work, walk to the dining room, walk to the commissary, and in some cases participate in physically demanding labor. According to Marquart et al. (2000), the most important aspect is the opportunity to work alongside men of various ages. Maintaining a structured routine can serve as a stimulating experience for older inmates and perhaps slow down mental and physical decline.

Inmates have generally found that the number of work opportunities available is rather limited (Caes, 1990). This is particularly true for aging inmates living in special-needs facilities. Older, frail inmates who have been transferred from the general prison population to a special-needs unit frequently complain about having to give up income-earning jobs (Marquart et al., 2000). Some units may house up to 500 aged and infirm inmates, and finding appropriate jobs for every inmate whose health permits it is virtually impossible. The scarcity of prison industry jobs and other work or programming tends to result in the underassignment of inmates to workactivities. Some older inmates with limited physical capabilities may be capable of working only a very short schedule. Only so many light housekeeping jobs can be invented for this special population. Of course, many aging inmates are unable to perform any work. They are, in essence, considered retired.

Some older inmates may work in cottage industries, which provide a legitimate community contribution as well as a limited income. Correctional facilities also require maintenance tasks and services in order to function, a few of which are janitorial work, construction, food preparation, nonconfidential clerical work, repair, laundering, landscaping, and serving as orderlies. As the aging prison population continues to increase, prison officials must be more creative in producing useful activities for them. Currently, numerous activities go on in most institutions as part of its illegitimate economy. For example, inmates provide services for each other such as tailoring, legal research, correspondence, and shoe shining. Cowles (1990) has suggested that if such activities could be legitimized and controlled, they could contribute to the smooth operation of the institution. At the same time, they would provide meaningful activities and a viable occupation for long-termers and other aging inmates. Pushing other inmates' wheelchairs, helping other inmates get dressed, bathe, or feed themselves, and writing letters, for example, all could be defined as regular "prison jobs." Many prison systems are now providing hospice services employing volunteer inmates. Such jobs could be formalized and inmates could receive some compensation for the specialized service.

Religious Activities

Religious groups and activities attract more inmate participation than any of the other prison programs. Imprisonment can be a lonely, soul-searching experience, and religious activities can make prison life more tolerable. Finding structure in religion provides many offenders with the internal stability that enables them to make either a successful adjustment to the prison subculture or a satisfactory transition back to society. Research indicates that religion can function to give hope, meaning, optimism, and a sense of security to those doing "hard time" (Williams, 1989).

In the first study that has examined religious background, religious ideology, and religious behavior, Koenig (1995) has disclosed some interesting links between religiosity and the level of emotional adjustment in prison. Koenig's study of ninety-six male inmates aged 50 and over confined to a federal correctional institution found that religious background, belief, activities, experience, and intrinsic religiosity are important factors in the adjustment and behavior of older prisoners. A large proportion of inmates in the study held conservative Christian religious beliefs, with 82 percent reporting belief in a personal God, and 86 percent believe that Jesus is the divine Son of God. These findings are similar to those reported by community-dwelling older adults (Atchley, 2000). Koenig also found that attendance at chapel services or other religious meetings was quite common in this group of older inmates, with 37 percent attending at least once per week (and 13 percent attending several times per week). Other forms of unorganized religious activity were equally important for coping with imprisonment. Fifty-one percent of inmates reported being involved in private religious activities such as prayer, meditation, or Bible study every day (and 19 percent several times per day). Church attendance and private religious activities were found to be more frequent among men who had been incarcerated less time, and these activities gradually declined as time spent in prison increased. The author hypothesized that as inmates become better adjusted to the prison life, they may find less need to participate in religious activities.

One-third of the older inmates reported having a religious experience that changed their lives, and 77 percent indicated that that experience had helped them cope with prison life. When this group was asked to rate on a scale from 1 to 10 the extent to which religion helps them cope, 40 percent reported an 8 or higher and 32 percent indicated a 10, "the most important thing that keeps them going." Additionally, 16 percent felt that religion helped them cope with the stressors of imprisonment. Although not statistically significant, the number of disciplinary actions for infractions of prison rules was found to be lower among more frequent church-goers as well as those who frequently engaged in private religious activities. Finally, this study concluded that religious affiliation, belief, and motivation served as important factors in reducing emotional duress. In contrast, depression scores were highest among inmates with no religious affiliation.

I also found that for most new elderly offenders in a small case study religion was most important in helping them cope with the pains of imprisonment. Most of the inmates in this study engaged in informal prayer and Bible reading, rather than the formal involvement in religious activities in prison. The following is typical of many of the responses regarding the role religion plays in the lives of older inmates (Aday, 1994):

I have a strong belief in God and feel that God will answer my prayers....I don't attend church in here because this outward sign by other inmates is for show only and does not reflect true dedication to Christian life. I watch Sunday morning Christian programs on television instead. (p. 87)

Those who felt religion was not important in their lives fell into two basic categories. One group indicated that religion was never really important in their lives. The second group, for whatever reasons, had drifted away from God and religion. Some inmates in their anger may blame God for their immediate incarceration and may continue to drift away from a religious life.

The available research suggests that religious activities are important in helping older inmates to more effectively adjust to prison life. Religious activities seem to provide an improved mental outlook, perhaps reducing anxiety, depression, and management problems. Koenig (1995, p. 229) has suggested that "religious activities should be made available to inmates, opportunities to practice their faith expanded and research conducted on how religion many enhance rehabilitation and prevent recidivism." Some other ways to strengthen the role that religious activities play in the lives of older inmates are encouragement to form prayer or scripture study groups among themselves and providing outside religious speakers. Some states have cut back chaplain services to contain costs (Bailey, 1991); but such services should continue because of the important role religion plays in the lives of older prisoners. If chaplains are unavailable, pastors in the community should arrange to conduct services and minister to the spiritual needs of older inmates.

Prison Pastimes

Remaining engaged in the social environment can compensate for some of the negative consequences of growing old in prison. Social integration has been considered one of the essential ingredients for successful aging. Although considered an important dimension or process of aging, the provisions of prison programming for social integration into the prison community vary from prison to prison and state to state. Inmates frequently complain about the lack of stimulating activities designed for the older inmate. As often occurs in the outside world, most prison activities are designed for the younger population. As we have discussed earlier, longer sentences have shock effects on some older inmates. Initially, older inmates will desire more formal activitities to buffer themselves against hopelessness and despair. As older inmates serve their lengthy sentences and are able to accept their fate, they will require less environmental stimulation.

Typically, older inmates prefer safety, privacy, and structure to achieve equilibrium as time advances and they move toward old age (Walsh, 1990).

Older inmates, as a group, normally prefer to engage in more passive activities to pass the time. Watching television, visiting with other inmates, sleeping, reading, walking, playing cards, engaging in religious activities or simply trying to find a place to be alone are activities many older inmates prefer. Inmates may also spend considerable time writing letters and making phone calls as permitted. Since many prisons are shifting to smoke-free environments, going for smoke breaks is becoming another common structured activity.

Marquart et al. (2000) reported a similar range of activities when assessing two separate groups of older inmates serving time in the Texas prison system. One group resided in the geriatric unit and the other in the general prison population. When asked to describe their daily routine, inmates in the geriatric unit indicated that watching television was again the most popular way to pass the time. In addition to eating meals, inmates visited with friends or acquaintances; a few wrote letters, read papers or magazines, snacked, or napped; and a small minority went outside for fresh air. Mealtimes were reported to be the most important activity of the day. The importance of the meal revolved not so much around the food, but the enjoyment received from inmate camaraderie. Inmates in geriatric unit sample did admit that they refrained from engaging in activities outside the facility because of the required strip search on entry and exit from the unit.

Prison Relationships

Both kin and nonkin relationships are important in old age. Some community studies have revealed nonkin relationships to be stronger predictors of well-being among the elderly than kin relationships (Aiken, 1995). Because they are voluntary and because inmates are isolated from the outside world, friendships in prison may be even more highly valued than kin relationships. Wood and Robertson (1978) provided strength for this argument when they found that life satisfaction in old age is more closely related to interactions with friends than to interactions with relatives. Most older adults report having friends who are similar to them in age, status, values, interests, and experiences. Also, friends in later life generally live in close proximity to each other.

Friends function as a source of emotional support, information, and entertainment, and hence can contribute to the older person's sense of belonging and meaningfulness (Aiken, 1995). Friends provide important emotional support in a time of crisis. Close personal relationships with friends can help cushion the shock of physical deterioration, the loss of loved ones, and other sources of stress in the prison environment. The prison social structure can provide an antidote to loneliness and loss of status in old age.

Our culture's definition of friendship is ambiguous, and defining friendships in prison can be even more uncertain. Do we consider someone a friend with whom we have regular sociable contact or someone with whom we have developed a great degree of intimacy, trust, and loyalty? Older prisoners may not fully recognize some of their ties as friendships even though such ties have many properties similar to pure friendship, because the prisoners see the relationship as a consequence of common participation in the prison environment rather than a relationship they purposefully selected for companionship. The conclusion to be drawn is that the more an inmate sees a relationship and its parameters as defined by a prison context or routine, the less likely that inmate is to recognize the relationship as a true friendship. Another important structural quality of what constitutes a friendship is reflected in the tendency for people in a relationship to occupy similar positions within the social structure. People are drawn together when they meet people whose life circumstances are similar to their own.

Older inmates' health also has important repercussions for their patterns of sociability and friendship. Many older inmates suffer from infirmities or disabilities that influence their opportunities for involvement with friends. While such conditions can restrict social interactions and limit opportunities for fostering friendships, physical handicaps can also act as friendship resources in some instances. Older inmates who are restricted from working may pass the time by engaging in more frequent contact with others in similar circumstances.

The number and intensity of friendships among older inmates in prison vary with a variety of factors. Older men, unlike older women, are less likely to have deep and long-lasting friendships. As a whole, older men tend to have "associates" with whom they share activities and experiences. Also related to the number of friendships in old age are length of incarceration and the number of older people who are housed in the same vicinity. Prison can in its own way provide a better opportunity to develop friendships with one's own age group. Older inmates frequently seek out each other's company in preference to that of younger inmates. Gallagher (1990) found that inmates ranging in age from 45 to 87 had significantly more friends in prison than younger inmates and were more likely to have a confidant inside the prison.

I included a variety of questions on prison friendships when interviewing a group of older inmates residing in the Mississippi Correctional System (Aday, 1995). Aging prisoners were asked, "In regard to your friendships here, how frequently do you talk to other inmates here about...." And a list of topics of conversation was presented. Respondents were more likely than not to discuss food or other conditions, feelings about being in prison, religious feelings, their health or illnesses, and life outside of prison. Respondents were less likely to discuss things they were sad about, things they were ashamed of, their financial situations, loved ones who have died, or their own feelings about death. Most inmates agreed that they had at least one confidant they depended on for intimate conversation and daily friendship.

Age also plays an important role in shaping perceptions of inmate–staff relations. Older inmates have been credited with providing stability to the prison environment. As inmates increase in age, they are more likely to report satisfactory relationships with prison staff (Hemmens & Marquart, 2000). When aging inmates face an increasing number of physical functional impairments, they become more dependent on their immediate support system. Some older inmates find significant institutional support from benevolent staff persons who serve as surrogate family members. This tendency increases as the length of sentence increases and outside contacts dwindle.

SUMMARY

This chapter has raised a number of important issues on prison adjustment, which has become a major concern for correctional officials. The diversity of the growing number of older offenders must also be recognized and incorporated into rehabilitative programs. For example, the elderly first offender should be integrated into prison life differently from the repeat offender. The first offender is likely to be more anxious, fearful, depressed, and suicidal than the chronic offender. To aging inmates coming into an institutional setting late in life, the realization that prison may be their final home can be a tremendous shock. Other inmates imprisoned for long periods of their lives may be fearful of returning to the free world.

In other situations, locating family members who will accept an aging inmate as well as providing necessary care-giving tasks may be difficult. Some family members are also aged and in poor health. The nature of the crime may have created a conflict among family members, resulting in a break in kinship ties. Such inmates may have few or no visits from close friends or relatives on the outside. The lack of a supportive social network can adversely affect the incarcerated elderly, since significant others are key buffers against the negative effects of incarceration. Of equal importance for correctional officials is the creation and maintenance of safe environments for older inmates with declining health. Older offenders, who are fearful, depressed, and anxious about being placed in a prison environment at a time when their health is declining, will need special programs to assist in their transition to prison life.

Inmates who have been imprisoned for the best part of their adult lives often become stereotypes in the public mind and are thought of as evil persons. As a result, many long-termers have been forgotten and neglected. To counteract the devastating effects—social, psychological, and emotional—of long-term incarceration, maximum effort must go into the development of programs better suited for this group. Creating relevant recreational, social and health promotion activities designed for the elderly not only will enhance prison adjustment, but could be cost effective by improving the overall health of older inmates.

Not everyone will have the aptitude or the essential skills to work with elderly inmates. Careful selection with sensitivity to the unique needs of the long-term geriatric inmate should be an important consideration. Training for prison staff, counselors, and health providers should develop a better knowledge of growing old and how this affects those who have spent most of their lives incarcerated.

REFERENCES

Adams, M. E., & Vedder, C. (1961). Age and crime: Medical and sociological characteristics of prisoners over 50. *Journal of Geriatrics, 16*, 177–180.

Aday, R. H. (1994). Aging in prison: A case study of new elderly offenders. *International Journal of Offender Therapy and Comparative Criminology, 38*(1), 79–91.

Aday, R. H. (1995). *A preliminary report on Mississippi's elderly prison population*. Parchman: Mississippi Department of Corrections.

Aday, R. H. (2001). *A comprehensive health assessment of aged and infirm inmates*. Nashville: Tennessee Department of Correction.

Aday, R. H., & Nation, P. (2001). *A case study of older female offenders*. Nashville: Tennessee Department of Correction.

Aday, R. H., & Rosefield, H. A. (1992, Winter). Providing for the geriatric inmate: Implications for training. *Journal of Correctional Training, 12*, 14–16, 20.

Aday, R. H., & Webster, E. L. (1979). Aging in prison: The development of a preliminary model. *Journal of Offender Rehabilitation, 3*(3), 271–282.

Aiken, L. R. (1995). *Aging: An introduction to gerontology*. Thousand Oaks, CA: Sage Publications.

Anderson, D.C. (1997, July 13). Aging behind bars. *The New York Times Magazine, 146,* 28–33.

Anderson, J.C., & Morton, J.B. (1989). Graying of the nation's prisons presents new challenges. *Aging Connection, 10,* 6–7.

Atchley, R.C. (2000). *Social forces and aging.* Belmont, CA: Wadsworth.

Bailey, J. (1991). Legislature approves budget cuts: Cuts also endanger Central State chaplaincy program. *Milledgeville, GA: Union Recorder,* p. 1.

Barnard, D. (1984). The personal meaning of illness: Client-centered dimensions of medicine and patient care. In R.F. Levant & J.M. Shlien (Eds.), *Client-centered therapy and the person-centered approach: New directions in theory, research, and practice* (pp. 337–351). New York: Praeger.

Beck, A.J. (1997). Growth, change, and stability in the U.S. prison population, 1980–1995. *Corrections Management Quarterly, 1*(2), 1–14.

Caes, G. (1990). Long-term inmates: A preliminary look at their programming needs and adjustment patterns. In *Long-term confinement and the aging inmate population* (pp. 5–8). Washington, DC: U.S. Department of Justice.

Clemmer, D. (1958). *The prison community.* New York: Holt, Rinehart and Winston.

Coe, R.M. (1962). *Institutionalization and self-conception.* Unpublished doctoral dissertation. Washington University, St. Louis.

Cohen, S., & Taylor, L. (1972). *Psychological survival: The experience of long-term imprisonment.* New York: Pantheon.

Cowles, E.L. (1990). Program needs for long-term inmates. In *Long-term confinement and the aging inmate population* (pp. 17–26). Washington, DC: U.S. Department of Justice.

Douglass, R.L. (1991). *Oldtimers: Michigan's elderly prisoners.* Lansing, MI: Michigan Department of Corrections.

Dugger, R.L. (1990). Life and death in prison. *The Prison Journal, 7*(1), 112–114.

Flanagan, T.J. (1982). Correctional policy and the long-term prisoner. *Crime and Delinquency, 28,* 82–95.

Flanagan, T.J. (1985, September). Sentence planning for long-term inmates. *Federal Probation, 69,* 23–28.

Flanagan, T.J. (1992). Long-term incarceration: Issues of science, policy and correctional practice. *Forum for Corrections Research, 4*(2), 19–24.

Gallagher, E.M. (1990). Emotional, social, and physical health characteristics of older men in prison. *International Journal of Aging and Human Development, 31,* 251–266.

Georgia Department of Corrections. (2001). *Georgia's aging inmate population.* Atlanta, GA.

Goetting, A. (1983). The elderly in prison: Issues and perspectives. *Journal of Research in Crime and Delinquency, 20,* 291–309.

Goetting, A. (1984). The elderly in prison: A profile. *Criminal Justice Review, 9*(2), 14–24.

Goffman, E. (1961). *Asylums: Essays on the social situation of mental patients and other inmates.* Garden City, NY: Doubleday.

Ham, J.N. (1980, July–August). Aged and infirm male prison inmates. *Aging,* 24–31. Washington, D.C.: U.S. Department of Health and Human Services. 24–31.

Hemmens, C., & Marquart, J.W. (2000). "Friend or foe? Race, age, and inmate perceptions of inmate–staff relations." *Journal of Criminal Justice, 28,* 297–312.

Johnson, R., & Toch, H. (1982). *The pains of imprisonment.* Belmont, CA: Sage Publications.

Koenig, H.G. (1995). Religion and older men in prison. *International Journal of Geriatric Psychiatry, 10,* 219–230.

Krane, J. (1999). Demographic revolution rocks U.S. prisons. </www.apbon-line.com/cjsystem/behind_bars/oldprisoners>.

Kratcoski, P.C. (2000). Older inmates: Special programming concerns. In P.C. Kratcoski (Ed.), *Correctional counseling and treatment.* Prospect Heights, IL: Waveland Press.

Kratcoski, P.C., & Babb, S. (1990). Adjustment of older inmates: An analysis by institutional structure and gender. *Journal of Contemporary Criminal Justice,* 6, 139–156.

Kratcoski, P.C., & Pownall, G.A. (1989, June). Federal Bureau of Prisons programming for older inmates. *Federal Probation, 53*(2), 28–35.

Krebs, J.J. (2000). The older prisoner: Social, psychological, and medical considerations. In M.B. Rothman, B.D. Dunlop, & P. Entzen (Eds.), *Elders, crime, and the criminal justice system* (pp. 207–228). New York: Springer.

Lawson, D.P., Segrin, C., & Ward, T.D. (1996). The relationship between prisonization and social skills among prison inmates. *Prison Journal, 76,* 293–309.

MacKenzie, D.L., & Goodstein, L. (1985). Long-term incarceration impacts and characteristics of long-term offenders. *Criminal Justice and Behavior, 12,* 395–414.

Marquart, J.W., Merianos, D.E., & Doucet, G. (2000). The health-related concerns of older prisoners: Implications for policy. *Aging and Society, 20,* 79–96.

McShane, M.D., & Williams, F.P., III. (1990). Old and ornery: The disciplinary experiences of elderly prisoners. *International Journal of Offender Therapy and Comparative Criminology, 34*(3), 197–212.

Mishel, M.H. (1988). Uncertainty in illness. *Image: Journal of Nursing Scholarship,* 20, 225–232.

Moore, E.O. (1989). Prison environment and their impact on older citizens. *Journal of Offender Counseling, Services and Rehabilitation, 13.* 175–192.

Richards, B. (1978). The experience of long-term imprisonment. *British Journal of Criminology, 18,* 162–169.

Rieske, R.J., & Holstege, H. (1996). *Growing older in America.* New York: McGraw-Hill.

Royer, A. (1995). Living with chronic illness. *Research in the Sociology of Health Care, 12,* 25–48.

Sabath, M. J., & Cowles, E. L. (1988). Factors affecting the adjustment of elderly inmates in prison. In B. McCarthy and R. Langworthy (Eds.), *Older offenders: Perspectives in criminology and criminal justice* (pp. 178–195). New York: Praeger.

Santos, M. G. (1995). Facing long-term imprisonment. In T. J. Flanagan (Ed.), *Long-term imprisonment* (pp. 36–40). Thousand Oaks, CA: Sage Publications.

Sapsford, R. J. (1978). Life-sentence prisoners: Psychological changes during sentence. *British Journal of Criminology, 18,* 128–145.

Sheppard, R., Demont, J., Jenish, D., Nicol, J., & Macqeen, K. (2001, April). Growing old inside: After decades behind bars, how can aging, ailing inmates adjust to life in the real world? *Maclean's, 114,* 30–34.

Silverman, M., & Vega, M. (1996). *Corrections: A comprehensive view.* New York: West.

Smyer, T., Gragert, M. D., & LaMere, S. H. (1997). Stay safe! Stay healthy! Surviving old age in prison. *Journal of Psychosocial Nursing, 35(9),* 10–17.

Stinchcomb, J. B., & Fox, V. B. (1999). *Introduction to corrections.* Upper Saddle River, NJ: Prentice-Hall.

Sykes, G. M. (1958). *The society of captives: A study of a maximum security prison.* Princeton, NJ: Princeton University Press.

Townsend, P. (1962). *The last refuge.* London: Routledge and Kegan Paul.

Vega, M., & Silverman, M. (1988). Stress and the elderly convict. *International Journal of Offender Therapy and Comparative Criminology, 32,* 153–162.

Vito, G. S., & Wilson, D. G. (1985). Forgotten people: Elderly inmates. *Federal Probation, 49(1),* 18–24.

Walker, S. A. (1993, August). South Carolina volunteer agency plays vital role in corrections. *Corrections Today, 55,* 99.

Walsh, C. E. (1991). *Needs of older inmates in varying security settings.* Unpublished doctoral dissertation. New Brunswick, NJ: Rutgers University.

Wikberg, R., & Foster, B. (1989). The long-termers: Louisiana's longest serving inmates and why they've stayed so long. *The Prison Journal, 80.* 9–14.

Williams, G. C. (1989). *Elderly offenders: A comparison of chronic and new elderly offenders.* Unpublished master's thesis. Murfreesboro: Middle Tennessee State University.

Wilson, D. G., & Vito, G. F. (1986). Imprisoned elderly: The experience of one institution. *Criminal Justice Policy Review, 1,* 399–421.

Wood, V., & Robertson, J. F. (1978). Friendship and kinship interaction: Differential effect on the morale of the elderly. *Journal of Marriage and the Family, 40,* 367–375.

Wright, K. N. (1993). Prison environment and behavior outcomes. *Journal of Offender Rehabilitation, 20,* 93–113.

Wright, K. N. (1988). The relationship of risk, needs, and personal classification systems and prison adjustment. *Journal of Research on Crime and Delinquency, 26,* 67–89.

Yates, J., & Gillespie, W. (2000). The elderly and prison policy. *Journal of Aging and Social Policy, 11*(2–3), 167–175.

Zamble, E., & Porporina, F. (1988). *Coping behavior and adaptation in prison inmates.* New York: Springer-Verlag.

Zemzars, I. S. (1984). Adjustment to health loss: Implications for psychosocial treatment. In S. E. Milligan (Ed.), *Community health care for chronic physical illness: Issues and models* (pp. 44–48). Cleveland, OH: Case Western Reserve University.

Chapter 6

Housing and Programming for Aging Inmates

Aging in place refers to the phenomenon of elderly persons remaining in their current living environment despite increasing frailty. Whether housed in a maximum-, medium-, or minimum-security facility, the elderly inmate faces numerous challenges in his or her living environment. Many prison environments are currently being adapted to meet the needs of the frail. While chronological age does not necessarily imply poor health, the probability that one will develop chronic illnesses increases with age. With advanced age comes the greater possibility of physical and mental decline, frailty, and loss of independent functioning. Although recent correctional literature strongly advocates the development of supportive prison programs and facilities for older inmates, it also raises questions about which environmental models would be best suited for optimum aging.

The number of older prisoners is currently manageable in most states, but the growth in the aged inmate population is raising questions of crucial significance for correction programs in the coming decades. Many states are faced with a greater number of aging prisoners than they are used to who are in need of acute or chronic medical care. Many older offenders need corrective aids and prosthetic devices such as eyeglasses, dentures, hearing aids, ambulatory equipment, and special shoes (Wikberg, 1988). Because of the circumstances such as these, correctional systems are forced into making necessary adjustments to accommodate the special needs of aging inmates. Special diets, around-the-clock nursing care, building new facilities or remodeling old ones, and restructuring institutional activities are becoming more frequent topics of discussion.

The Americans with Disabilities Act of 1990 (ADA) prohibits discrimination against disabled inmates. As a result, all inmates must have
access to the same programs, services, and other activities. Those who are
formally considered disabled are defined "as individuals with a physical or
mental condition that substantially impairs one or more life activities"—
e.g., caring for oneself, completing basic tasks, seeing, hearing, breathing,
walking, or working (Morton, 1992, pp. 10–11). Disabled inmates are frequently placed in a special-needs category and are referred to as "noninte-
gratable" because their condition has either prevented or impaired their
successful integration into the general population. Failure to respond to
inmates with special needs could prove costly to correctional systems in
terms of legal expenditures as well as staff resources. According to prison
officials, expenditures are significantly reduced when older offenders are
housed in an environment without stairs and when a specially trained staff
can recognize and treat problems before they become severe.

In this chapter, I provide a comprehensive discussion of the special facilities and programs for aging prisoners. I present the pros and cons of
grouping aging inmates in specialized housing units. The environmental
press theory is introduced as a model that highlights the importance of providing an environment suitable for older inmates' functional capabilities.
In response to the daily functioning needs of this special population, this
chapter describes several model geriatric facilities and programs. The emergence of prison nursing homes and hospice care are also discussed.

SPECIALIZED VERSUS MAINSTREAM HOUSING

Maintaining an optimum environment for the frail elderly inmate presents a significant challenge for prison officials in that the physical condition and architectural structure of the institution create significant problems for the elderly inmate. Prison systems are designed to house primarily
young, active inmates. The cold and dampness of the prison environment
often cause considerable discomfort to older, frail offenders, and distance to
the cafeteria or health facilities in many facilities poses a problem to those
with low mobility. Other environmental issues such as stairs to negotiate,
limited tempature control, and lack of adequate lighting also present problems for older or disabled inmates. Inmates with little mobility may find the
physical design of many prisons too stressful to negotiate, and they simply
withdraw into isolation. The typical prison management and environmental system is an evident mismatch with the needs of the elderly.

Older prisoners differ from younger inmates not only in their need for
medical care, but also in their psychosocial needs. Walsh (1989) found that

older male inmates expressed a greater need for privacy and for access to preventive health care and legal assistance than younger men. Older inmates are often unable to cope with the fast pace and noise of a regular facility (Anderson & Morton, 1989). Wilson and Vito (1986) also found that older inmates had difficulties with a lack of privacy and complained they could not escape from the continuous noise and distracting activities of other inmates. As a result, several elderly inmates reported high levels of anxiety and nervousness.

Studies have found that older inmates report feeling unsafe and vulnerable to attack by younger inmates and expressed a preference for rooming with people their own age (Marquart, Merianos, & Doucet, 2000; Walsh, 1990; Williams, 1989). The new elderly offender can feel particularly unsafe, coming into an unfamiliar environment late in life and ripe for potential victimization. Vega and Silverman (1988) reported that abrasive relations with other inmates were the most disturbing incidents elderly prisoners had to cope with while incarcerated. Fifty-five percent of their respondents indicated that abrasive incidents occurred every day. As one older inmate said, the worst part of doing time as he grows older is the younger, bolder prisoners: "They call you names. You go to the prison store, they snatch the bags from your hands as you leave. You've living in a jungle among savages" (Vega & Silverman, p. 155).

An inmate's perception of the risk of abuse may intensify as the inmate ages. The simple "fear of victimization" by younger inmates is extremely prevalent among elderly inmates. Wilson and Vito (1986) found that inmates housed in a geriatric unit felt vulnerable because the most dangerous and unpredictable inmates were held close by. Elderly inmates assumed that their financial status, for one thing, made them potential targets. The authors felt that the physical and mental problems of the geriatric unit elders magnified their concerns: Few specific incidents of victimization were mentioned other than harassment, teasing, or minor incidents. Still, the effect of the perception was extreme. For example, the authors reported that a number of geriatric unit inmates were so fearful that they would not leave the immediate area of the unit. Several refused to venture out into the yard, and when older inmates from the unit did go out on the yard, they traveled in pairs to increase their safety.

On the other hand, it has been suggested that inmates who have aged in prison may have developed a certain degree of bravado to protect an increasingly fragile self-image (Smyer, Gragert, & LaMere, 1997). As time passes and the disabilities increase, the false bravado may produce chronic stress, with more isolation and distrust the result. At some point, the frail inmate is no longer strong enough physically or emotionally to fend off potential attackers, producing an extremely fearful situation that can take a significant psychological toll.

The small amount of research that has been conducted has found that older females have fewer safety concerns in their respective prisons (Aday & Nation, 2001; Walsh, 1990). These studies have shown that older females fail to see younger female inmates as likely threats to their physical or psychological safety. While noise from younger offenders may produce some friction, as a rule older inmates feel safer in a sheltered environment. Only infrequently would older female inmates receive physical threats or be robbed in prison. Walsh also reported that older females made easier role transformations to a "senior inmate" from a senior citizen, having their status in prison better defined for them by other inmates and staff.

When comparing older inmates who were mainstreamed with those in a special facility, Marquart, Merianos, & Doucet (2000) discovered that most prisoners from both groups overwhelmingly supported the idea that older offenders required sheltering from the general prison population, especially from young inmates who might victimize them. Sixty-one percent of those housed in the geriatric facility agreed that older inmates would have difficulty making it in the general prison population. Among older inmates in the general population, 65 percent agreed that if their health condition declined, they would feel more comfortable housed in a more sheltered geriatric prison facility. Moreover, 74 percent of the geriatric facility inmates felt safe in their unit compared with 57 percent of those in the general population. One-third of the latter group had been victimized since their arrival at the integrated unit. It should be mentioned that underreporting is also common among older inmates because of intimidation and the fear of being victimized repeatedly. Medical staff also voiced support for the specialized unit and felt that the geriatric facility provided necessary protection and easier mobility for the aging inmates.

There has been considerable support for addressing the special needs of elderly inmates, but opponents of segregating them have raised questions about the detrimental effects of placing elderly inmates into specialized units or facilities (Fattah & Sacco 1989). It has been argued that some inmates placed in specialized units and facilities suffer from isolation and boredom, especially if of the facility provides no appropriate programming to keep inmates occupied (Marquart et al., 2000). As I mentioned in Chapter 5, it is almost impossible to provide enough suitable jobs in specialized units for older inmates who may desire to work. Some older inmates may feel comfortable remaining integrated with inmates of other ages. Like the elderly in the free world, they are familiar with life in the general population and perceive that it has a mark of independence.

Fattah and Sacco (1989) further suggest that although segregation is often justified, it could easily have the effect of age discrimination. Elderly inmates might be deprived of services and enrichment opportunities available only in the general prison population. Being grouped in a special facility, aging inmates may be viewed as old, weak, helpless, and in need of specialized care. For this reason, removing frail inmates from mainstream prison life and work opportunities may only serve to heighten their sense of inadequacy and enhance their institutional dependency. For some older inmates, the move to a prison facility for elderly inmates may have the same symbolic meaning as entering a nursing home in the free world and would be viewed in the same negative terms.

Other, structural arguments have been made to support the appropriateness of integrating older prisoners with the main prison population. For some older inmates, entering a specialized unit could move them further away from family and friends and result in fewer outside visits. Prison administrators have also consistently stressed the stabilizing effect older inmates can have on the general prison population. They point to research showing that older inmates present fewer problems with correctional staff, demonstrate more respect, commit fewer rule infractions, and in general get along better with other inmates (Fattah & Sacco, 1989; Hemmens & Marquart, 2000). In this sense, aging inmates can serve as important role models for younger inmates and can possibly have a positive influence on those who are adrift in the system.

Although the debate on the advantages and disadvantages of both mainstreaming and segregation will continue, Fattah and Sacco (p. 101) state, "Concern for their safety and the need to protect them against victimization, exploitation and harassment outweigh any stabilizing effect their integration might have." Although some may argue that few older offenders are victimized, research has proven otherwise (Smyer, Gragert, & LaMere, 1997; Vega & Silverman, 1988). For frail elderly inmates, harassment and verbal abuse can create undo fear and mental stress regardless of whether physical abuse or theft occurs. As older inmates become more vulnerable to victimization, correctional officials incur greater responsibility to provide protection. Of course, as the size of the aging inmate population escalates, it may be prove challenging for correctional officials to provide a sheltered environment for all older inmates who may desire one. Numerous states offer very few beds in geriatric facilities, and in some cases the demand has far exceeded the supply as demonstrated by the number of inmates waiting for a geriatric facility assignment. For example, Texas and Kentucky have only approximately 60 beds available at their geriatric units, and Texas has over 13,000 inmates who are 50 years of age or older. Other

states such as Oklahoma, Arkansas and California have no units designated strictly for geriatric inmates although their older inmate populations
are significant.

ENVIRONMENTAL PRESS THEORY

One way to view the effects of incarceration is what has been described
as the social environmental perspective (Gibbs, 1991). This approach includes the dynamic interactions of the physical and psychological characteristics of the aging individual with the social and physical environment.
Environmental press refers to the demands that the social and physical environments make on the individual to adapt, respond, or change. The social environmental perspective suggests that the environment changes con-
tinually as the older person controls what can be manipulated and adjusts
to conditions that cannot be changed. Adaptation in prison implies a dual

Figure 6.1
Diagram of the Behavioral and Affective Outcomes of Person-Environment
Transactions

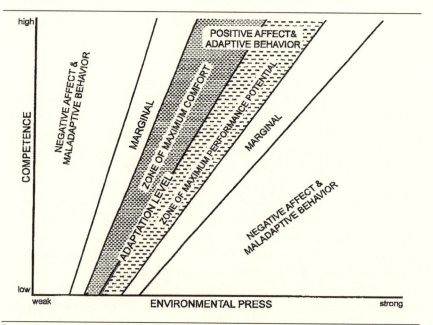

Source: Lawton, M.P., and Nahemow, L., (1973). Ecology and the Aging Process. In C.E. Eisdorfer &
M.P. Lawton (Eds.). *The psychology of adult development and aging*. Washington, DC: American Psychological Association. Reprinted by permission of the American Psychological Association.

process in which the older offender adjusts to physical conditions of the prison as well as the social dynamics of prison life. Lawton and Nahemow's (1973) ecological model is based on the premise that a person's behavioral and psychological stage can be better understood with knowledge of the physical environment in which the individual lives. Individual competence may decline because of losses in the cognitive or sensorimotor functions and general health, but prison architects can develop ways to make physical environments more accessible for older people with disabilities. If there is an imbalance between person and environment, the situation may lead to various degrees of adaptive behavior, which often can have a negative effect on the psychological well-being of the aging inmate.

As noted in Figure 6.1, the amount of press in an individual's living situation may range from minimal to quite high. Very little environmental press is present in an institutional setting where an individual is not responsible for self-care and has few resources to stimulate the senses or challenge the mind. Other prison environments can create a great deal of press. For example, some maximum-security prisons may offer significant physical challenges in that they are designed for younger, healthier inmates. Living in a familiar prison environment with few available activities generates low levels of environmental press. Sharing a crowded and noisy living arrangement would increase the environmental demands. As the demands change, the older inmate must adapt to the changes in order to maintain a sense of well-being. Individuals cope best when the environmental press slightly exceeds the level to which they adapt. In other words, the environment challenges them but does not overwhelm them. If the level of environmental demand becomes too high, the individual experiences excessive stress or overload. On the other hand, when the environmental press is below the individual's adaptation level, sensory deprivation, boredom, learned helplessness, and dependence on the prison environment may result. This may explain why, when either extreme occurs, some older inmates withdraw and exhibit significant signs of depression.

Personal safety and security are major concerns of the elderly. Factors such as poor vision, balance problems, hearing difficulties, and slower reaction time may put older individuals at greater risk in their living environments. A prison environment that provides a great deal of safety and security is likely to have less privacy, independence, and choice. A closed environment might guarantee absolute security with a great deal of control by correctional management, but it would also minimize autonomy. Clearly, a balance between autonomy and security is needed.

A facility's physical environment can affect older inmates' behavior and their ability to cope. Walsh (1990) introduced the importance of structure in the lives of older inmates, which serves as another illustration of optimum environmental press and its role in explaining successful coping. Structural concerns revolve around environmental stability and predictability. As a rule, older people prefer stability and predictability more than younger individuals do, who find change stimulating. Prisons provide structure to the extent that they provide guides for action, with penalties for noncompliance and rewards for compliance. Older inmates also prefer stability as they age in place. Although stability may contribute to replication of their daily routines, according to Walsh, older inmates are willing to trade some boredom for dependency and consistency. Older inmates also prefer predictable behavior on the part of others. This outward continuity provides a sense of emotional well-being and is motivated by the desire for predictable social support.

As either time to be served or time served increases, the older inmate's need for structure increases. Longer sentences necessitate a regulated lifestyle to compensate for an unpredictable future. The passing of predictable events is a useful benchmark for successfully "doing time." As older inmates proceed in the service of their sentence, they become more attached to the defined prison structure. For this reason, inmates become increasingly obsessed with the desire to maintain predictable prison routines. In essence, the elderly become more rigid and less flexible in their behavior. Locus of control becomes more important with increasing age. As we experience personal losses (decline of physical health and death of family members), more control is required over our immediate social world.

Application of Environmental Press Model

Moore's (1989) research on a group of older inmates in Michigan provides an illustration of the environmental press theory. His research describes a sample of older males incarcerated at the State Prison of Southern Michigan who were relocated to a special-needs facility. In this group of older inmates, 83 percent reported at least one chronic health problem with 49 percent having three or more chronic health problems. Moore's study was a follow-up to examine health-care needs and demands as well as the influence that the environmental change had upon these older relocated inmates. In contrast to the much larger state prison facility, the special-needs facility is a converted mental hospital facility housing approximately a hundred men. The author reported that the inmates who participated in the study ranged in age from 50 to 80 and were housed in double bunks in a dorm room. Each room had a window and a radiator controlled by the inmates. Overall, the facility provided a more intimate environment, with dayrooms on each floor, pool tables, card tables, and television viewing area. Laundry facilities and storage facilities were provided in each building for inmate use.

Moore attributed numerous changes in the older inmates' welfare to changes in the environment. Many concrete improvement in overall well-being occurred. After the move to the special-needs facility, 69 percent of the sample reported an improvement in mood level, 25 percent experienced fewer incidents or confrontations after the move, and 26 percent indicated that they now had a good friend in their new facility after having had no good friends while at the state prison. Overall, 75 percent of the men were generally more satisfied after the move to this more sheltered environment. The physical environment (physical arrangement and cleanliness) was frequently mentioned (63 percent) as an important factor contributing to their satisfaction. Another 45 percent reported that being segregated with other inmates of a similar age was important. Older inmates tended to feel more comfortable in the special-needs facility, as illustrated by the 16 percent who were hassled less and felt safer. Sixteen percent of those relocated to the facility liked the quieter environment.

Moore further suggests that while the needs of the elderly inmate are the same as those of any other prisoner, they are more critical. Aging inmates are less able to cope, and trying to accommodate those special needs in the typical prison setting presents complex problems. Moore envisions a number of design implications that seem consistent with the environmental press theory. Implementing his recommendations would provide the older inmates with the optimum level of functioning.

- To accommodate the physical limitations of older inmates, one-story living areas would be most desirable.

- Provisions for a minimal examination room and space for certain health-care-delivery services would be desirable near or in the housing unit.

- All areas should be wheelchair accessible, including cells, water fountains, and toilet and bathing facilities. It may be necessary to modify equipment (such as dining hall tables or noncontact visitation cubicles, for example) to facilitate walkers, wheelchairs, or other physical units.

- Housing areas should specify placement of handrails and follow barrier-free guidelines.

- Where possible, rooms with doors for all elderly prisoners would provide privacy and quiet for resting, as well as adding a measure of security for the elderly.

- Provisions for therapeutic activities such as gardening, woodworking, or similar activities are recommended.

Table 6.1
Available Facilities, Services, and Challenges for Geriatric Inmates

	Grouped or in Geriatric Facilities	Programs or Recreational Opportunities	Special Work Assignments	Hospice/ End-of-Life Programs	Medical or Compassionate Release	Early Release Planning
Alabama	✔	✔	✔	✔	✔	✔
Alaska					✔	✔
Arizona	✔	✔			✔	✔
Arkansas	✔		✔		✔	
California		✔		✔		✔
Colorado					✔	✔
Connecticut	✔	✔				
Delaware						
D.C.						
Florida	✔	✔	✔	✔	✔	✔
Georgia	✔	✔		✔	✔	
Hawaii	✔	✔			✔	
Idaho						
Illinois	✔	✔		✔	✔	
Indiana		✔	✔	✔	✔	✔
Iowa		✔				✔
Kansas				✔	✔	✔
Kentucky	✔	✔	✔	✔	✔	✔
Louisiana	✔		✔	✔	✔	✔
Maine		✔				✔
Maryland		✔		✔	✔	✔
Massachusetts		✔				
Michigan	✔	✔		✔	✔	✔
Minnesota			✔	✔	✔	✔
Mississippi					✔	✔
Missouri		✔			✔	✔
Montana		✔			✔	
Nebraska					✔	✔
Nevada						✔
New Hampshire	✔		✔			
New Jersey		✔				
New Mexico	✔					
New York				✔	✔	✔
North Carolina	✔	✔	✔			✔
North Dakota	✔	✔		✔		✔
Ohio	✔	✔			✔	✔
Oklahoma	✔				✔	
Oregon		✔			✔	✔
Pennsylvania	✔	✔				✔
Rhode Island					✔	✔
South Carolina	✔	✔	✔		✔	✔
South Dakota				✔	✔	✔
Tennessee	✔		✔		✔	✔
Texas	✔	✔	✔	✔	✔	✔
Utah		✔	✔	✔	✔	✔
Vermont					✔	✔
Virginia	✔				✔	✔
Washington	✔	✔		✔	✔	✔
West Virginia	✔	✔	✔		✔	✔
Wisconsin	✔	✔	✔		✔	✔
Wyoming	✔				✔	✔

A major problem for many aging inmates currently serving time is the fact that physical layouts of most facilities were primarily designed to control young, violent inmates and for the administrative convenience of the prison staff (Formby & Abel, 1997). Much of the discussion, especially in public forums, rests on the view that prisons should be designed for punishment and not for comfort. When prison policy conforms to this view, aged and infirm inmates are left to adapt to a physical environment which offers little flexibility. As a whole, however, aging inmates adjust better to their surroundings and stay healthier when physical plants are designed or adapted to meet their needs.

Grouping inmates with similar health-care needs can also be more cost-effective as well as providing prison officials the opportunity to cater more efficiently to the unmet needs of elderly prisoners. Specialized staff members are able to identify, monitor, and treat geriatric health problems as they arise. Separate facilities can also be cost-effective from a security standpoint. Since most elderly inmates do not pose a high security risk to management, reduced custody facilities for older inmates can free up high-security beds for younger, more violent offenders. Further cost reductions can occur from a reduction in the number of correctional officers for a lower-security facility.

THE GROWTH OF GERIATRIC FACILITIES

Numerous nationwide surveys conducted during the past decade have focused on proliferation of separate housing and services for elderly inmates (Aday, 1999; American Correctional Association, 2001; Flynn, 1992; National Institute of Corrections, 1997). Their findings show that an increasing number of correctional systems routinely house older inmates apart from the general population and offer them unique programming or services. Since the 1980s many states have built special-needs facilities or secure nursing homes to accommodate the increasing number of older inmates. Other states have converted old tuberculosis or mental health hospitals into special facilities for aged and infirm inmates. In about half the states, elderly inmates are either grouped together or housed in separate units often described as "aged/infirm," "medical/geriatric," "disabled," or simply "geriatric" (see Table 6.1). Most of these units mix older inmates with younger disabled ones.

Whenever possible, inmates of the same age are grouped together in dormitory-style cells. Generally, those states reporting some form of special housing have one or two facilities within their prison system where older inmates are normally placed. Fifteen states provide some type of consolidated medical care at one or more main prison sites. The most frequent special medical care provided for elderly inmates are preventive care, chronic care clinics, and more frequent physical examinations. A number of assisted-living units are maintained for the chronically or terminally ill. Of course, handrails, lower bunks on main-floor tiers, elevated toilets, and wheelchair accessibility are provided in most special housing facilities.

PRISON PROGRAMMING

As in the case of the physical design of prisons, correctional programs have been developed primarily for younger inmates. The approach has been realistic, since the majority of inmates are in their 20s and 30s. Educational and vocational programs were initially designed to provide young inmates with opportunities to improve their educational skills or acquire some vocation that could facilitate a successful transition back to society. Walsh (1992) reported that younger inmates generally desire more freedom, social and recreational activity (e.g., basketball, weightlifting), and mental stimulation. Recreational programs have provided inmates a way to alleviate boredom, help pass the time, and work off excessive energy. The rising median age has resulted in larger groups of aging inmates being housed together, and it now becomes necessary to provide relevant programming for this older population. Many of the aging prisoners will never be released from prison and most do not possess the health, interest, or energy to participate in sports and recreational activities developed for their younger counterparts. Rather, their needs are directed toward more preventive care, orderly conditions, safety, and emotional feedback and support from prison staff.

Keeping older inmates active is important. Correctional systems are slowly beginning to recognize the importance of introducing specific programming that successfully offsets the effects of institutionalization. In the recent past, correctional systems have been more eager to provide suitable housing (bricks and mortar) but neglected to add creative programming. Few prison systems have any sort of systematic plan for those individuals serving for extended periods of time that frequently range from five years to life. The general assumption seems to be that regular programs—academic programs, vocational training, and some sort of counseling or psychotherapy—should serve very well, particularly for the first few years. Improving or implementing new programs and opportunities for those individuals who have been subjected to the highly ineffective punishment of long-term confinement remains a challenge. The urgency is further underscored by the strong public sentiment for imposing more severe penalties, and more and more people will be caught up in long-term prison confinement.

Although Goetting (1983) reported that prison staff was unwilling to place older prisoners in educational and vocational programs, numerous states now have expanded the program to accommodate the elderly (Aday, 1999; Flynn, 1992). As Table 6.1 indicates, rehabilitative, recreational programs, and work opportunities for elderly inmates now exist in numerous states. As these programs demonstrative their effectiveness, other states will probably follow suit in designing more appropriate programming. A few facilities now employ psychologists and counselors with professional training in geriatrics, so there is a greater awareness of the unique social, psychological, and emotional needs of elderly inmates.

The elderly inmate population is frequently characterized as having diverse interests and abilities. More individualized programming is necessary to address the diversity. Rather than emphasizing vocational activities, the focus should be upon leisure activities, a cottage industry or part-time work, volunteer activities within the institutions, or recreational activities such as gardening, woodworking, ceramics, and other craft activities (Anderson & McGhee, 1991).

Group work with the elderly inmates as a planned program activity can be an effective intervention strategy in the prison environment. If given the choice, many older inmates would be satisfied to remain in a passive state or vegetate rather than become involved in recreational, social, and educational activities (Kratcoski, 2000). Many older inmates are depressed, have a number of chronic illnesses, and really see no value in participating in specialized prison programs. The use of groups can be ideal in overcoming loneliness and facilitating positive personal changes. Toseland (1995, pp. 18–19) has identified numerous benefits of group work:

- Group participation provides feelings of belonging and affiliation and helps older adults to overcome social isolation and loneliness.
- Group participation helps to validate and affirm the experiences of the participants.
- Groups give members an opportunity to share and to learn new information.
- Groups provide participants with unique opportunities for interpersonal learning.
- Groups offer older adults the opportunity to resolve problems with the help and support of fellow members.

There are three categories of older adults for whom groups are particularly beneficial: (1) older adults who are socially isolated, (2) older adults who have interpersonal problems, and (3) older adults who need assistance in identifying and participating in new social roles. Older inmates transitioning into prison as well as those coping with the effects of long-term imprisonment can benefit greatly from effective group participation. The following sections provide examples of specific group types.

Support Groups

Those inmates who will remain incarcerated until they die need special programming. Working with elderly offenders in group therapy settings can provide excellent treatment. One of the significant phenomena in the health and mental health fields in recent years has been the development of groups in which members provide mutual help in dealing with shared difficulties. These groups, generally called mutual help, support, or self-help groups, are all similar in their function. Counseling groups in the prison setting are sometimes structured around this concept, with one or more groups composed totally of those serving life sentences. Such groups attempt to serve a variety of functions related to the aging process and the debilitating effects of long-term deprivation.

One aspect of the process of the support group is to minimize the social isolation somewhat by the sharing of the experience, for any negative experience seems less negative if shared with others. Another aspect is to provide a vehicle for more social interaction. Guest speakers and sometimes visits outside the prison can be arranged. Activities of this sort can only be beneficial in their normalizing effects. Other creative activities such as writing can serve as a focus for a group. In particular, writing therapy can be effective with elderly prisoners by encouraging them to express and share feelings and memories.

Support groups for those dealing with grief or loss of a loved one may be helpful in alleviating the emotional pain of those incarcerated with no opportunity for structured grief. Other areas for topic-specific groups might be assertion training, alcoholic support, coping with loneliness and problems of institutionalization, physical and cognitive impairments, religious convictions, ethnic pride, and dying in prison. Some such groups take on projects of value to the prison, to other inmates, or to society. They might, for example, repair toys for children, accept responsibility for painting and decorating the mess halls, or plant flowers.

Reminiscing Groups

Reminiscing groups can have a number of informal and beneficial therapeutic effects for aging inmates. The process of reminiscence involves "a way of reliving, re-experiencing or savoring events of the past that are personally significant" (Burnside & Schmidt, 1995). Clinical experience suggests that in peer groups, many older adults spend time talking about their past and swapping stories about what life has been like for them. This is especially true if they are not engaged in activities that keep them involved and that help them to replace lost roles with new ones. Older adults often derive much satisfaction from recalling and reliving past experiences. Some inmates, of course, have had painful life experiences, and reminiscing may cause them to recall unpleasant experiences. Some elderly prisoners, however, may learn to discard their feelings of embarrassment or shame about their current life situation through reminiscing.

Reminiscing groups may also be successful in allowing members to increase their interpersonal involvement and social skills. Reminiscence groups have been found to increase life satisfaction and self-esteem, improve morale, enhance ego integrity, and increase control of the environment (Cully, LaVoie, & Gfeller, 2001). The active sharing of specific events and details can allow the members to regain a sense of their own uniqueness and individuality, which is often lost with the process of prisonization. Burnside and Schmidt (1995) have indicated that remembering can lift spirits and can entertain. Other benefits include mental stimulation and enjoyment.

Remotivation Groups

Remotivation therapy is "a group technique introduced for the purpose of stimulating and revitalizing individuals who are no longer interested and involved in either the present or the future" (Burnside & Schmidt, 1995, p. 153). This type of group was originally designed to remotivate patients with mental illness and is currently used with nursing home patients and those who suffer from alcoholism and depression. Remotivation could be useful in working with older offenders to increase their sense of reality and to produce changes in self-concept.

Remotivation therapy could function as the first important step in motivating individuals to gain maximum benefit from other therapeutic programs (Janssen & Giberson, 1988). For example, aging prisoners might benefit more from physical therapy if they were motivated to change. Remotivation therapy offers older inmates an opportunity to practice healthy roles and to realize a more objective self-image. An awareness of one's own potential for growth and the motivation to work toward positive change are two significant achievements commonly derived from participating in this type of group. Remotivation is useful in encouraging re-

gressed older inmates to reinvolve and helps them maintain a sense of purpose in participating in the activities of daily living.

Psychotherapy Groups

Aging inmates frequently have deep feelings of fear, guilt, loneliness, stress, or anxiety, which they may keep to themselves. Kratcoski (2000) stressed that many older inmates commit offenses that are extremely up-setting for the family, for the community, and for the offender as well. For example, inmates who commit sexual crimes against children often suffer from extreme guilt and depression. Counseling groups can provide a place to identify and express these feelings and to find support from other in-mates who share similar feelings.

It is essential for prison practitioners who work with older inmates to become thoroughly familiar with the process of grieving. Loss is a theme that frequently emerges when working with older inmates. Loss of free-dom, health, work roles, identity, family members, marriage partners, or prison acquaintances is quite common. Group time is often spent in sup-porting inmates who have had a recent loss or are attempting to work though the grief process. Group therapy can provide the means for elderly inmates to accept and resolve longstanding attitudes and feelings related to their life in prison. Psychotherapy is also helpful, since it can expand older inmates' coping strategies.

SELECTED STATE FACILITIES

As I mentioned earlier, about half the states provide geriatric facilities and programming for elderly inmates. Flynn (1992) succeeded in identi-fying twenty-two states and the federal system as providing special pro-gramming or housing for long-term and aging offender populations. When conducting a similar study in 1999, I found a similar number of states of-fering special services to the geriatric inmate (Aday, 1999). The special units in most states frequently mix older inmates with younger disabled ones. Special considerations are usually given to accommodate safely the handicapped and less physically able. Georgia, Kentucky, Louisiana, Mary-land, Nevada, New Jersey, Oklahoma, Tennessee, and Wyoming have re-ported that they are in various stages of planning new facilities or ex-panding old ones or initiating new policies or programs for the elderly prison population. Other states have appointed committees to assess the special needs of older inmates or have long-range plans to do so. The fol-lowing states provide a representative sample of how various correctional systems are responding to their aging prison population. Research information provided by each state respectively.

South Carolina

One of the first and more comprehensive facilities to accommodate elderly inmates was developed in South Carolina. In 1970 prison officials began providing special facilities for the elderly. The state, renowned for its harsh sentencing practices, has always had a large number of long-termers growing old behind bars. When it needed more space, the state's prison for the elderly moved into a former tuberculosis hospital at State Park in 1983. When State Park was opened, certain ground rules were established: (1) Handicapped or disabled inmates are mainstreamed as long as they function in the general population. (2) All inmates work within their medical limitations. (3) Inmates aged 65 and over can retire but cannot collect earned work credits. The majority of minimum-custody inmates are housed at the State Park Correctional Center, which has 100 male beds and 11 female beds for handicapped elderly. South Carolina is the only state that has reported housing their frailest older female prisoners in a special geriatric facility.

Twenty-four-hour medical coverage is available at State Park. Thirteen nurses working in shifts are on duty around the clock. A doctor is assigned to the facility full-time and writes an average of 925 prescriptions a month. In addition to providing two daily sick calls, a pill line, and emergency and routine treatment, the medical staff provides educational programs geared to the needs of the residents. Those inmates on dialysis and chemotherapy are bused daily to a nearby hospital.

Residents are expected to go to meals and participate in other routine activities of daily living. Educational, recreational, craft, horticultural, literacy, and work-release programs are some of the offerings at State Park. South Carolina has recently initiated a trial work-release program for older, low-risk inmates as well as a prerelease training program to assist participants in adapting as they make the transition to the outside. Units other than State Park also house the geriatric population and offer them special recreational, educational, and counseling programs.

North Carolina

North Carolina has also been a leader in providing special housing and medical services for its aging population. The McCain Correctional Hospital received national attention during the 1990s for its innovative programming. In 1983 the North Carolina Department of Corrections assumed control of a state-owned tuberculosis hospital, complete with staff and budget. A major goal of the facility was to provide a hospital setting, which would include medical treatment for the handicapped and geriatric population. McCain Hospital is licensed by the state as a hospital and as a hospital-based skilled nursing facility, with forty-seven infirmary beds.

This facility provides a great variety of medical services to the inmates housed there. In addition to access to twenty-four-hour nursing care and frequent physician contact, the facility provides a pharmacy, a medical laboratory, an X-ray machine, physical and respiratory therapy equipment, and urology services. The physical therapy department has been highly beneficial to the geriatric offenders. The exercises and treatments, such as range-of-motion exercises, help the stroke inmates become more independent by aiding them in regaining a degree of their productivity and ADLs. Geriatric and other disabled inmates are given outpatient medical care and are housed on the first floor of the facility. No in-patient surgery is provided, however; patients who are critically ill are sent to a community hospital for treatment.

Recreational personnel provide a geriatric walking program three times a week as well as other low-impact sports activities. Older offenders frequently interact with members of the community outside the prison and have an opportunity to talk about life on the outside. Eligible inmates may attend off-site ballgames and movies and meet monthly with a local senior citizens group. Rehabilitation therapy, gardening therapy, and woodworking classes are also provided at McCain. A local community college provides instructors for the gardening program. Rehabilitation therapy, provided by institutional staff, offers ceramics, artwork, collages, and painting. Some other supervised activities are board games, horseshoes, and bingo.

McCain's psychologist and social workers provide case management, mercy parole recommendations, nursing home placement, and other special care not normally provided by case managers. Social services personnel at McCain manage a variety of self-help support groups and reminiscence therapy to keep the inmates' minds active. Older inmates are also encouraged to participate in literacy classes to promote mental alertness. The social workers help maintain family contacts, which can be quite difficult, since it is common for family members of the elderly to have grown ill or died. McCain also provides an active hospice program with appropriate counseling services for the inmate and family members. Social services personnel also arrange for appropriate aftercare to elderly inmates who are released.

Pennsylvania

More recently, Laurel Highlands, a minimum security facility located in the backwoods of Pennsylvania, was opened to care for aging inmates. Converted from a state mental hospital into a prison in 1996, this hospital-like prison maintains a high level of cleanliness. SCI Laurel Highlands is a security level 2 facility and, after a recent renovation, now can accommodate approximately 900 adult male inmates. Laurel Highlands provides special services to inmates with special needs.

Inmates may be referred to SCI Laurel Highlands Long-Term Care Unit if they have a significant medical condition or illness that requires active nursing and medical care; have a physical or mental condition that prevents them from independently caring for their own ADLs; or need intermediate or skilled nursing care. The Bureau of Health Care Services in consultation with the Bureau of Inmate Services, the medical director, and the Long-Term Care Admission Committee make the final decision to admit the inmate. The age criterion for participation in the geriatric inmate program is 55 years of age. Upon arrival, inmates are housed according to need: general population, wheelchair-bound, geriatric, or long-term illness.

The substance abuse programs for geriatric inmates follow the same general twelve-step principles used with the general substance abuse population. Treatment is based on each inmate's history of abuse. Geriatric inmates are included in drug and alcohol education seminars, Alcoholics Anonymous/Narcotics Anonymous groups, coping skills groups, individual and group counseling sessions, outpatient treatment programs, and relapse prevention programs. To address drug and alcohol treatment plans for geriatric inmates, the facility takes special pains with training staff in identification of addiction in the elderly, generational attitudes, physical changes in the elderly, managing prescribed medications, and basic interpersonal skills. The Geriatric Substance Abuse Program assists the individual in a holistic recovery.

The psychological services at the facility have been designed for the geriatric inmate. Utilizing a needs assessment approach, staff will conduct interventions to combat depression, stress, anger, and other symptoms common during incarceration. Inmates can learn to deal with their psychological reactions to health issues, problems with their spouses, adjusting to prison life, and strained relationships with children and grandchildren. Specialized evaluations are also conducted for geriatric inmates who have symptoms of Alzheimer's disease. Individual counseling on death, dying, and bereavement is also available.

To accommodate end-of-life concerns for aging inmates, psychologists work closely with the chaplain to coordinate counseling services. Religious services are conducted by the chaplain in a designated area of the Long-Term Care Unit for inmates who are unable to attend regular services in the chapel. For those unable to participate in either of these services, a private service is provided in keeping with the inmate's faith. The chaplain also supervises spiritual relaxation group sessions consisting of videos, films, trivia games, and recorded music for mobile inmates.

Ohio

Some of the most ambitious programs for the older offender have been developed by the Ohio Department of Rehabilitation and Correction. The Ohio prison system houses over 3,000 inmates who are 50 years of age or older (about 5 percent of whom are females). Educational services are available to all inmates through the Ohio Central School System. The Department of Educational Services plans to increase vocational programming for older inmates who will be released to the community with an expected to have ten to fifteen working years remaining in their lives. Examples of training provided are desktop publishing, entrepreneurial skills, and real-estate license preparation.

The Hocking Correctional Facility houses 450 medium-security inmates, three-fourths of them aged 50 or older. One-third of all inmates are enrolled in an educational enrichment program. Many of the inmates housed at Hocking have only third- or fourth-grade reading skills. Permitted to work in slower-paced classes among inmates their own age and with the aid of large-print books, the inmates thrive. Thirty to forty earn their GEDs each year (Beane, 1999). Hocking also offers building maintenance programs, college-level courses in business management, and culinary arts training. In prerelease programs, prisoners are instructed about Medicare, Social Security, and how to apply for jobs. Plans are developed for those needing support services in the community upon release.

The Department of Correction has implemented recreational programs for older inmates at other institutions in the system as well. The department supports joint programming between medical services and recreation with a major emphasis on health and wellness. Aging and infirm inmates have the opportunity to exercise with others of their own age group. This encourages them to compete without being subject to ridicule, which is frequent in the general prison population. One successful program in this area is the Jogger/Walker Fitness Program. The program stresses good physical and mental health and is conducted during the summer. Participants are encouraged to monitor their progress and to keep tabs on the total miles completed. Participatory awards and achieved goals are displayed. Other examples of recreational programming for older offenders include weight-machine work, Whiffle ball, and team sports such as intramural basketball and softball leagues.

PRISON NURSING HOMES

It appears that nursing homes and assisted living facilities within prison walls will become common in the future. Numerous states are developing nursing home–like settings within the prison environment, which provide a greater degree of shelter and accommodation. For example, Mississippi has a geriatric unit that houses eighty-five offenders (Aday, 1995). In 1987 an old prison hospital was remodeled and specifically designed as a nursing home in a correctional setting. In this unit, twenty-four-hour nursing care is provided and sick call is available once a week. A physician checks with the unit every day. In addition to the nursing staff, a psychiatric assistant provides recreational activities, and a case manager is also assigned to the unit.

In 1995 the Kentucky Department of Corrections opened the fifty-five-bed, skilled-care nursing facility to house geriatric and infirm inmates. A licensed nursing home administrator supervises the facility. Officials believe it to be the only licensed nursing care facility inside a medium-security correctional facility in the United States, and the unit is being expanded with another thirty beds. The facility is responsible for on-site physical therapy and dialysis for the inmate population and contracts with specialists who visit the institution every week to conduct clinics (American Correctional Association, 2001).

Virginia has been one of the most recent states to open a new facility designed for ailing and aging prisoners. Build to accommodate over two hundred inmates, the Deerfield Correctional Center will specialize in providing care to inmates who need assisted-living or skilled nursing home care. Inmates eligible to enter this facility are those considered to be medium-security risks with no more than twelve years left on their sentences. The majority of inmates housed at Deerfield are older than 55 and need assistance with at least one or two ADLs, such as dressing or bathing. Correctional officers have received training in nursing assistance and are formally considered treatment officers rather than guards. The medical staff also includes a physician and registered and licensed practical nurses (Baker, 1999).

A number of private companies are opening and operating penal nursing homes for aging and ailing prisoners. Just Care, Inc., was the first private company to open a facility, and others, such as National Corrections Corporation and Wackenhut Corrections Corporation, are exploring the possibility of opening geriatric facilities (Beiser, 1999). One such facility recently opened in South Carolina. From a business standpoint, private geriatric prisons offer promising financial gains for "prisons for profit." Beiser has predicted that with the number of elderly prisoners skyrocketing, the southeast market alone will need ten to fifteen of these facilities in the next few years. It is still unclear whether such facilities can provide health services to this population more cheaply than state-run institutions. According to Beiser, private health companies claim to provide a wider range of treatment to inmates than most traditional prison clinics do, but the claim has not yet been supported by a thorough study. Some experts fear that private prisons will negligently skimp on services to boost profits, and as a result, neglect the frail geriatric population.

EMERGENCE OF HOSPICE PROGRAMS

Since 1980 hospice programs have become common in communities around the country. The movement has now found its way into state, federal, and municipal prison systems. A 1997 survey by the National Institute of Corrections found that one-third of all state corrections departments provided some type of hospice services (see Table 6.1). The six medical centers of the U.S. Bureau of Prisons have made available 1,500 hospice beds to serve their prison population of over 135,000 inmates (National Institute of Corrections, 1998). In addition, Idaho, New Hampshire, and Vermont indicate that hospice care is available if funded by the inmate, the inmate's family, or an insurance policy held by the inmate (National Institute of Corrections, 1997, p. 5).

Formal hospice programs are governed by policies and procedures that give criteria for admission, specify special privileges for terminally ill inmates, and stipulate requirements for housing in hospice settings, do-not-resuscitate orders, and the role of prison volunteers, among other issues (National Institute of Corrections, 1997). The decision to formally admit an inmate to a prison hospice program is made in a variety of ways. In about half the states with hospice programs, admission decisions are made jointly by medical and security staff. In other states, the decision to admit an inmate is made by medical staff and the hospice coordinator. As in community hospices, admission requires a doctor's certification that the patient has a terminal condition with an approximate life expectancy of six months or less. Hospice participants are required to sign informed-consent statements, whose provisions vary by correctional system.

Hospice patients have access to special privileges above and beyond those of a general prison population (Seidlitz, 1998). The most common of these privileges is a relaxed visitation policy. For example, hospice patients at Angola Prison in Louisiana can designate up to ten people on a list and receive two visitors for up to two hours each seven days a week. Visitors may include nonfamily members and may include persons inside or outside the prison. Another hospice benefit is special food requests such as chocolates, fresh fruit, or other culinary yearnings, which are provided to those in the final stages. Hospice patients often can keep additional personal property such as special clothing, pillows, and lotions, and, in some correctional facilities, may have smoking privileges. The services of clergy and social workers as well as the opportunity to plan their memorial services are usually included in prison hospice services.

Many correctional agencies allow inmates who have been admitted into a formal hospice program to remain in the general prison population as long as their health permits. The medical profession is improving palliative care gradually as stronger drugs are developed to combat the pain and special clothing and shoes are designed to promote greater comfort. Of course, prison hospices must be placed in a location where family members can have easy access, especially as the end of life becomes near. South Carolina, for example, makes an effort to place terminally ill inmates in the hospice closest to their families. The National Institute of Corrections has identified ten states that also provide family members of terminally ill inmates counseling on issues of death and dying (National Institute of Corrections, 1997).

The transition of the hospice philosophy into the prison setting is not without controversy. Table 6.2 provides a summary of advantages and disadvantages of hospice programs produced from a national survey of correctional facilities. Even with the special privileges afforded hospice patients, meeting every need is impossible. Requests for pain medication can take time to receive official medical approval, and clearing a request for a visitor can take too long from the inmate's perspective. Prison hospice programs may create high expectations that in a correctional setting cannot entirely be met. Of course, a number of barriers exist in many communities; some lack proper links to community hospice programs and some communities oppose the idea.

The growth of the prison hospice movement has put medical providers who are interested in compassion and comfort for their patients at odds with the often rigid security concerns and procedures of the corrections environment. Helping to break down the divide between the objectives of compassionate medical care and maintaining the boundaries of incarceration is

Table 6.2
Summary of Advantages/Disadvantages of Prison Hospice Programs

Advantages	Disadvantages
Provides death with dignity and pain management	Lack of prison space for hospice program
Improves continuity of care	Inmates are distrustful of prison staff
Improves family relationships	Need better links to community programs
Decreases custodial problems	Staffing requirements and turnover
Is a rewarding experience for inmate volunteers	Inmates sometimes refuse to accept terminal diagnosis
Reduces trips to outside hospital	Family gaining frequent access to prison
Cost effective without increases in staff or funding	Security issues sometimes override hospice management issues
Team management concept improves cooperation and health care	Misperceptions by security staff of mission or value of hospice in a prison setting
Compassionate program in a harsh setting provides evidence of caring	Lack of community support for specialized programs
Improves inmate morale for recipients	Regulating drugs and other special favors
Provides good community relations	Unrealistic expectations from patients

Source: National Institute of Corrections, U.S. Department of Justice.

one of the important functions of the National Prison Hospice Association. Regardless of the disagreements, dying patients in correctional facilitates need mental and spiritual preparation for the natural process of dying.

Identifying and meeting the needs of dying inmates is a challenge filled with contradictions and pitfalls. Prisons as a rule have promoted conformity rather than individuality. Prisons frequently dehumanize a person and convey the idea that inmates have little worth. Prison is a place where even simple platonic gestures are often discouraged. Simple human contact such as touching a patient's hand or shoulder during an assessment is often frowned upon. Some security and medical staff may have misperceptions about the mission and value of hospice in a prison setting. Physicians have been especially slow to accept hospice programs. Other security staff may believe the inmate does not deserve a dignified death. Staff turnover necessitates a constant retraining of the hospice team members.

SUMMARY

Those who support the segregation of older inmates believe it is necessary to protect elderly and other weak inmates against victimization, exploitation, and harassment by younger, more aggressive inmates. As a rule, older inmates prefer to reside in age-segregated environments, which are more likely to be quieter and more conducive to developing social relationships. Engaging in age-specific activities within the institution can be beneficial to the mental health of older inmates. Participating in reminiscence therapy and other support groups has proven successful in helping inmates cope with incarceration. Social interaction among fellow elderly inmates can help them to avoid loneliness and reduce the effects of institutionalization.

The success of aging in place in the prison environment requires a case management approach and coordinated care. Inmates should receive a comprehensive assessment of their functional and cognitive capacities, strengths, abilities, limitations, and existing supports upon incarceration. After incarceration, staff should monitor inmates and adjust services and prison environments as health care needs change. Problems such as incontinence, dementia, victimization, and cancer contribute to the older offender's loss of competency and suggest a need to relocate the inmate to a more sheltered environment. Careful monitoring can allow inmates to be placed in an appropriate prison environment and prevent many of the negative outcomes associated with prisonization.

It becomes apparent from the discussion in this chapter that correctional officials are just beginning to recognize the special needs of incarcerated senior citizens. While specific programs have been opposed in some states by popular sentiment and budget limitations, many of the programmatic changes could be implemented at little cost but with great benefit for inmates and their families and corrections health providers. As the number of elderly inmates continues to increase, it will not only become cost-justified but also increasingly necessary to implement specialized programs and facilities.

Habitual offender statutes that sentence to life without parole and mandatory minimum sentencing will increase the number of inmates serving long sentences and pose new and costly problems for corrections departments. Additional research is needed to assist correctional officials in their decision making and the implementation of quality programs and facilities. Special attention to current needs can prevent the need for crisis management in the future. Prisons, like other social institutions in society, must be prepared for the graying of America.

REFERENCES

Aday, R. H. (1999). *Golden years behind bars: A ten-year follow-up*. Paper presented at the annual meeting of the Academy of Criminal Justices Sciences, Orlando, FL.

Aday, R. H., & Nation, P. (2001). *A case study of older female offenders*. Nashville: Tennessee Department of Correction.

American Correctional Association. (2001). Elderly inmates: Survey summary. *Corrections Compendium, 26*(5), 7–21.

Anderson, J. C., & McGhee, D. (1991, August). South Carolina strives to treat elderly and disabled offenders. *Corrections Today, 53*, 53–124.

Anderson, J. C., & Morton, J. B. (1989). Graying of the nation's prisons presents new challenges. *Aging Connection, 10*, 6.

Baker, D. P. (1999, July 3). Virginia opens special prison for aging inmates.

Baumann, M. A. (1990). *The effect of reminiscence group therapy on personal control of institutionalized elders*. Unpublished master's thesis. Augusta: Medical College of Georgia.

Beane, B. (1999, Winter). As time goes by. *Jubilee Magazine, 14*. 6–12.

Beiser, V. (1999, May 17). Pensioners or prisoners: Private penal nursing homes. *Nation, 268*, 28.

Burnside, I., & Schmidt, M. G. (1995). *Working with older adults*. Sudbury, MA: Jones and Bartlett.

Cavan, R. H. (1987). Is special treatment needed for elderly offenders? *Criminal Justice Policy Review, 2*, 213–224.

Cully, J. A., LaVoie, D. & Gfeller, J. D. (2001). Reminiscence, personality, and psychological functioning in older adults. *Gerontologist, 41*, 89–95.

Fattah, E. A., & Sacco, V. F. (1989). *Crime and victimization of the elderly*. New York: Springer-Verlag.

Federal Bureau of Investigation. (1990). *Uniform crime reports*. Washington, DC: U.S. Government Printing Office.

Flynn, E. E. (1992). The graying of America's prison population. *The Prison Journal, 16*, 77–98.

Formby, W. A., & Abel, C. F. (1997). Elderly men in prison. In J. K. Kosberg & L. W. Kaye (Eds.), *Elderly men: Special problems and professional challenges*. New York: Springer.

Gibbs, J. J. (1991). Environmental congruence and symptoms of psychopathology: A further exploration of the effects of exposure to the jail environment. *Criminal Justice and Behavior, 18*, 351–374.

Goetting, A. (1983). The elderly in prison: Issues and perspectives. *Journal of Research in Crime and Delinquency, 20*, 291–309.

Hemmens, C., & Marquart, J. W. (2000). Friend or foe? Race, age, and inmate perceptions of inmate–staff relations. *Journal of Criminal Justice, 28*, 297–312.

Janssen, J. A., & Giberson, D. L. (1988). Remotivation therapy. *Journal of Gerontological Nursing, 14*(16), 31–34.

Kratcoski, P. C. (2000). Older inmates: Special programming concerns. In P. C. Kratcoski (Ed.), *Correctional counseling and treatment*. Prospect Heights, IL: Waveland Press.

Lawton, M. P., & Nahemow, L. (1973). Ecology and the aging process. In C. E. Eisdorfer & M. P. Lawton (Eds.), *The psychology of adult development and aging* (pp. 660–681). Washington, DC: American Psychological Association.

Marquart, J. W., Merianos, D. E., & Doucet, G. (2000). The health-related concerns of older prisoners: Implication for policy. *Aging and Society, 20,* 79–96.

McCarthy, M. (1983, February). The health status of elderly inmates. *Corrections Today, 45,* 64–65, 74.

Moore, E. O. (1989). Prison environments and their impact on older citizens. *Journal of Offender Counseling, Services and Rehabilitation, 13,* 175–191.

Morton, J. B. (1992). *An administrative overview of the older inmate.* Washington, DC: U.S. Department of Justice.

National Institute of Corrections. (1997). *Prison medical care: Special needs populations and cost control.* Washington, DC: U.S. Department of Justice.

National Institute of Corrections (1998). *Hospice and palliative care in prisons.* Washington, DC: U.S. Department of Justice.

Seidlitz, A. (1998). Fixin to die: Hospice program opens at LSP-Angola. *NPHA News, 5,* pp. 1, 3–5.

Smyer, T., Gragert, M. D., & LaMere, S. H. (1997). Stay safe! Stay healthy! Surviving old age in prison. *Journal of Psychosocial Nursing, 35*(9), 10–17.

Toseland, R. K. (1995). *Group work with the elderly and family caregivers.* New York: Springer.

Vega, M., & Silverman, M. (1988). Stress and the elderly convict. *International Journal of Offender Therapy and Comparative Criminology, 32,* 153–162.

Walsh, C. E. (1989). The older and long term inmate growing old in the New Jersey prison system. *Journal of Offender Counseling, Services and Rehabilitation, 13,* 215–248.

Walsh, C. E. (1990). *Needs of older inmates in varying security settings.* Unpublished doctoral dissertation. New Brunswick, NJ: Rutgers University.

Walsh, E. E. (1992). Aging inmate offenders: Another perspective. In C. A. Hartjen & E. E. Rhine (Eds.), *Correctional theory and practice* (pp. 197–208). Chicago: Nelson-Hall.

Wikberg, R. (1988). The longtermers. *Angolite, 13,* 3–24.

Williams, G. C. (1989). *Elderly offenders: A comparison of chronic and new elderly offenders.* Unpublished master's thesis. Murfreesboro: Middle Tennessee State University.

Wilson, D. G., & Vito, G. F. (1986). Imprisoned elders: The experience of one institution. *Criminal Justice Policy Review, 1,* 399–421.

Chapter 7

Older Women in Prison

Women in prison represent a much-neglected population. Only recently has it become apparent that the number of older female offenders is beginning to pose significant problems for correctional officials. Correctional officials are beginning to assess what new prison policies they will have to implement to address emerging health needs, programming, and security issues for the geriatric female offender (Caldwell, Jarvis, & Rosefield, 2001). Developing strategies to better manage this diverse group of offenders is now taking place in some correctional systems and will probably surface in others soon.

Because this topic has emerged as a vital concern so rapidly, any systematic research focusing on this special population is almost nonexistent. This chapter will explore the many issues facing officials responsible for women who are aging in prison. When addressing this topic, it will be necessary at times to interpose what is known about aging and older women in general with issues relevant to female offenders. This chapter will initially provide a descriptive view of the older female offender. I will include a discussion of the influence of drugs and alcohol on patterns of female offending as well as a general overview of incarcerated female offenders. Understanding how older female inmates adapt to prison life will form another focus. I will address topics such as health issues, friendship patterns, and prison activities. I will conclude with how correctional systems can better respond to the special needs of older female offenders. The discussion will revolve around health and housing issues, work opportunities, and special programming.

Only recently has the older women's involvement with crime and criminal justice agencies received close scrutiny (Steffensmeier & Allan, 1996). The special needs of female inmates have been largely overshadowed by preoccupation with the predominantly male prison population. While the rate of increase in the number of women in prison has been great, male inmates continue to constitute the majority of prisoners. The fact that female inmates account for only a fragment of the total prison population has been used to excuse the system's failure to meet the needs of female offenders (Phillips & Harm, 1998). As a result, correctional planning often is driven by the overwhelming profile of the predominant male population. It has also been observed that male inmates receive most of the programs, including health services. In many state correctional systems, female offenders have become an afterthought.

For the past several years, the National Institute of Corrections (NIC) has sponsored intensive educational programs focusing on "Critical Issues in Managing Women Offenders" (DeCostanzo, 1998). Such workshops have provided correctional personnel with an opportunity to learn more about the special needs of the older female inmate. NIC and numerous other researchers have shown that female offenders' needs are notably different from men's (Coll, Miller, Fields, & Mathews, 1998; Cranford & Williams, 1998; Owen & Bloom, 1995; Pollock, 1998; Ross & Lawrence, 1998). Fifty-seven percent of female offenders have experienced some form of physical or sexual abuse prior to incarceration, and about half were unemployed at the time of arrest and 64 percent failed to complete high school (Beck, 1999). As a result, female offenders have much greater physical and mental health care needs than male inmates. Other gender differences have been identified in the areas of inmate–staff relations, communication, prisonization, family background, and criminal activity, to mention a few. These important issues have sometimes been overlooked in correctional planning and supervision (DeCostanzo, 1988).

OLDER FEMALE OFFENDERS

Greenfield & Snell (1999) have estimated that one million women are under the care, custody, or control of correctional agencies. About 85 percent of them are being supervised in the community by probation or parole agencies. While women make up a small percentage of incarcerated adults in the U.S. prison system, the number of women in prison is increasing at a much faster rate than that of men. At the end of 1999, women as a whole represented about 6.4 percent (90,668) of all federal and state inmates (General Accounting Office, 2000). Of this number, 9,206 were housed in federal institutions. Almost 24,000, or about 25 percent of the women incarcerated, were imprisoned in Texas and California. In 1990 Texas housed only 2,196 female offenders, compared with 12,502 in 1999. Local jails confine over 63,000 females, representing 10.8 percent of the jail population (Beck, 1999).

Of the total number of women imprisoned in U.S. prisons in 1999, some 2,078 were between the ages of 55 and 74. Another 130 females currently serving time in state and federal prisons were over the age of 75 (*Corrections Yearbook*, 2000). Older female offenders represent only about 5 percent of the total older inmate population. As a whole, the majority of older prisoners are non-Hispanic whites, but a disproportionate number of older inmates are African American. Few older incarcerated females are married. Well over half of older female offenders are widowed or divorced, and approximately 25 percent single, separated, or in common-law marriages (Georgia Department of Corrections, 2001). The vast majority enter prison without a high school education. For example, 77 percent of older female offenders in Georgia over the age of 55 had failed to reach high school, and only 2 percent had completed the twelfth grade (Georgia Department of Corrections). The majority of older inmates in this age group were tested as reading at the sixth-grade level, and over one-third of the older female population had intelligence quotients below 70. In contrast, older offenders in Tennessee were more likely to be high school graduates and one-third had attended some college (Aday & Nation, 2001).

Two-thirds of the women in all prisons and jails are incarcerated for nonviolent crimes such as property offenses and drug offenses, which means about one-third are in prison for violent crimes (Curry, 2001). Approximately three-fourths of older female inmates serving time in prison had never been incarcerated prior to the current offense (Aday & Nation, 2001; Georgia Department of Corrections, 2001). Violent offenses such as murder and manslaughter constitute the majority of this group's criminal activity. Drugs and drug trafficking also account for the incarceration of an increasing number of older female offenders, followed by forgery, theft, and robbery. As a result of the serious crimes committed by older inmates in their 40s and 50s, a significant number are serving life sentences. In Georgia, the average sentence (excluding life) for the female 55 and over age group was 14.26 years compared with 10.46 for those between the ages of 40 and 54. The average sentence for the entire 2,620 women serving time in Georgia prisons is 9.16 years.

The establishment of longer mandatory sentences, the war on drugs, and the abolition of parole in some states are some of the factors contributing to the increasing number of both male and female long-term inmates

(Cranford & Williams, 1998; Henderson, Schaeffer, & Brown, 1998). Another simple explanation for the increase in the older female population is that there are now more older females to commit crime (Colsher, Wallace, Loeffelholz, & Sales, 1992; Ellsworth & Helle, 1994). According to McQuaide and Ehrenreich (1998), welfare reform will reduce the legal means available for those at poverty level to support their families, and this could lead to an increase in the number of poor single parents and elderly women committing crimes. Also, there appears to be a greater willingness to put women in prison for their crimes (Immarigeon & Chesney-Lind, 1992) and to give them harsher sentences (Curry, 2001). Continuing to issue life sentences without parole will change the general age composition of prisons (LaMere, Smyer, & Gragert, 1996). Cranford and Williams (1998) note that the female prison population is growing older, much as the male prison population is.

HEALTH-CARE UTILIZATION AND NEEDS

Prisons are faced with tremendous demands on their health-care systems. Older people typically need more health care than their younger counterparts, and women need more than men. It follows that geriatric female inmates will likely use medical services more than other inmate categories (Caldwell et al., 2001). These pressures are coming when many correctional systems have already been criticized for their consistent indifference to the special needs of female offenders. Despite severe fiscal constraints and societal unwillingness to spend resources on inmate care (Young, 1998), numerous physical and mental health concerns of older female inmates—including Alzheimer's disease, other forms of dementia, and other physical disabilities—are becoming a major concern for prison health-care officials. Diabetes, hypertension, menopause, arthritis, dental problems, HIV/AIDS, and cancer of all types—especially lung, breast and cervical—also are of concern to the older female prison population (Caldwell et al., 2001; Cranford & Williams, 1998). Additionally, Morton (1993) has cited that hysterectomies can cause dramatic physical and psychological problems with which women offenders must cope.

One measure of health status is the extent to which health care is utilized. Previous research specifically among women prisoners shows heavy utilization of health services (Goldkuhle, 1999; Koons, Burrow, Morash, & Bynum, 1997; Young, 1998). Koons et al. reported in a secondary analysis of 1980s data (N = 3,090) that 42.8 percent of women reported receiving medical services in prison. Ingram-Fogal (1993) also found in her sample that female inmates made frequent sick-call visits (mean = 12.5

over a six-month period). In addition to sick-call visits, Ingram-Fogal's sample made an average of 2 visits to physicians and 6.5 visits to nurse practitioners or physician assistants.

Young (1998) conducted an assessment of the health of all women in Washington state's women's prison who entered prison between September 1, 1995, and April 30, 1996. A final sample of 129, or about 21 percent of the women incarcerated at the women's prison, was included in the study. In a review of self-reported health information, the author noted that over half the women (53.5 percent) were on medication when they entered prison and almost 73 percent of the sample smoked, which is about three times as high a percentage as among women in the general population. Just over 60 percent of the sample reported at least one significant medical problem and over one-fifth indicated a physical limitation. Self-reported limitations included hearing loss, inability to get around without medical equipment such as crutches, or any physical condition that hinders one's ability to perform regular daily activities, including work. The most frequent health problem cited was asthma (30.8 percent), followed by back or neck pain (15.8 percent), and heart conditions (9.2 percent).

Health-care utilization was quite remarkable for this sample. Young (1998) reports that 2,869 medical services for the 129 women in the sample were received over four months. Over 85 percent of the sample received some form of treatment in the period: a total of 735 medications and 656 medical examinations. Health education (351), health status reviews (348), medical tests (236), and referrals (190) were received by well over half the participants in the study. In addition, the inmates received a number of medical services outside the prison setting. About 36 percent of these services were for chemotherapy, radiation, or dialysis for three women. Young (1998, p. 98) concludes, "the health service utilization is extensive whether one considers the actual number of requests for medical services, number of actual medical services provided, or number of visits to outside medical providers." These findings are consistent with findings on women in the general population, who reportedly suffer from more chronic health conditions resulting in interference with daily functioning than men and require more frequent medical services than men (Hooyman & Kiyak, 1999).

As the number of incarcerated women continues to grow, correctional health officials can expect significant challenges because of their diverse needs. Although not life-threatening, there are many chronic conditions that affect the quality of life of the female offender. Eighty-five percent of women suffer from some type of chronic disorder, a higher incidence than among their male counterparts (Kaye, 1997). For example, Hooyman and

Kiyak (1999) have concluded older women have a higher incidence of certain debilitating diseases than older men, including strokes, visual impairments, arthritis, hypertension, most digestive and urinary problems, incontinence, most types of orthopedic problems, depression, and diabetes. Women also face health problems specifically associated with their reproductive functions, such as breast, cervical, and uterine cancers—occurrences of all of which have risen in recent years. Since 1977, the chances that a woman will develop breast cancer have grown from 1 in 16 to 1 in 9 (Ebersole & Hess, 1998). Of those diagnosed with the disease, approximately one-third will die as a result.

Complications from hysterectomies are also common among older women. Compared with their male counterparts, older women experience more injuries and more days of restricted activity and bed disability. Osteoporosis, a degenerative bone condition affecting older women, causes them to be three to five times as likely to suffer from hip, back, and spine impairments as men are. It has been reported that 20 percent of women aged 50 and older have osteoporosis in both hips and spine (Speroff, Rowan, Symons, Genant, & Winborn, 1996). The higher incidence of wrist, spine, and hip fractures related to postmenopausal osteoporosis has been linked to the number of injuries and days of restricted activity among older women. An estimated 75 percent of postmenopausal women will fracture a hip and approximately 35 percent will suffer spine shortening and often painful vertebral fractures (Speroff et al., 1996).

Heart disease is also becoming more prevalent among older women. Heart disease is the primary killer of older women, and the disease is more likely to be fatal among women than among men. The reasons for this discrepancy are fourfold: Women are typically older than men at the time of their first heart attack, and many of the tests designed to detect heart disease were developed for men and are not very accurate when used to diagnose women. Doctors also frequently overlook the symptoms associated with female heart attacks, which can be very different from those for males. Finally, women themselves often overlook the symptoms of a heart attack (Ebersole & Hess, 1998).

AIDS poses a special threat to older women specifically because of the infrequency and invisible profile of AIDS carriers. Most women feel that older males are not a major risks and they fail to take preventative measures. There are currently as many HIV-positive women as men worldwide. At the end of 1997, 3.5 percent of all female state prison inmates were HIV-positive, compared to 2.2 percent of male state prisoners (Bureau of Justice Statistics, 1998). The incidence of new cases among persons over age 50 has increased at a rate of about 10 percent annually (Kaye, 1997).

Health-care providers have failed to acknowledge the sexual activity of older women as well as the possibility of contacting the disease through drug usage. Because of misconceptions about what constitutes normal aging, many early symptoms of the disease are casually passed off as signs of old age. This policy frequently results in delayed treatment (Watchel & Stein, 1995).

HEALTH STATUS OF OLDER FEMALES

Cox (1982) examined self-perceived health and aging of a group of older female inmates and found a number of important health issues. While their physical health was somewhat problematic, she found the majority of her respondents to be emotionally and spiritually sound. The data clearly demonstrated that a significant weight gain occurred among her respondents after several months of incarceration. Her finding has particular implications for older women who may be more likely to suffer from hypertension, a slowing metabolism, and higher risk of heart disease. Cox also reported concerns about the subjects' poor eating habits, insufficient exercise, stress resulting from confinement, lack of understanding of disease, and need for spiritual outlets.

One of Cox's case studies was of an older female inmate 60 years of age, serving a life sentence for murder. The case study provides an illustration of coping with deteriorating condition. This female inmate was unable to work because of pleurisy and a continuing problem with a hiatal hernia and hypertension. Functionally, the inmate was limited in bending and lifting motions and was on medication for balance problems. The inmate indicated that the food was not adequate, especially for "older folks." She cited a lack of proteins and insufficient time for older inmates to eat. She also complained that appropriate exercise opportunities were not available for older women. As she stated, "Who would want to jog with heart trouble?" "Who can run with arthritis?"

In a more extensive sample of older female prisoners over 50, Kratcoski and Babb (1990) discovered that a significantly large proportion of the older female inmates claimed their health was poor or terrible. In fact, 47 percent of the women stated that their health was either poor or terrible, compared with 25 percent of the men. Only 12 percent of the older women claimed that their health was excellent. Persistent health problems were of both a physical and a psychological nature. For this group of older female inmates, substance abuse, overeating, worry, depression, heart, respiratory, and degenerative illnesses were quite common. Mental health issues frequently mentioned included worry and depression.

In an exploratory study of twenty-nine older females aged 50 or older housed at Tennessee's Prison for Women, Aday and Nation (2001) also found significant health problems. Of this group, 20 percent considered their health to be poor and another 51 percent reported their health as only fair. The women report the chronic health problems shown in Table 7.1. Hypertension (65 percent) was the most prevalent chronic illness, followed by arthritis (55 percent), and over one-third (41 percent) suffered from a heart condition. Depression is also quite prevalent in the sample, which might be expected with the excessive number of health conditions reported coupled with prison confinement. Approximately one-third of this sample felt that their health would worsen over the next year. Over half (54 percent) admitted that they currently smoked and over one-fourth (29 percent) reported having a previous drug or alcohol problem that was exacerbating their worsening health. Although the sample was small, it provides a vivid description of the many health problems in this age group.

An older female offender described some of the common health problems she faces:

> I'm 73 years of age and serving life in prison for committing a murder 17 years ago. My health is poor and I think it is steadily getting worse. . . . My health problems include arthritis, emphysema, and sigmoid hypothyroidism. I also have a hiatal hernia, ulcers, hypertension and circulatory problems. . . . My mental health is also poor and I suffer from anxiety disorder and depression. I take approximately a dozen medications, including Prozac. (Aday & Nation, 2001, p. 14)

Although this inmate does not require frequent sick-call assessments, she voiced her concern and worry about getting sick in prison. Because of her poor health, she has mobility problems and can't walk long distances or stand for long periods of time. Her case is typical of many older female inmates who have acquired a number of health conditions while incarcerated. Developing a case management strategy that is responsive to the health needs of this growing frail population while maintaining adequate cost controls is a challenge most prison systems are facing.

More studies are needed to evaluate the effectiveness, efficiency, and consequences of programs and services for female offenders. Research that compares health status and service use among women of all ages and stages of incarceration would be helpful in fully understanding service need and utilization. It has been suggested that those recently incarcerated may have greater need for health-care services because much medical attention is often required to bring their health up to that of other inmates after years of neglect (Yergen, LoGerfo, Shortell, Bergner, Diehr, & Richardson, 1981;

Table 7.1
Self-Reported Chronic Illnesses of Older Female Inmates 50+ in Tennessee (N = 29)

Health Condition	Percentage
Hypertension	65.5
Arthritis	55.0
Emphysema/Asthma	44.7
Depression	42.7
Heart disease	41.3
Menopause problems	31.0
Stomach/intestinal ulcers	31.0
Nervous system disorders	24.1
Skin problems	17.2
Blood disorders	13.7
Diabetes	10.3
Urinary tract problems	10.3
Respiratory system disorders	6.9
Stroke	6.9
Cancer	3.4
Cirrhosis/liver disease	3.4
Kidney disease	3.4
Pulmonary disease	3.4

Young, 1998). In particular, it is more common for older women to be poor and less likely for them to have medical and financial support programs or insurance (Morton, 1993). This is true even more often for minority women. As older female offenders "age in place," their health needs will grow, and no plans are in place to expand prison programs and services to meet the needs.

PRISON ADAPTATION AND COPING

Research on inmate adjustment to prison has focused largely on the experiences of men. Older offenders and female offenders both frequently being referred to as "forgotten" subgroups, older incarcerated women are doubly overlooked in the literature (Negy, Woods, & Carlson, 1997). Research has demonstrated that the experience of incarceration is much different for women than for men (Cranford & Williams, 1998). As the authors write:

> Women are not men, and they should not be treated as if they are. But if we've heard it once, we've heard it a thousand times, that "an inmate is an inmate is an inmate." The fact is that female behavior is different than male

behavior, and just because a woman enters prison, it doesn't make her less a woman. (p. 130)

It has been suggested that correctional staff should keep the unique needs of women offenders in mind as they assist them in coping with their incarceration.

Coping refers to the cognitive and behavioral responses an individual employs to manage or tolerate stress (Lazarus & Folkman, 1984). Determining how to develop a means of successful coping can be more challenging in a prison setting than in others. As I mentioned in an earlier chapter, the prison environment creates such stressors as crowded living conditions, loss of privacy, excessive noise, feelings of isolation, boredom, health concerns, and possible personal threats. Goffman, in his classic work on asylums (1961, p. 257) stated, "the inmates undergo a series of abasement, degradations, and humiliation of self in a total institution." Common stress relievers used on the outside, such as reading, watching movies, and listening to music, for example, may be limited or engaged in under adverse conditions with little privacy. Some women overeat and gain weight in prison or perhaps use available drugs, including prescription drugs. Female offenders incarcerated with mental problems are especially at risk when confronted with the stressors of growing old in a prison environment.

The pains of imprisonment for women are plentiful. Female offenders enter the system overwhelmed with issues of low self-esteem, the stigma and shame of incarceration, and histories of abuse (DeBell, 2001). While for some older female offenders prison can provide a measure of consistent health care, there are also inherent environmental conditions, which contribute to increased stress and anxiety. Women's prisons are frequently built in predominately rural areas, resulting in family isolation. In many states, there is only one facility for women in the state, requiring all classification levels to reside together in one institution. As a result, all female offenders, even those classified as minimum custody, live under higher security levels to accommodate inmates with high security classification (Pollock, 1998). The entry into and adaptation to prison can be a difficult transition for many older women. Coping with chronic illness and losses associated with aging can further induce stressful reactions.

Concerns of Declining Health

Genders and Player (1990), in a study of women lifers, provide a comprehensive account of the experience of growing old in prison. They report that the experience of female lifers is accompanied by an over-whelming fear of deterioration in their physical health and psychological well-being. Older females in their sample complained of a cessation of men-struation and an increase in premenstrual tension. They tended to suffer from skin and weight problems that were attributed to a lack of fresh air and a poor diet. The poor diet is reflected in the fact that women offend-ers serving sentences in excess of eighteen months typically report gaining an average of 20 pounds over a three-year period. The greatest concern, however, was the anxiety that accompanied the large number of hysterec-tomies and the fear of gynecological referrals.

Female lifers have also expressed fears of physiological deterioration that were linked to their low sense of self-esteem, dread of institutionalization, loss of self-concept, and inability to conceive of a future (Greco, 1996). Their fears associated with being reduced to a passive mental state can be a significant stressor for many of the female offenders. As one older female stated:

> I had a real fright when I first arrived and saw the mental state of some of the women in here. They can't think beyond the prison and they can't talk about anything important anymore.... There's something about the place that takes all the maturity away from you. You retreat into a childhood state. It is so easy to lose sight of your real self.... It is terrifying. It really is. (Gen-ders & Player, 1990, p. 54)

The major anxiety seems to be traced to the fear that they would lose all motivation and sense of self through prisonization. Female offenders in the Greco study discussed the signs of deterioration in others and harbored a tremendous fear that institutionalization would take its toll on them as well. The Genders and Player (1990) study provided particularly telling comments from their respondents that demonstrated the uncertainties as-sociated with the indeterminacy of their sentence.

Acoca (1998) provides support for the picture of the aging female in-mate's condition in the following description:

> In a Southern maximum security prison for women, an older inmate who has had both legs amputated due to advanced circulatory disease sits out-side in her wheelchair. Correctional staff, attending to other duties, have left her alone in the baking midday sun, which she cannot avoid because she is too debilitated to operate the chair herself. Diagnosed terminally ill, she and her family have asked for her compassionate release so that she may die at home. This request has been denied. (p. 49)

This scene raises some of the complex issues surrounding women's health in correctional settings and the realistic consequences of what it means, for some, to see their bodies gradually waste away. At this time there is little dignity left in life, and loss of health and dignity is a common fear among those inmates severing long sentences.

Family Relationships

Inmates may adapt to prison life in a variety of ways. Kratcoski and Babb (1990) conducted a comprehensive comparative institutional and gender study in eight U.S. Bureau of Prison facilities. The older inmates' adjustment to the institutional setting was measured with questions on visitors, institutional activities, health problems, relations with other inmates and staff, feelings of fear, and victimization by other inmates. Findings indicate that older women, when compared to older men in this sample, are less likely to be married and living with their spouse before being institutionalized. Similar results were reported by Aday and Nation (2001), who found about one-third of their sample was widowed and another 25 percent divorced. Kratcoski and Babb feel that this fact provides a useful explanation of why older women received few visitors. More than 50 percent of the women in their sample stated that they never had visitors, compared with 25 percent of the older men. In addition, only 18 percent of the women reported that they received visitors at lease once a month compared with 33 percent of the men housed in facilities at similar security levels.

However, other research discovered that some older offenders prefer not to have frequent visits and rely more on letters and phone calls to stay in touch with family members (Aday & Nation, 2001). In Aday and Nation's small sample, 27 percent indicated that they had living parents, 86 percent had children, and 65 percent grandchildren. Almost all (93 percent) said that they remained in contact with family members. While only 10 percent of this group received visits weekly, over 70 percent talk each week on the phone to family members. This is indicative of how geographical distance can serve as a barrier to family visits for those who desire them. Over 80 percent indicated they feel a strong emotional closeness with their family and friends on the outside. Almost all feel that they have family or friends on the outside whom they can depend on for support. And only 14 percent are not satisfied with their present family relationships. Well over half (65 percent) indicated a very high degree of satisfaction.

Being separated from family members can prove to be difficult for many older female inmates. Not being able to fulfill the role of parent or grandparent every day can be frustrating. Some older female inmates serving life sentences have been unable to interact with their grandchildren in the free world. It can be a tremendous stigma for a grandmother to know that her grandchildren have always had to live with the fact that grandma is in prison. For some older inmates serving long sentences, visitation from family or friends on the outside can cause a continuous grief reaction with each visit. For these inmates, it becomes easier to do the time by maintaining a degree of social distance from their families and the outside world. They turn to an inner circle of inmate friends for social support. This technique of compartmentalization is one way some older females cope with long-term incarceration and family separation (Aday & Nation, 2001).

Prison Friendships

Prison friendships are important for older incarcerated females because they serve as a buffer against role losses and reduced social interaction with the outside world. Therefore, friendships formed in prison may aid in adapting to prison life. Gutheil's (1991) findings suggest that nursing home residents use their friendships as a coping strategy for adapting to institutional living, and it is suspected that prison friendships may be even more important. Issues normally discussed with family or outside friends are now shared with other inmates. Friends made in the prison setting may also act as socializing agents for adapting to new roles for which an individual is not prepared (Crohan & Antonucci, 1989; Gutheil, 1991). Inmates who have already experienced the transition to prison are important in helping incoming older inmates relinquish former roles and behavior patterns.

Prison friendships and support networks are also important when inmates face personal crises. For example, as older offenders age in place, they frequently outlive family members on the outside. When those tragic losses occur, the prison is not an ideal environment to process grief and cope with personal losses. In a focus group setting, I asked older females at the Tennessee Prison for Women, "How do you cope when family members on the outside die?" The consensus seemed to be that when such losses occur, inmates create a supportive environment conducive to processing the associated grief. As one older female stated, "when an inmate loses a family member to death, we become very protective of that person....Normally, a close friend will serve as a buffer to her. We try to provide as much privacy as possible and to assist in any way we can." Approximately three-fourths of the subjects in the group felt that they have fellow inmates they can depend upon and share similar social activities, interests, and concerns. A similar number frequently provide some type of assistance to a fellow inmate, and most are satisfied with their prison friendships. It is obvious that these close ties are important, for they contribute significantly to the formation of emotional closeness and social bonding within the confines of the prison.

As important as friends may be for the establishment of a supportive social network in the confines of prison, not all older inmates are able to find suitable friends who provide companionship. Some older female offenders are cautious about forming extremely close friendships. While they may visit frequently, they may be protective about discussing intimate topics. As a whole, I found that only 25 percent of our sample felt free to discuss almost any personal matter with a fellow inmate: some 37 percent were willing to discuss some personal matters, but only 4 percent would discuss all personal issues (Aday & Nation, 2001). In their specific conversations, they are more likely to discuss nonthreatening topics such as food or other prison conditions and things they are, in general, happy about.

Prison Activities

Passing time is an important part of coping with prison life. Available prison activities and work opportunities are key ingredients in developing successful coping strategies. Of course, being motivated to participate in prison programming is equally important. Older women are significantly less likely to be involved in various forms of sporting and recreational activities. As expected, watching television and working are popular ways to pass time in prison. Television provides a useful, and to some the only, link to the outside world. Work, on the other hand, provides a sense of usefulness and an opportunity to earn a small, but significant, amount of money. Writing letters is also an important activity, since it is the medium through which many inmates communicate with family and friends. Few older female inmates engage in educational programs, who as a group have had little opportunity for the educational preparation necessary to benefit from them or enjoy them (Kratcoski & Babb, 1990). Aday and Nation (2001) found that some female inmates regretted the lack educational opportunities for those who were college graduates.

When older females do socialize or make conversation with their fellow inmates, most do so when they are working, eating, watching television, or helping others, in that order. Religious activities, cards, arts and crafts, and other recreational games are also popular ways to interact with others (Aday & Nation, 2001). About one-third also socialize when they are taking a smoke break. Over 50 percent stated that they never or almost never participated in social activities such as watching television with others or playing cards or other games. Passivity in coping with confinement is most often the response of the older female inmate. Being alone, when possible, can also be a rewarding activity.

Prison Environment

The physical condition and structure of the institution can also create significant problems for older female inmates. Few of the older inmates in either Aday and Nation (2001) or Kratcoski and Babb (1990) report being satisfied with their living conditions. Older, frail offenders often find the prison environment oppressive with poor lighting and ventilation. Stale air from smokers, top bunking, and being housed too far away from the dining room and bathrooms were also viewed as significant environmental problems. Although we found that a significant majority (96 percent) of our sample could walk independently, well over half reported having difficulty walking long distances or standing in line for periods of fifteen minutes, as they sometimes were required to do (Aday & Nation, 2001). As Table 7.2 illustrates, the majority of older female inmates in this sample require ground-level housing and need a lower bunk. These findings are consistent with statistics produced by the Georgia Department of Corrections (2001), which indicates 65 percent of female inmates 55 years of age or older have major functional limitations.

Like older males, older female inmates housed in the general prison population often express a need for greater privacy. We discovered in our sample that approximately three-fourths of this sample found the current housing situation to be crowded, unpleasant, uncomfortable, and very noisy. In particular, the older inmates found younger inmates to be too noisy and most inconsiderate. These findings are consistent with other studies reporting that many of the older inmates of both sexes prefer to live with people of their own age (Cox, 1982; Walsh, 1989; Williams, 1989). Kratcoski and Babb (1990) found that older female inmates were much more likely to see other inmates as aggressive and violent than were older male inmates. The older women were also more likely to have little or no interaction with other inmates. As one older inmate reported, "Older residents are hassled by the younger ones and they receive little, if any, of the attention that older people need" (Cox, 1982, p. 74). As one older female offender stated about the "new" younger inmates, "These younger drug offenders come in and serve their time and then they are gone. . . . They don't care about the prison environment while they are here. . . . They just want to watch MTV and create problems" (Aday & Nation, 2001, p. 20). A significant number (30 percent) of the older female inmates stated that they were either occasionally, frequently, or always afraid (Kratcoski & Babb, 1990). This is contrary to previous studies, which reported that women inmates are much more likely to establish intense personal relationships with other inmates and less likely to be involved in violent confrontations (Carp & Schade, 1993).

Table 7.2
Self-Reported Functional Health Status of Older Female Inmates 50+ in Tennessee (N = 29)

Functional Status	Percentage
Need a lower bunk	87.5
Vision problems	87.5
Capable of going up/down stairs	70.8
Difficulty stand in line up to 15 minutes	66.7
Require ground-level housing	60.9
Difficulty walking long distances	58.3
Smoke regularly	54.2
Wear corrective eye lenses	54.2
Require a flat, even walking terrain	45.8
Hearing problems	29.2
Past drug/alcohol problem	29.2

RESPONDING TO OLDER FEMALE OFFENDERS

Female offenders make up a little more than 6 percent of the total state and federal prison population (General Accounting Office, 1999). The female over the age of 50 represents an even smaller percentage of the prison population. This underrepresentation of the female offender significantly reduces the availability of special housing, programs, and services provided to them (Bonta, Pang, & Wallace-Capretta, 1995). Programs and services for this small group are extremely limited. Oddly enough, female inmates have responded well to the few programs offered them. Many female offenders want to gain economic independence and are eager to learn new skills

Research by Morash, Bynum, & Koons (1998) cited major differences between male and female offenders, indicating the need for different policies and programs. Their survey of jail and prison administrators and programmers sponsored by the National Institute of Justice reported 242 programs in 33 states designed specifically for female offenders. Sample programs they cited were substance abuse programs, work training programs, child visitation and parent education programs, and a variety of transition, aftercare, education, and health programs. Survey respondents also cited the need for more programs providing drug treatment and mental health services. Correctional officials were in agreement that prison management styles for female offenders should be different from those for men. Effective managerial characteristics mentioned included the capacity to respond to expressions and emotions and the ability to communicate openly with female offenders.

Many states, particularly those with small female offender populations, have made no special provisions in management or programming for meeting the needs of incarcerated women. The special circumstances of female offenders, together with the general increase in the number of women in prison and jail, point to the need for different approaches to management and programming. In addition, responding to the increasing number of older women in jail and prison is most challenging because of the negative effects of crowding, lack of space, and constant movement in and out of institutions. Except for states with females inmate populations of 1,000 or more, classification and assessment are often unrelated to where women are housed or what programs they can participate in.

Housing and Health Needs

As the number of older female offenders increases, placement in special units specifically designed for or adapted to meet the special needs of aging inmates should be considered by correctional officials. Older offenders with chronic illnesses are increasingly housed for the long term in special-needs medical units. For example, California has a licensed skilled nursing facility in the women's prison that provides constant, direct nursing care for its aging and infirm prisoners (Nadel, 1998). Correctional policy should clearly define the goals and objectives of special units and should develop specific criteria for admission. Combining similar populations, such as older female inmates with serious physical disabilities, can provide the protected environment old inmates may need to reduce environmental stressors.

Morton (1993) has called for an increase in planning of medical services to meet the needs of older female offenders. Such planning would include special diets and physical therapy to counter osteoporosis and other potentially debilitating conditions. Other health services such as regular mammograms, Pap smears, and other diagnostic work should be offered in accordance with prevailing community standards. With increasing percentages of elderly inmates, prison health care providers will acquire the additional responsibilities of observing and reporting changes in the health of the elderly inmates and assisting and encouraging them to better manage their health problems (Booth, 1989). Frequent staff observations are important because the health of elderly prisoners can deteriorate rapidly. Older inmates are often unaware of changes in their health, or they may be reluctant to disclose health information about themselves. Prison staff training should include an awareness that it is easy to attribute certain symptoms to old age, which can result in overlooking serious medical problems. Monitoring for any changes in the older female's health is a responsibility that should be assumed by those who have frequent contact with the inmates.

Nadel (1998) has also called attention to the fact that women's needs for emergency and health services differ from men's, in that they have a greater demand for health services and different medical exams and tests. Inmates in Nadel's study reported marked delays in treatment. This creates tremendous anxiety for older, frail inmates. Planning for twenty-four-hour medical support that enables emergencies to be handled efficiently and effectively can relieve the anxiety of staff and older inmates. According to Morton (1993), such planning can, in the long term, reduce the number of emergency calls. Also, women typically have more medical problems upon entering prison and require more follow-up tests and lab services than men. Pharmacies must be able to prepare and store appropriate medications for female-related medical problems. Of course, co-payments (even those as low as $3–$5) implemented by managed-care organizations can serve as a barrier to health-care access.

Work and Training Assignments

Kratcoski and Babb (1990) reported that interviews with prison staff indicate that the most difficult task for prison administrators is to find ways to keep older inmates busy. Correctional officials recently reported a variety of work training programs, in-prison industries, and other work programs in various states. About half these programs were in work training (Morash, Bynum, & Koons, 1998). However, Carp and Schade (1993) have pointed out that the majority of available training emphasizes traditional female occupations that reinforce homemaker or low-skilled worker skills. The result is that female inmates often receive training in job skills like the ones that led them to being economically deprived in the first place. Work and training assignments are a critical phase of a female inmate's incarceration experience and plays an important role in helping inmates to maintain their maximum productivity and highest self-worth.

Many older inmates are incapable of successfully completing work assignments or training programs. Chronic health problems may prevent older female offenders from participating in normal work or training assignments. Prison officials must be more imaginative in programming for this subgroup. In facilities designed solely for older, special-needs offenders, finding suitable work assignments for everyone may prove difficult. Sometimes contacts with outside agencies can provide new opportunities for older, frail inmates. However, the location of women's prisons in isolated areas can hinder such programming. Regardless, correctional officials have to be creative in work programs. Sheltered workshops and modified prison industry programs designed specifically for female offenders should be developed.

Staff Training

Women's prison administrators have pointed to high turnover and the need for better-qualified staff (Caldwell et al., 2001). It is important that correctional agencies provide prison environments that are more gender-sensitive as well as appropriate staff training that permits successful outcomes with female geriatric inmates. Selecting and training staff to deal effectively with older female offenders will be an increasingly important challenge. Understanding the unique social environment found in a women's correctional facility is critical. Women offenders generally are not likely to challenge for control and power over their social setting. Females are more content to have someone else be in charge (Cranford & Williams, 1998). Female offenders in general, and older offenders in particular, do not see the prison experience as a contest between staff and inmates. Rather, they feel more in control of their environment through the process of communicating and sharing with others, including staff members. It may be necessary for prison officials to develop a new skill set to work effectively with women.

In addition, not everyone who works in a correctional environment may have the aptitude or the essential skills to manage elderly people. Correctional staffs that provide services to older inmates need to be knowledgeable, sensitive, creative, and flexible when responding to their special needs. Special sensitivity training may be necessary to adequately prepare staff to work with the aging population (Morton, 1993). Staff, particularly medical personnel, who work with this population should have extensive training in gerontological health issues (Morton, 1992). I have found that inmates frequently report that younger staff members frequently have very little patience when working with elderly inmates. Older inmates complain that they are treated like the younger, more violent inmates. As one older female stated, "they yell and scream and at us.... Although we treat them with respect, they have no respect for us" (Aday & Nation, 2001).

When prison officials design correctional health service programs, staffing patterns should take into account that supervising older women is frequently more time-consuming because of health impairments and other special needs. Overall, older inmates, both men and women, are more dependent on staff than younger ones are, demanding more staff time, assistance, and energy. Because older inmates are less involved in the inmate subculture, they often turn to staff members for help in dealing with a personal crisis. Kratcoski and Babb (1990) found a general consensus among prison staff that older inmates tend to have more complex and more frequent health problems. Training of administrative personnel, line security staff, and health providers should improve their knowledge of growing old and how aging specifically affects the elderly in a prison environment. In addition, the use of knowledgeable outside health consultants and community volunteers will greatly improve the ability of correctional officials to deal effectively with older incarcerated offenders (Morton, 1992).

Special Programming

The process of imprisonment encourages inmates to become dependent on the institution in which they live. Passivity is also highly encouraged and rewarded. As a result, many older offenders are reluctant to assert themselves with medical staff or in other prison programs. Prison staffs have indicated that it is more difficult to get older women involved in educational, recreational, or exercise programs (Kratcoski & Babb, 1990). Some of this reluctance has been attributed to cultural conditioning that emphasizes passivity in women. However, the authors also found that many of the women had never been employed outside the home and were not interested in pursuing a career. Therefore, the educational programs were viewed as irrelevant for them.

Programs in prison range from landscape maintenance to confrontational group therapy. Some authors have considered educational programs, medical services, leisure activities, religious services, and educational programs to be rehabilitative in nature (Pollock, 1998). However, few programs have been specifically designed for the older female inmate. Nearly 24 percent of female state prison and local jail inmates, and 22 percent of female probationers, were identified in a recent study as possessing mental health problems (Ditton, 1999). They are likely to be poor, lack education, and possess few work skills. Many have backgrounds of abuse and enter prison with considerable anger and resentment. Older female inmates bring health problems and anxieties concerning their own aging in addition.

As Chapter 6 described, various types of group therapy activities have become an important tool for renewing power and improving the overall quality of life for the elderly (Toseland, 1995). Group programs have reportedly relieved anxiety, stress, anger, and depression and have improved personal connections and interaction. Support groups have been particularly successful in helping older women to cope with the many changes of aging. Support groups have proved useful in helping older adults and their relatives learn to cope with medical procedures and devices such as kidney dialysis, respirators, wheelchairs, and artificial limbs. Acceptance of physical limitations or chronic conditions resulting from illness such as stroke, heart attack, cancer, HIV, or lung disease has been facilitated by discussion and support in groups with similar conditions.

In support groups, members are bonded together by the knowledge that they share concerns that are often not well understood by untrained prison staff. Older female offenders can take pride in having information to offer each other that is derived from life experiences and from their ongoing efforts to cope with stressful life events related to imprisonment. Meetings of support groups are characterized by interaction among members. Members can participate at their own pace, revitalizing, adjusting, and enhancing coping capacities that they have developed over a lifetime. In particular, for older inmates, support groups provide a sense of hope and can counterbalance situational depression arising from losses. They provide normative guidelines for later life development that are often lacking or unclear. Table 7.3 is a modified list of support group topics frequently used for older women (Kaye, 1997, p. 99).

The Ohio Department of Rehabilitation and Correction (1999) has implemented several programs designed solely for older female offenders, one of them a program in assertiveness training. The program teaches older offenders how to get their needs met in an assertive manner without major conflict or confrontation. Issues of loss from chronic illness and death are addressed in other department programs. Providing appropriate care for dying prisoners is a growing problem for the Ohio prison system, and the program Heart to Heart provides a support system for offenders who are struggling with issues of their terminal illness. It provides information on living wills and other end-of-life concerns. The program also improves the quality of life for dying offenders through interaction in an emotionally supportive environment. Another program, Life Beyond Loss, also teaches participants about the grieving process and how to apply techniques of grief resolution. Hospice care is now provided in many correctional facilities. Such programs provide counseling, crisis intervention, and closure in the form of funeral or memorial services.

Florida is another state that has experienced a significant growth in its number of older female offenders. In response, Florida Corrections Commission has announced the opening of a special unit for its older female inmates. In the department's Operational Plan for Female Offenders (Florida Department of Corrections, 1999), one of the major goals was to promote health and wellness services for aging female inmates. In con-

Table 7.3
Support Group Topics for Older Women

Topics Addressing Personal Development
    Loneliness
    Mortality
    How to make each moment count
    Self-esteem
    Future fears and desires
    Life transitions
    Ageism
    Drug/alcohol abuse
    How to maintain independence
    Energy level changes
    Anger management
    Lack of mobility
    Isolation
    Weight gain
Topics Addressing Daily Life Issues
    Work activities
    Learning to live in prison
    Getting along with others
    Learning to live with chronic illness
    Legal issues
    Financial concerns
    Environmental stress
Topics Addressing Family and Social Relationships
    Desertion by families
    Children and grandchildren
    Sexuality and relationships
    Prison friendships
    Social issues
    Abusive relationships
    Death of family and friends

Source: L.W. Kaye, *Self-Help Support Groups for Older Women* (Washington, DC: Taylor & Francis, 1997), p. 97.

junction with institutional program staff, volunteers lead support groups and other activities that address special issues and needs of female inmates over 50 years of age. Special needs of this population were identified to include depression, death and dying, health, exercise, menopause, wills and trusts, nutrition, stress, and life skills, to mention a few of the issues relevant to the aging female.

CONSCIOUSNESS-RAISING PROGRAMS

An increased emphasis on self-care is another initiative that has been offered as a possible solution to the growing number of older female offenders. The popular appeal of alternative therapies such as special diets, upbeat exercise routines, meditation, and other practices of self-observation and self-treatment can serve as an important source of empowerment for female offenders. Educational programs in group settings can be of equal importance in heightening awareness to practice healthful behaviors. Research by Negy, Woods, and Carlson (1997) showed that prisoners who took a "proactive stance" toward problems, planned specific courses of action, reinterpreted stressful events in a positive way, and accepted unpleasant events felt better about themselves and were less depressed or anxious.

To enhance prison adjustment and personal autonomy, Greco (1996) established the CRP (Consciousness-Raising Program) at a maximum-security prison in New York. The purpose of the program was to increase the older women's empowerment and their awareness of ways they could improve their health and their quality of life while in prison. The program included twelve seminar sessions on three subject categories (1) biological topics focusing on physical changes, women's health issues, HIV/AIDS and older women, exercise, and nutrition; (2) psychological topics centered on religion, mental health, sexuality in later life, and creativity; and (3) social issues including intergenerational relationships and grandparenthood, social policy, and alcoholism in later life. Regardless of the topic, experts conducted each session with a comprehensive approach to the issue of women aging in prison. The women who participated in the CRP volunteered from the inmate population of the Bedford Hills Correctional Facility in Westchester County. The participants' ages ranged from 50 to 67, with a mean age of 56.5 years.

The intent of such programs is not only to lengthen life but, more importantly, to improve the functional independence of the aged. Several participants in the program began to accept responsibility for their own health and began to lobby for preventive health-care measures and more elaborate medical procedures in the prison. As a result of the assertive measures taken by program participants, a doctor was assigned specifically to address the needs of women over 50. The CRP provided the women with new information that was easily incorporated into their everyday lives.

The program, like others, enabled older female offenders to discover ways to overcome the anonymity and dehumanization of prison life. Participating in the CRP permitted the women to disclose, and in the process to affirm, their identities. Participants reported greater self-confidence. The consciousness-raising seminars provided a new emotional and intellectual experience for the previously passive aging female offenders. Encouraged by the mental health specialists leading the awareness-increasing sessions, older female inmates reported that their attitudes toward other prisoners became more favorable.

Finally, the CRP provided the participants with the opportunity to examine their own aging process while in prison. Providing the women with new information enabled some participants to distinguish more clearly between normal and pathological symptoms. By sharing their personal experiences of aging, numerous participants began to design new life activities and experiences for themselves. Behavioral changes included more exercise, eating a healthier diet, and losing weight. As one women explained, "the seminars gave me a way to embrace the idea of aging. And accept it, get into it and explore it rather than deny it.... It was like a bridge into a new stage of my life" (Greco, 1996, p. 17).

SUMMARY

The number of older offenders in our prisons is gradually rising as a result of the increasing number of states with mandatory life sentences and as a result of the graying of the population as a whole. As a result, a variety of designated units have been developed for older males. While the growth will continue to be more dramatic for males, prison administrators would do well to plan for increasing numbers of older females. When planning for older female inmates, recognition of their health-care needs is important. The size of the facility and the number of health-care beds should be influenced by the projected increases of aging females. As older female inmates' health deteriorates and they leave the general prison population, alternative facilities or services could include assisted-living-type prison facilities, which would include full-time nursing staff.

Like older male offenders, older women in prison may be in prison for the first time late in life or may be growing old in prison as a result of long sentences. It is difficult, however, to draw firm conclusions about the experiences of older women in prison because there is so little available literature. We do know that women in general and older women in particular have a broad variety of health-care needs. Neglecting the needs of older women in prison simply on the grounds of numerical rarity does not seem to be ethically justifiable. Crime by older female offenders needs to be taken more seriously. Comprehensive strategies will be necessary to adequately respond to the special needs of the increasing number of older female offenders.

REFERENCES

Acoca, L. (1998). Defusing the time bomb: Understanding and meeting the growing health care needs of incarcerated women in America. *Crime and Delinquency, 44*, 49–70.

Aday, R. H., & Nation, P. (2001). *A case study of older female offenders*. Nashville: Tennessee Department of Correction.

Aday, R. H., & Rosefield, H. A. (1992, Winter). Providing for the geriatric inmate: Implications for training. *Journal of Correctional Training, 12*, 14–16.

Beck, A. J. (1999). *Prisoners in 1999*. Washington, DC: U.S. Department of Justice.

Belknap, J. (1996). *Access to programs and health care for incarcerated women*. Washington, DC: Administrative Office of the United States Courts.

Bloom, B., Chesney-Lind, C., & Owen, B. (1994). *Women in California prisons: Hidden victims of the war on drugs*. San Francisco: Center on Juvenile and Criminal Justice.

Bonta, J., Pang, B., & Wallace-Capretta, L. (1995) Predictors of recidivism among incarcerated family offenders. *Prison Journal, 75*, 277–295.

Booth, D. (1989). Health status of the incarcerated elderly: Issues and concerns. *Journal of Offender Counseling, Services and Rehabilitation, 13*, 193–214.

Bureau of Justice Statistics. (1998). *Prisoners in 1997*. Washington, DC: U.S. Department of Justice.

Caldwell, C., Jarvis, M., & Rosefield, H. (2001). Issues impacting today's geriatric female offenders. *Corrections Today, 65*(5), 110–113.

Carp, S. V., & Schade, L. S. (1993). Tailoring facility programming to suit female offenders' needs. In *Female offenders: Meeting needs of a neglected population* (pp. 37–42). Laurel, MD: American Correctional Association.

Coll, C. G., Miller, J. B., Fields, J. P., & Mathews, B. (1998). The experiences of women in prison: Implications for services and prevention. *Women and Therapy, 20*(4), 11–28.

Colsher, P., Wallace, R., Loffelholz, P., & Sales, M. (1992). Health status of older male prisoners: A comprehensive survey. *American Journal of Public Health, 82*, 881–884.

Corrections Yearbook. (2000). South Salem, NY: Criminal Justice Institute.

Cox, J. (1982). *Self-perceptions of health and aging of older females in prison: An exploratory group case study*. Unpublished doctoral dissertation, Southern Illinois University.

Cranford, S., & Williams, R. (1998, December). Critical issues in managing female offenders. *Corrections Today, 60*, 130–135.

Crohan, S. E., & Antonucci, T. C. (1989). Friends as a source of social support in old age. In R. G. Adams & R. Blieszner (Eds.), *Older adult friendship: Structure and process*. Newbury Park, CA: Sage Publications.

Curry, L. (2001, February). Tougher sentencing, economic hardships and rising violence. *Corrections Today, 63*, 74–76.

DeBell, J. (2001). The female offender: Different, not difficult. *Corrections Today, 63*, 56–61.

DeCostanzo, E. T. (1998, December). Why women offenders? *Corrections Today, 60*, 8.

Ditton, P. M. (1999). *Mental health and treatment of inmates and probationers*. Washington, DC: Bureau of Justice Statistics.

Ebersole, P., & Hess, P. (1998). *Toward healthy aging*. St. Louis: Mosby.

Ellsworth, T., & Helle, K. A. (1994). Older offenders on probation. *Federal Probation, 68*(4), 43–50.

Epp, J. (1996, October). Exploratory heath care needs of adult female offenders. *Corrections Today, 58*(6), 96–100.

Flanagan, L. (1995). Meeting the needs of females in custody: Maryland's unique approach. *Federal Probation, 59*(2), 49–53.

Florida Department of Corrections. (1999). *Operational plan for female offenders*. Tallahassee, FL.

Genders, E., & Player, E. (1990). Women lifers: Assessing the experience. *Prison Journal, 80*(1), 46–57.

General Accounting Office. (1999). *Women in prison*. Washington, DC.

Georgia Department of Corrections. (2001). *Georgia's aging inmate population*. Atlanta, GA: Author.

Gilliard, D. D., & Beck, A. J. (1997). Prison and jail inmates at midyear, 1996. *Bureau of Justice Statistics Bulletin*. Washington, DC: U.S. Department of Justice.

Goffman, E. (1961). *Asylums: Essays on the social situation of mental patients and other inmates*. Garden City, NY: Doubleday.

Goldkuhle, U. (1999). Health service utilization by women in prison: Health needs indicators and response effects. *Journal of Correctional Health Care, 6*(1), 63–83.

Greco, R. (1996). "I'm in prison, my mind is not!" *Prospective on Aging, 25*(2), 25–27.

Greenfield, L. A., & Snell, T. L. (1999). *Women offenders*. Washington, DC: Bureau of Justice Statistics.

Gutheil, I. A. (1991). Intimacy in nursing home friendships. *Journal of Gerontological Social Work, 17*(1–2), 59–74.

Henderson, D., Schaeffer, J., & Brown, L. (1998). Gender-appropriate mental health services for incarcerated women: Issues and challenges. *Family and Community Health, 21*, 42–52.

Hooyman, N., & Kiyak, H. A. (1999). *Social gerontology*. Boston: Allyn & Bacon.

Immarigeon, R., & Chesney-Lind, M. (1992). *Women's prisons: Overcrowded and overused.* San Francisco: National Council on Crime and Delinquency.

Ingram-Fogel, C. (1993). Hard time: The stressful nature of incarceration for women. *Issues in Mental Health Nursing, 14,* 367–377.

Kaye, L. W. (1997). Self-help support groups for older women. Washington, DC: Taylor & Francis.

Koons, B. A., Burrow, J. D., Morash, M., & Bynum, T. (1997). Expert and offender perceptions of program elements linked to successful outcomes for incarcerated women. *Crime and Delinquency, 43,* 512–533.

Kratcoski, P. C., & Babb, S. (1990). Adjustment of older inmates: An analysis by institutional structure and gender. *Journal of Contemporary Criminal Justice, 6,* 139–156.

LaMere, S., Smyer, T., & Gragert, M. (1996). The aging inmate. *Journal of Psychosocial Nursing, 34*(4), 25–29.

Lazarus, R., & Folkman, S. (1984). *Stress, appraisal, and coping.* New York: Springer.

McKensie, D. L., Robinson, J., & Campbell, C. (1989). Long term incarceration of female offenders. *Criminal Justice and Behavior, 16,* 223–238.

McQuaide, S., & Ehrenreich, J. H. (1998). Women in prison: Approaches to understanding the lives of a forgotten population. *Affilia: Journal of Women and Social Work, 13,* 233–246.

Morash, M., Bynum, T., & Koons, B. (1998). *Women offenders: Programming needs and promising approaches.* National Institute of Justice research in brief. Washington, DC: National Institute of Justice.

Morton, J. B. (1992). The older female offender. In *Female offenders: Meeting needs of a neglected population* (pp. 80–84). Laurel, MD: American Correctional Association.

Morton, J. B. (1993, February). Training staff to work with elderly and disabled inmates. *Corrections Today, 55,* 44–47.

Nadel, B. (1998, October). BOP accommodates special needs offenders. *Corrections Today, 60,* 76–80.

Neeley, C., Addison, L., & Craig-Moreland, D. (1997, August). Addressing the needs of elderly offenders. *Corrections Today, 59,* 123–127.

Negy, C., Words, D., & Carlson, R. (1997). The relationship between females, coping and adjustment in a minimum security prison. *Criminal Justice and Behavior, 24*(2), 224–233.

Ohio Department of Rehabilitation and Correction (1999). *A comprehensive approach to addressing the needs of aging prisoners.* Columbus, OH.

Owen, B., & Bloom, B. (1995). Profiling women prisoners: Findings from national surveys and a California sample. *Prison Journal, 75*(2), 1765–1785.

Phillips, S. D., & Harm, N. J. (1998). Women prisoners: A contextual framework. *Women and Therapy, 20*(4), 1–9.

Pollock, J. M. (1998). *Counseling women in prison.* Thousand Oaks, CA: Sage Publications.

Ross, P.H., & Lawrence, J.W. (1998). Health care for women offenders. *Corrections Today, 60,* 122–128.

Roth, E.B. (1992, July–October). Elders behind bars. *Perspectives on Aging, 21,* 25–31.

Speroff, L., Rowan, J., Symons, J., Genant, H., & Winborn, W. (1996). The comparative effect on bone density, endometrium, and lipids of continuous hormones as replacement therapy: A randomized controlled trial. *Journal of the American Medical Association, 276,* 1397–1403.

Steffensmeier, D.J., & Allan, E. (1996). Gender and crime: Toward a gendered theory of female offending. *Annual Review of Sociology, 22,* 459–488.

Toseland, R.K. (1995). *Group work with the elderly and family caregivers.* New York: Springer.

Walsh, C.E. (1989). The older and long term inmate growing old in the New Jersey prison system. *Journal of Offender Counseling, Services and Rehabilitation, 13,* 215–248.

Watchel, W., & Stein, M.D. (1995). HIV infection in older persons. In W. Reichel (Ed.), *Care of the elderly: Clinical aspects of aging* (pp. 214–227). Baltimore: Williams & Wilkins.

Williams, G.C. (1989). *Elderly offenders: A comparison of chronic and new elderly offenders.* Unpublished master's thesis. Murfreesboro: Middle Tennessee State University.

Yergen, J., LoGerfo, J., Shortell, S., Bergner, M., Diehr, P., & Richardson, W. (1981). Health status as a measure of need for medical care: A critique. *Medical Care, 19,* 57–68.

Young, D.S. (1998). Health status and service use among incarcerated women. *Family and Community Health Journal, 21,* 1–16.

Chapter 8

Responding to Aging Offenders

Correctional officials consider that age will be one of the most important factors in managing the criminal justice system well into the 21st century. The baby boomers swelling the ranks of those reaching older adulthood have forced new prison policies to emerge. For example, in addition to building new geriatric facilities, many correctional systems have also introduced hospice and managed care into the prison setting in an attempt to control health care costs.

Other polices are sure to emerge in the future as the crisis associated with the graying of America's prisons steadily worsens. Although few standardized policies may be based solely on age alone, criminal justice agencies are likely to utilize unwritten or informal policies to deal with our aging population, which is likely to result in considerable variation from state to state or jurisdiction to jurisdiction. Local variation is already evident today in the diversity found between states in the strictness of their sentencing laws. It is important to review some of the existing policies from the time older offenders are apprehended until they leave the system.

This chapter will explore important policy issues in the treatment of elderly offenders in the criminal justice system. It will examine previous literature to identify any policy trends in response of the various arms of the criminal justice system to the elderly offender. I will address (1) the use and extent of police discretion, (2) the role of the courts in developing sentencing mandates, (3) current prison policies on age, and (4) alternatives to incarceration. As the final chapter of the book, Chapter 8 will conclude with important research questions and discuss some of the challenges to the implementation of new policies for the aging inmate.

POLICE DISCRETION

Most police departments operate on an "incident-based" response policy (Terry & Entzel, 2000). In other words, the police respond to incidents case by case, as each is telephoned in. Incident-based response is not very well suited to understanding the special needs or unique characteristics of certain groups, such as the elderly. Procedural rules in police training manuals on the apprehension of elderly offenders are almost nonexistent.

While the criminal justice system purports to treat people equally regardless of their age, sex, race, or social class, it may be impossible for those who work in criminal justice (whether law-enforcement officials, lawyers, or judges) to be totally objective and impartial in their response to the general public. Individuals who work in the criminal justice system are products of society and may hold certain negative or positive biases toward various groups. Police officers who have the responsibility of arresting elderly lawbreakers may see a similarity between the offender and his or her own grandparents. It has also been suggested that some members of the police force might respond more harshly toward the older offender. In areas where large enclaves of elderly reside, police may enact more restrictive controls. Some justice officials may be outraged at a multiple recidivist who continues to commit crime in his later years without any remorse. Others may be incensed when a respectable elder in the community with no previous criminal record participates in the sale of drugs or engages in sexual abuse of an unsuspecting child (Fattah & Sacco, 1989). Insofar as such biases operate, elderly offenders may be treated differently by those in gate-keeping positions in the criminal justice system.

Research indicates that the police decision to arrest depends on offender characteristics and demeanor and incident characteristics. For example, Ebersole and Hess (1998) described a 70-year-old woman who was arraigned for selling marijuana to schoolchildren. She was simply admonished to discontinue. Likewise, an 80-year-old threatened police with an ax while they attempted to evict her. Again, charges were not filed in the case. These examples demonstrate that old lawbreakers often receive preferential treatment. Frequently, the elderly, children, and the sick are not expected to fully adhere to performance standards of the rest of society. These vulnerable populations are not held fully accountable because their actions are considered less significant (Ebersole & Hess, 1998). The legal system is at present unable to adequately distinguish responsible older violators from those unable to fully comprehend their crimes.

Bachand (1984) suggests that community priorities, the offender's age, and gender can influence the police officer's decision to apprehend a suspect. He reported that elderly offenders would receive less enforcement attention as long as their criminal activity did not exceed in either seriousness or incidence the criminal participation of the more youthful offenders. He further suggests the following situational factors that tend to influence elder arrests (p. 47):

- The elderly will be arrested less often for law violations, since offense pattern data suggest their criminal activity is concentrated in the less serious crime categories.
- The elderly offender's age combined with a respectful attitude toward the police will result in lower arrest rates.
- Elderly shoplifters generally will not be arrested as often as younger shoplifters because the elderly are less likely to be perceived as suspects and store owners are generally less willing to prosecute older offenders.

While the community is concerned about such issues as shoplifting, family violence, and drunken driving, the public generally retains great sympathy for the elderly (Fyfe, 1984). Geriatric delinquents who are vagrants, alcoholics, or simply confused are viewed as merely in need of supervision. Evidence suggests that police respond to these minor offenses committed by older people primarily in terms of their harmlessness and their need for protection (Alston, 1986). While they may be considered a nuisance and an occasional inconvenience to the police, they are not normally viewed as criminals. In the abstract, the public may support forceful policies to deal with such offenses. These concrete instances, however, frequently provoke a feeling more of sympathy, and in some instances the public perceives the police as responding too severely when arresting some elderly offenders commiting minor offenses.

Atchley (2000) proposes that the reduction in arrest rates of older people has been influenced by recent changes in societal reactions to specific crimes. For example, as a result of a less punitive approach to alcohol abuse in the 1980s, older people picked up for drunkenness are now more likely to be held without arrest until they sober up and then be released. Conversely, Atchley asserts that shoplifting and drunken driving are being handled more punitively. He suggests that in the 1980s both these offenses came to be viewed more seriously by society. A national campaign against drunk drivers and a greater willingness of retailers to prosecute shoplifters have contributed to more frequent arrests of older adults for these criminal activities.

Newspapers and television reporting of arrests of the elderly give the impression that the more serious crimes of the elderly are viewed by police and by the general public with greater tolerance than those of juveniles (Cohen, 1985). The impression is reinforced by a study of reactions to hypothetical acts of theft involving young and older adult offenders. A sample of elderly people, college students, and law enforcement officers viewed elderly offenders more positively than their young counterparts. All respondent groups indicated that the elderly offenders should receive less severe punishment than juvenile offenders receive (Silverman, Smith, Nelson, & Dembo, 1984).

Bachand (1984) argues that the literature on police discretion generally supports the hypothesis that the criminal justice system affords the elderly preferential treatment in prearrest situations. Further, among the elderly, women have been found to receive leniency more often than males, and there is mixed evidence that white offenders may be treated more leniently than blacks and other minorities (Visher, 1983). Shichor (1984) noted from arrest patterns that elderly females might be handled more leniently than younger females in arrests for minor offenses. On the other hand, Fyfe (1984) advocated that the police need even more discretion to divert incompetent elderly offenders from the criminal justice system to alternative social welfare agencies. He argues that the inflexibility of the prescribed arrest process may subject elderly offenders to the trauma of detention before court appearances without accomplishing anything.

On the whole, the discretion that police can exercise in both misdemeanor and felony cases appears to have diminished. The tougher attitude toward crime today, even toward offenses such as shoplifting, may result in greater arrest rates of older adults even if their offense rates remain the same (Alston, 1986). In addition, because newspapers, television, and radio have focused significant attention on the criminal activity of the elderly, the elderly will receive more attention as suspects of crime. As the elderly population grows, police officers may have fewer opportunities to exercise the day-to-day discretion in making arrests. Today, the public has far less tolerance for sexual offenses and other crimes of violence committed by the new elderly offender. The shift in attitudes toward all types of crime will influence discretion policies and decrease the previous flexibility afforded those responsible for monitoring and controlling crime.

THE COURTS AND SENTENCING

With a growing interest in elderly criminality, a number of studies have addressed the basis, operation, and consequences of elderly justice (Feinberg & McGriff, 1989; Finkel & Macki, 2000; James, 1992). From these studies, a recurring question has emerged: Should advanced age and health be used as a discriminating factor buffering the defendant from more punitive reaction of the court? Answering the question is not easy. The complexity of the crimes committed and the diverse characteristics of the perpetrators make it extremely difficult to establish uniform policy. Those working in the criminal justice system also have different ideologies and life experiences, resulting in differences of opinion on whether to sentence elderly offenders more leniently than younger offenders.

A number of research studies support the suspicion that criminal justice decisions makers give elderly offenders sentencing breaks. For example, Champion (1989) found that for minor offenses such as shoplifting, elderly offenders tended to be prosecuted less frequently in general than other age groups. Similarly, Cutshall and Adams (1983) reported that prosecutors were more lenient in their treatment of older shoplifters, being more willing to dismiss minor charges against them than they were to dismiss those of younger adult shoplifters. Shichor (1985) also determined that from female arrest patterns it appears elderly offenders apparently were treated more leniently than younger ones where minor offenses are concerned. The authors contended that advanced age may be a mitigating factor in the enforcement of legal norms, at least with respect to minor criminal offenses such as misdemeanor shoplifting.

Feinberg and McGriff (1989) also investigated the defendant's advanced age as a proponent status when charged with misdemeanor theft crimes. Using records of the Dade County Court, Eleventh Judicial Circuit of Florida, the authors found age to be one of the most significant determinants of sanctions for convicted misdemeanor theft defendants. Although the majority of elderly theft defendants were convicted (57 percent), the conviction rate was significantly (p. <.05) lower than among their younger counterparts (66 percent). The elderly were more likely to be fined and were less likely than their younger offenders to do jail time as a result of their theft accusation. Some 31.8 percent of elderly misdemeanor theft offenders were placed on probation compared with 20.2 percent of offenders under 25 years of age. In sum, elderly misdemeanor theft defendants were found to receive more lenient treatment than younger offenders. The elderly were more likely to receive pretrial interventions, receive withheld adjudications, and were, generally speaking, less likely to be convicted. On the other hand, older offender acquittal rates were also much lower than those enjoyed by younger theft offenders.

For more serious offenses, Champion's (1988) research focused on the sentences defendants received both from plea bargaining and from judges in the sentencing portion of trials. He found that offenders aged 18 to 29 received sentences of 23 percent of maximum penalty, while offenders aged 60 and up received only 10 percent of the maximum penalty. In cases where trials were conducted and convictions were obtained, Champion found the discrepancies were even greater. Champion's findings are also supported by additional research. For example, Helms (1997) reviewed felony sentencing in county courts in Oregon. His analysis of court decisions and sentence types for offenders receiving incarceration found that older offenders were more likely to receive court leniency than younger, adult offenders.

In contrast, Bachand (1984) contends that elderly defendants, contrary to common belief, are not only more likely to be convicted than comparably accused younger defendants, but they are also more severely sanctioned than comparably accused younger defendants. Feinberg and Kholsa (1985) observed that of the ninety-seven judges they surveyed (1) almost 50 percent are not especially sympathetic toward the elderly; (2) most sanction elderly shoplifters with fines despite beliefs that their thefts are motivated by economic need; and (3) older judges are not more likely than younger colleagues to favor special treatment for elderly defendants.

Wilbanks (1985) reported that the courts up to the sentencing stage treat older offenders more severely, at which point the elderly appear to benefit from lenient treatment. Elderly criminals aged 60 and over were more likely than younger offenders to be incarcerated for crimes such as aggravated assault with a weapon, negligent manslaughter with a vehicle, motor vehicle theft, dangerous drugs, molestation, disturbing the peace, and fraud. However, Wilbanks reported that older offenders were less likely to be imprisoned for homicide, rape, robbery, simple assault, burglary, larceny, and forgery. In sum, Wilbanks found little evidence that the elderly are treated more leniently than younger offenders.

Furthermore, Jackson (1996) examined factors that affect the severity of sentencing for sexual offenders, a common crime among older adults. Her research investigated sentencing child molestation, sexual assault, sexual abuse, and sexual conduct with a minor. Jackson found that older offenders with no prior contact with their victims received the most severe sentencing recommendation. Thus, for cases where no previous contact had taken place, age was an important discriminatory factor.

In comparison, Lindquist, White, and Chambers (1986) produced mixed results in their study of felons and misdemeanants, with some classifications of older misdemeanants actually receiving more severe sentences than their younger counterparts. In their examination of the two constituent parts of the criminal justice system, prosecution and adjudication, they found that the elderly fared much better at the hands of prosecutors than at the hands of judges. For example, over 70 percent of the cases they observed involving elderly defendants never appeared in the courtroom, compared to less than 55 percent of the cases in which the defendant is under age 55. When they get to court, younger defendants (98 percent) are almost certain to be found guilty, while the elderly have a 17 percent chance of going free.

According to Alston (1986), of importance here is the issue of criminal responsibility. While our legal system has never established age as an indicator of reduced capacity, Cohen (1985) argues that "functional impairment that may be associated with a physical or mental condition suffered by the elderly accused" could possibly serve as a mitigating factor at sentencing. For example, older people can suffer from organically based disorders that interfere with logical thought. Ebersole and Hess (1998) have suggested that the legal system is unable to adequately distinguish responsible older violators from those unable to fully comprehend their crimes. With the significant number of older offenders continuing to commit violent crimes, the criminal justice system will need to become more adept at differentiating the competent from the impaired elderly offenders (Ogloff, Roesch & Eaves, 1995). The involvement of mental health professionals in adjudicating legal issues, such as dementia and competence to stand trial, has been the subject of extensive debate. While the core definition of competence is legal, all state and federal competence-to-stand-trial statutes define that competence in terms of mental function. An Interdisciplinary Fitness Interview (IFI) developed by Roesch and Golding (1985) has proved successful for professional teams in evaluating competence. Although not developed specifically for the elderly, the assessment tool could prove useful in evaluating them.

A basis for believing that older people should be treated less harshly is that similar punishments have different severity at different ages. By this logic, older offenders may be treated with more leniency than younger offenders because they feel punishments with disproportionate effect. This line of reasoning raises the question of whether a five-year prison term to a 25-year-old is the same as a five-year sentence for a 70-year-old, which in turn introduces another important issue revolving around what constitutes "fair punishment." To give one example, a five-year sentence to an advanced age offender may be the equivalent of a life sentence (Alston, 1986; Sherwin, 1990). For example, in State v. Waldrip, the judge reduced a 67-year-old defendant's sentence for voluntary manslaughter from five years to life to five to ten years. The judge argued that even the minimum term of five years could in effect be a life sentence because of the defendant's age (James, 1992).

Federal court decisions focus more on the initial sentence appropriate for the crime, rather than using age as a mitigating factor (James, 1992). James in her research on the sentencing of elderly criminals provides several illustrations demonstrating the courts' reluctance to provide lighter sentences on the basis of age. For example, Melvyn R. Paisley, aged 67, was convicted for fraudulent activities. His sentence was a $50,000 fine and four years in prison. However, Paisley argued that he should be given home detention because of his age and his battle with cancer. In this case, the court ruled that the defendant was neither elderly nor infirm. James concludes that a defendant is considered infirm only if he or she is at the present time suffering from an adverse medical condition as opposed to merely having a serious and perhaps fatal diagnosis. According to federal sentencing guidelines, to be elderly and infirm, a defendant would need to be at least 60 years of age and currently experiencing the effects of a debilitating disease (United States Sentencing Commission, 1989).

The discretion that has been built into our criminal justice system probably results in considerable variation in the disposition of the cases of older offenders according to the type of offense and the individual judge. At the same time, mandatory sentencing and the "get tough on crime" policy have reduced some of the judicial discretion utilized in the past. The population composition of the community may also play a role in sentencing. It is possible to handle older offenders more leniently in communities where their numbers are relatively small. Small numbers and low offense rates mean that older offenders rarely come before the court. Their cases are more likely to appear to be unique and therefore to call for alternative solutions.

In contrast, there are reasons to expect older offenders to be dealt with more harshly. It has been argued that the older offenders should know better and are, therefore, more culpable than young people (Cohen, 1985). Judges may also hold that the older person who violates the law is hopelessly obdurate and that society has no choice other than incarceration. Black (1980) further suggests that marginality increases vulnerability to the law. He notes that "A marginal man is ... more likely to have the police called against him, to be arrested, prosecuted, to have heavy damages demanded of him, or to be severely punished" (p. 51). Finally, as we have discussed, because many older offenders may have received special treatment at earlier stages of police or court processing, only the most serious older offenders actually reach the sentencing stage. In this regard, earlier leniency in the criminal justice system may lead to what appears to be harsh treatment by the sentencing judge (Steffensmeier, Kramer, & Ulmer, 1995).

Steffensmeier and Ulmer (1995) further argue that older persons are better able to reform themselves and that they are less likely to have the pervasive criminal tendencies or physical skills that characterize younger offenders. For these authors, society is less likely to view older offenders as a comprehensive criminal threat, and their criminal activity is more typically viewed as idiosyncratic. Criminal activities of aging offenders can be explained away as resulting from external forces outside their control, such as extreme social and environmental circumstances or health problems associated with advanced age. It appears that older offenders are viewed as less dangerous and less likely to commit crimes in the future. Frail elderly may be able to influence public opinion and thus sway the sentencing judge toward a more lenient sentence by showing remorse or the potential for rehabilitation. Overall, society views older offenders as less dangerous and as posing a lesser risk of danger to the community than younger offenders.

Such was the case of Ms. Egan, a 68-year-old mother who was acquitted by a jury of the attempted murder of her daughter ("Mother is Acquitted in Paralyzing Attack," *New York Times*, 1999). The police report indicated that Ms. Egan shot her daughter after hearing a conversation between her daughter and her daughter's boyfriend about putting her in a nursing home. As a result of the gunshot wound, her daughter was paralyzed from the neck down, was barely able to speak, and was incapable of swallowing or of controlling her bladder. She won the right to be taken off life support and died shortly thereafter. The state's attorney decided against bringing a murder charge, citing Ms. Egan's poor health and closeness to her daughter. The defense lawyer argued that Ms. Egan was involuntarily intoxicated from prescription drugs and did not intend to shoot her daughter.

James (1992) suggests that from a utilitarian perspective, reduced sentences for the elderly make sense if deterrence and rehabilitation are ineffective for that population. Inasmuch as punishment is not viewed as an end in itself, severe punishment should not be implemented if it serves no real societal purpose. Judges may conclude that sentencing older offenders to a long prison sentence is financially costly and poses special problems for the prison system to provide special diets, medications, and so forth. By this reasoning, if an elderly offender is not presently a threat to society, perhaps it would be better to release these relatively harmless individuals into society than to keep them in prison and have taxpayers incur costly medical expenses. Yates and Gillespie (2000, p. 173) fully supports this view: "returning discretion to federal judges, at least for consideration of age and health in sentencing elderly offenders, is warranted."

AGE AND PRISON POLICIES

The specific written polices that address aged or infirm inmates are as few as are the policies that address sentencing the elderly. While correctional administrators report that the needs of older offenders in prison differ from those of younger inmates, few jurisdictions operate programs and services specifically designed for the older inmate (Edwards, 1998; Ellsworth & Helle, 1994). Typically, all inmates including the elderly are screened in the admission process. As a matter of practice, the needs of older inmates are addressed, to the extent possible, in the course of the screening process. In most states, for example, when older inmates are separated from the general population, it is usually because of medical and security reasons rather than because of the age of the inmate. In several states, older inmates have the option of requesting housing compatible with their health. Older inmates who suffer from many chronic health problems are granted special treatment because of their inferior health status, but not because of age alone.

Alaska, Illinois, Michigan, Mississippi, South Carolina, and Texas make some policy decisions based solely on age (Aday, 1999; Flynn, 1992). In addition, Minnesota, New Jersey, and Rhode Island, for example, report that age is frequently used unofficially as a means of making policy decisions. In Texas, the inmate is medically classified according to medical history, general health, physical findings, and age. Inmates 50 to 55 years of age receive a classification requiring lighter, slower duties. Inmates 55 and over are assigned a classification that restricts the inmate from harder, heavier work and may allow for fewer work hours. Alaska reports occasionally providing a modification in sentencing for disease onset in the elderly. In Mississippi, inmates over 50 years of age are housed in geriatric units if their security classification permits. In South Carolina, inmates may retire from work at age 65. Numerous states also provide annual physicals for inmates over the age of 50, rather than every other year for the general prison population.

Grouping Older Inmates

Chapter 6 addressed the risk of elderly inmates being victimized by younger felons. One way to improve the safety of vulnerable inmates is to provide separate housing (Rosefield, 1993). Those who support the segregation of older inmates believe it is necessary to protect elderly and other weak inmates against victimization, exploitation, and harassment by younger, more aggressive inmates. As a rule, older inmates prefer to reside in age-segregated environments, which are more likely to be quiet and conducive to developing social relationships. Engaging in age-specific activities within the institution can be beneficial to the mental health of older inmates. Social interaction among fellow elderly inmates can help them to avoid loneliness and reduce the effects of institutionalization.

Grouping inmates with similar health-care needs can be more cost-effective as well as provide prison officials the opportunity to cater more efficiently to the needs of elderly prisoners. Specialized staff members are able to identify, monitor, and treat geriatric health problems as they arise. Separate facilities can also be cost-effective from a security standpoint. Since most elderly inmates do not pose a high security risk to management, reduced-custody facilities for older inmates can free up high-security beds for younger, more violent offenders. Further costs reductions can occur because fewer correctional officers are needed to staff a lower-security facility.

For example, the Texas Department of Criminal Justice houses about half its approximately 5,000 inmates over the age of 55 in fourteen "elderly wings," which offer special limited programming for older inmates. Estelle Unit, the designated geriatric facility, houses inmates who require a sheltered environment to complete their ADLs. The Estelle Unit has a capacity of only 60 beds; another unit has 108 beds designated as "overflow" for inmates waiting transfer to Estelle. The department uses a geriatric center assessment to screen the elderly. Admission into the Estelle Unit depends on space availability and coordination between the facility's medical director and the Health Services Liaison Committee. The following criteria have been established to ensure proper placement: Inmates must (1) be 65 years old or older (requests for exceptions may be reviewed); (2) not require skilled nursing care; (3) find housing with the general population difficult because of age or health condition; (4) meet the prison's security requirements for living in a dormitory environment in accordance with the inmate classification policy.

In the state of Washington, inmates with infirmities related to old age are likely to be transferred to the state penitentiary, where a number of cells in one unit have been designated for their use. Older inmates with chronic illnesses would be considered for transfer to the assisted living facility at the Ahtanum View Correctional Complex, which houses aged and infirm inmates. The unit accepts only offenders scheduled for release within four years. In addition, inmates must be either 55 years of age or have a physical disability or illness, and they cannot be considered security threats. Older inmates who require long-term inpatient care would be considered for transfer to the state reformatory, which has the largest inpatient unit in the system.

Compassionate Leave

As of this writing, the courts have not recognized any constitutional right to compassionate or medical leave. Most states provide compassionate leave for those inmates who are terminally ill or are not capable of physically functioning in the correctional system (see Chapter 6), but not because of age alone. As a rule of thumb, the prognosis must usually be six months or less to live and specific criteria of custody classification and medical requirements must be met. Yates and Gillespie (2000) have made the point that prisons can reduce overcrowding and their health-care costs through medical parole programs for elderly inmates. The authors call for compassionate release that would go beyond the release for severely or terminally ill patients. They suggest that policies in most states drastically limit potential medical parole and as a result have little impact on prison overcrowding or rising medical costs.

One obstacle to widening compassionate release is the lack of a suitable community placement. Many families, who also may be dealing with aging issues, do not have the time or resources to adequately care for a released prisoner. Some states have nursing home placement as a practical alternative; on the other hand, nursing home administrators may not be favorable to the notion of accepting ex-prisoners who have life histories of crime and violence, even if they are quite ill. When compassionate leave is impossible because of the nature of the crime, correctional policy, or lack of available alternatives, prisons are developing policies and programs to better serve the terminally ill. Family members are permitted to spend extended periods of time with the dying inmate, and hospice supervisors work closely with the inmate and the family.

In 1998, the warden at Angola Prison in Louisiana began to make pine coffins as a cheaper and more dignified way to bury the growing number of inmate deaths on prison grounds. Until this policy change, local funeral homes contracted by the prison buried prisoners' bodies in cardboard boxes and packing crates (Cain & Fontenot, 2001). To add more dignity to prison funerals, inmates have also built an elaborate, old-fashioned hearse that is pulled by horses to the Point Lookout Cemetery (Krane, 1999). Inmates also sing songs and offer prayers on behalf of the deceased at prison funeral services. One older inmate who is a 73-year-old carpenter serving 119 years for armed robbery and possession with intent to distribute opium has been making coffins since the inception of the program.

DIVERSION, PROBATION, AND PAROLE

Using data on the "prefile" diversion review of 5,715 drug offenders residing in one county of Arizona, Johnston and Alozie (2001) explored the effect of age on criminal processing outcomes. Although their sample contained only sixty offenders over the age of 50, the findings are worth noting. The authors found that age was, indeed, a relevant variable in explaining the pretrial diversion review outcome in this sample. Up to a point, the results indicated something of a curvilinear pattern. For example, as age increased initially, offenders were less likely to receive a positive diversion review. As age increased to about 52 years, a positive age effect surfaced. Gender affected the prediction model, with older females more likely to receive a positive diversion review than older males. Prior arrest records also played a major role in the diversion review process. Offenders with more prior arrests were more likely to receive a negative diversion review. However, older whites with more arrests more likely to be treated more leniently than were blacks and Hispanics. These results introduce a significant caveat in the belief that all older offenders are treated more leniently in criminal processing. The authors conclude that older whites were more likely to be viewed as a group in need of help than are other racial groups.

As an increasing number of elderly offenders experiences various forms of mental illness or, at the very least, lacks substantial capacity to appreciate the criminality or wrongfulness of their behavior, not only should apprehension guidelines be reviewed, but also diversion alternatives should be considered by criminal justice officials. As Fattah and Sacco (1989) have suggested, the psychological trauma the elderly first offender is likely to experience when apprehended or appearing before a judge charged with a criminal offense warrants the establishment of alternatives to the current court system. Pretrial diversion is one of several alternative programs that have been successful with certain elderly offenders. Families of elderly perpetrators have also found diversion programs to be useful in reducing the stigma of criminal behavior in old age.

There have been numerous attempts to create special diversion programs for elderly offenders. The initial models generally focused on older offenders who were first-time offenders or who committed minor offenses. The Broward County Senior Intervention and Education Program has been offered as a community alternative to arrest in shoplifting cases. This model program removed the offender from the criminal justice process into a social agency trained to deal with senior problems. The major goal of the program is to provide courts with alternative means of dealing with the elderly offender without the stigma of a criminal record. The program offers individual counseling, social activities, and emotional support through group sessions. The offender who successfully completes the program has the charges dismissed with no court costs assessed and no criminal record created. Participation is voluntary, and the offender's enrollment in the program is brought to the attention of the court at the time of arraignment (Glugover & Zwetchkenbaum, 1980).

Another option available for handling the increasing number of older offenders is probation. McCarthy and Langworthy (1987) estimate that the number of older offenders under probation supervision may be four times the number of elderly in prison. Ellsworth and Helle (1994) estimate that 100,000 persons age 50 and over are on probation and under parole supervision, with an expected increase of 60,000 new offenders added to the count each year. Despite this strong representation, very little is known about the older offender on probation.

Several studies have, however, identified significant differences between younger and older probationers. For example, older probationers were less likely to have completed high school or a GED than were younger offenders (McCarthy & Langworthy, 1987; Shichor, 1988). Older offenders were less likely to be identified as drug abusers, but, as expected, older offenders were more frequently troubled with medical problems than were younger probationers (Ellsworth & Helle, 1994). Shichor (1988) further concludes that the older probationers appear to receive more lenient treatment by the system. He found that almost two-thirds of his sample of older probationers was being supervised at the medium and minimum levels. After examining numerous presentencing investigation reports, Shichor found evidence that a more severe punishment would have been justified if the offenders had been younger. Champion (1988) also reported in his extensive study of misdemeanant defendants that persons age 60 and over received probation recommendations 68 percent of the time as opposed to 16 percent of the time for younger offenders. It appears that age and poor health are frequently taken into account in sentencing recommendations and are also a factor in determining the offender's level of supervision (Ellsworth & Helle, 1994).

Some officials have called for earlier parole for elderly inmates judged to be no threat to society (Stock, 1996). Prison officials point to the need to relieve prisons of some of the severe overcrowding facing many states. Those in favor of this alternative argue that elderly parolees have low recidivism rates than younger parolees do. Age is considered by the U.S. Parole Commission to be the one accurate predictor of recidivism. It has been argued that elderly inmates represent a lower risk of reoffending than other prisoners do. According to state recidivism statistics, while 45 percent of those between the ages of 18 and 29 years returned to prison within one year of their release, only 3.2 percent of the 55 and above age group showed similar recidivism (Holman, 1998). The high costs of maintaining nursing homes within prison walls is another factor frequently mentioned by those in favor of alternative policies for older offenders.

In order to transfer elderly offenders back into the community, housing and financial assistance must usually be secured for inmates imprisoned for long terms and who have lost all contacts in the community. Parole decisions should be handled case by case. Prison staff should maintain good relationships with social service agencies, particularly Social Security officials and nursing home personnel. Older offenders will need assistance in getting their Social Security status reinstated and to determine whether they are eligible for Medicaid. Intervals for parole review of older inmates should be more frequent, especially in cases where terminal illnesses have been diagnosed.

PROJECT FOR OLDER PRISONERS

The Project for Older Prisoners (POPS), developed by Jonathan Turley of the George Washington University School of Law, has been advocating the early release of elderly prisoners since 1989. The development of POPS was inspired by the case of Quinton Brown, a 50-year-old drifter who stole $117 and a cherry pie from a convenience store in Morgan City, Louisiana. For this crime, he was sentenced to thirty years in a maximum-security prison. When Turley examined the case in 1989, Brown was 67 years old, a model prisoner, and suffering from bleeding ulcers and emphysema. With Turley's help, Brown won early release.

POPS is the first and only organization in the country to work exclusively with the elderly and infirm to influence their early release. Employing the services of hundreds of law students, the project is developing ways that states can lower expenses by acting on common geriatric problems. Although early release is clearly out of the question for some, many of the elderly fall into age and crime categories with a very low likelihood of committing new offenses. Since 1989, over 200 elderly inmates have been released as because of the efforts of the POP program. None has returned to prison for committing a new crime. Will (1998) speculates that the success of the POPS program is due to the careful selection of candidates for release aided by an extensive interviewing process that produces a ranking on a recidivism risk scale. The POPS program also interviews the victims or their families to ensure a consensus for the proposed parole. Another requirement is that the long-term inmates acknowledge their guilt.

POPS tries to place inmates who are able to work into jobs when they are released. This can prove difficult when many older lifers may have few skills to offer, but they at least are given an opportunity through the certification given by POPS. An alternative to full release would enable older prisoners to live in the community wearing an electronic bracelet. This device monitors the older parolee's whereabouts. Prisoners wearing the bracelet can continue to receive state benefits and utilize state hospitals for their care but not federal benefits such as Medicare and Social Security.

ARGUMENTS FOR ELDER JUSTICE

Several authors have suggested that at all stages of the criminal justice system the elderly offender may be treated differently from his or her younger counterpart (Cohen, 1985; James, 1992; Pertierra, 1995). In particular, the purpose of legal sanctions may be different for the elderly offender, leading to a deemphasis upon restraint, deterrence, and rehabilitation, given the mental and physical characteristics of the elderly. Some have urged that more drastic measures are needed in order to respond appropriately to the elderly offender. They have suggested putting in place a separate system for the aging population to fully recognize the distinct differences between extreme age groups (Clark & Mezey, 1997; Tucker, 1996). Newman & Newman (1984) have further argued that such an alternative would not be simply lenient justice, but a separate and distinct legal system that differs from the current adult system in philosophy, purpose, and technique.

Feinberg (1984) has suggested that an elderly justice system be constructed along the lines of the juvenile justice system. In such a system elderly law violators would be divided into four categories: (1) elderly in need of supervision; (2) neglected elderly; (3) elderly delinquents (those whose behavior lacks the spirit, maturation, and organization implied in criminal behavior but who have violated certain criminal laws); and (4) elderly offenders (those who have perpetrated a serious crime with the sophistication of younger adult law violators but who, by virtue of their chronological age, may need special processing). Justice objectives and procedures would then vary case by case. Feinberg suggests, however, that any elderly justice system should be created with caution. So drastic a change needs further research and more elaborate documentation before being launched.

Abrams (1984) also suggested the need for special courts to handle the elderly charged with crimes. Abrams sees the need for a court informed about geriatrics and gerontology that can assure the proper counseling services, the proper referral service, and the proper family and community support when dealing with the frail elderly caught in the judicial system. Today, thousands of elderly arrested on charges from shoplifting to violent crimes are shuffled into courts before judges who have little time, patience, or understanding. There is no inquiry into the impact of arterial blockage on cerebral functioning; the frustrations, fears, and confusion of elderly who may not be able to hear or see well; or undetected ministrokes that cause distortions in the elderly's perceptions of right and wrong.

A special senior citizens' court could provide insight into the problems of the aged offender. Special services might include referral and counseling for older offenders who are arrested. Adams (2000, pp. 97–98) has suggested that certain court accommodations for the frail elderly be given consideration:

- Offenders with hearing problems should be moved closer to the judge or provided amplification devices or visual transcription.
- Attorneys should be instructed to face the elderly person when talking and to speak in a low-pitched tone.
- Defendants with vision problems should be given a magnifying glass or exhibits should be enlarged.
- A proper time frame should be given for the offender to review court documents.
- Courtroom lighting should be designed to minimize or eliminate glare.
- Courtroom should be constructed with nonskid flooring, a minimum of stair steps, and well-marked areas to accommodate older people with mobility impairments.
- Court proceedings for those with dementia or memory problems should be held early in the day when mental confusion is at a minimum.

An example mentioned by Adams is the implementation of the Thirteenth Judicial Circuit's creation of the Elderly Justice System. The system was established to make the courts more accessible to those engaged in the legal process. The services provided include many of those mentioned above.

The debate over whether to develop special courts, change existing facilities to enhance the safety of older, frail inmates, enact more appropriate sentencing, or introduce more relevant programs will likely continue. Some authors (Adams, 1995; Champion, 1988) based the need for change on the failure to address the issue of an elder offender's criminal responsibility. The challenges of processing a growing population of defendants who make special demands on the criminal justice system and the financial burden of housing aging inmates for longer periods may eventually force states to review their current sentencing policies and force alternative sentencing.

FUTURE RESEARCH NEEDS AND CHALLENGES

Previous chapters have identified a number of areas where additional research is needed. Certainly, all phases of the criminal justice system need carefully conducted investigations from this field still in its infant stages of development. Research is needed to better determine why older offenders commit crimes late in life, and new theoretical models developed exclusively for the older offender would prove most useful in advancing knowledge in this area. Contemporary studies are also needed to identify the discretion that the police use when apprehending older offenders. Only a few studies have been conducted thus far on the successful outcomes of pretrial diversion programs for the older offender. Identifying more clearly how the court system responds to the elderly offender with physical or mental limitations is also an area ripe for investigation. Research would also be helpful in providing information about long-term inmates who have been paroled back to the community and how they are coping with the transition.

Researchers are beginning to address with more frequency the policy concerns associated with the aging prison population. Unfortunately, the body of knowledge on elderly inmates and the challenges posed to corrections systems in their special needs is not extensive. Burnett (1989) has noted that the conduct of original research on elderly offenders has been slow to develop for several reasons: (1) a lack of consensus on the definition of *old*; (2) few criminal offenders are classified in the upper, "older," categories of official arrest statistics; and (3) incomplete and inaccurate age data on defendants and inmates. It has also been suggested that most researchers and policymakers deem the crimes of youthful offenders as more serious and dangerous to the fabric of society than the crimes committed by older people. Research interest is expected to increase as policymakers and correctional officials seek information they need to respond the special needs of their older inmate populations.

In a survey of southern correctional facilities, Edwards (1998) found prison officials called for additional research in the following areas:

- Average annual medical costs for aged offenders
- Security levels necessary to protect both the community and the elderly housed in correctional facilities
- The impact of sentencing law changes on the size of the long-term inmate population
- The costs of long-term incarceration of infirm prisoners versus the risks of early parole or extended medical furlough
- The resources available for released older inmates
- Information on aging lifers without parole and the effects of long-term institutionalization
- Support measures for frail inmates and their special programming needs

Prison officials have also stressed that indicators are needed to more clearly identify model programs to meet the needs of the elderly inmate. For example, although a variety of programs and facilities have been introduced, a systematic way to evaluate them is needed. Important questions remain about their effectiveness in meeting the needs of the aging prisoner. Research, in this case, would emphasize (1) the living environment or custodial care, (2) humanitarian care, and (3) therapeutic care. An evaluation research design would focus on how effectively these programs currently meet the physical, medical, social, and mental needs of the aging prisoner.

Other research information desired by correctional officials includes (1) the general health-care needs of this special population, (2) the average annual medical cost for aged offenders, (3) the incarceration alternatives available for frail elderly inmates and data on the post-release success of elderly prisoners, (4) the nature of family relationships for those growing old in prison, and (5) the typical coping strategies of those who enter prison later in life. Scholars in the social and behavioral sciences can play an important role in assisting policymakers by providing the information they need to develop new program models.

In many ways, geriatric policies and programming is still in the developmental stage. While it is obvious that correctional officials are becoming more sensitive to the special needs of aging inmates, barriers continue to interfere with the ability of states to respond effectively. For example, most states are faced with the rising costs of medical care and general overcrowding, and about forty state prison systems are under court orders to rectify overcrowding (Will, 1998). In the 1990s, the war on drugs and tough mandatory sentencing laws has doubled the number of inmates. Overcrowding, AIDS, and other issues have hindered many states from implementing special programming for the aging inmate.

Another challenge in providing adequate care of aging inmates is a general lack of community support for specialized services. The arguments over special treatment of elderly inmates are still unresolved (Cavan, 1987). Some public sentiment is against providing special treatment or separate facilities for the older inmate (Edwards, 1998). Some correctional officials feel no need or responsibility to give special consideration to older offenders. The public also still disagrees about the ethical obligation to provide inmates with such acute care as arterial bypass surgery or kidney transplants when others in society may not have access to or the money for the same level of care. Thus, lack of space, philosophy, or costs may deprive some elderly inmates from specialized programming.

As Chapter 6 mentioned, the older offender may have to wait to be assigned to facilities providing special needs because slots are few. In particular, those states converting a small wing for older inmates may have long waiting lists. As the number of older inmates grow, it will become impossible to provide special housing for those who would qualify. Another major problem in meeting the special needs of older inmates is that many states still have a very small number of aging inmates. In those states, separate facilities or programs cannot be justified and correctional units have little choice but to mainstream elderly inmates.

Another obstacle in responding fully to the special needs of the aging inmate is the lack of adequately trained prison staff. Moreover, not everyone who works in a correctional environment may have the aptitude or the essential skills needed to manage elderly people. Careful selection for sensitivity to the unique requirements of geriatric inmates should be an important consideration. Training of administrative personnel, line security staff, and health providers should increase their knowledge of growing older and how the effects of aging interacts with the prison environment. Prison staffs need to be specifically trained to more fully understand the social and emotional needs of the elderly, the dynamics of death and dying, procedures for identifying depression, and a system for referring older inmates to experts in the community.

SUMMARY

The number of older offenders participating in the criminal justice system will continue to accelerate as the baby boomer population marches toward old age. While the aging inmates are the fastest growing group of inmates in both U.S. and Canadian prisons, the growth rate will rise even higher in the near future. Currently, the population of those aged 50 and over is growing at about 10 percent per year and the rate is expected to jump to 20 percent by 2010. In responding to the special needs of this group of offenders, policy issues will continue to come to the forefront for deliberation. The programs and policies now in place vary from state to state and this will most likely continue. Economic resources, sentencing guidelines, policy priorities, and the variation in the number and diversity of older offenders will contribute to this multiplicity.

As prison populations age, the problems confronting corrections departments will likely increase. In addition to health-care issues, work assignments, co-payments, nutritional requirements, concerns for victimization, end of life issues, and appropriate staffing are concerns that will have to be addressed in accommodating older inmates. In order to manage the onslaught of older offenders, some policymakers are calling for alternative sentencing solutions. Since bed space for frail inmates is already considered one of the major problems facing departments of corrections, the use of secure nursing homes, halfway houses, home monitoring, and other pretrial diversion programs will receive serious consideration.

Although older inmates have been recognized to have needs quite different from those of younger inmates, there is significant diversity within the group. Programs will need to be designed to accommodate the successful transition of new elderly offenders into the criminal justice system. Mental and physical assessment, counseling services, and other programming will be necessary. For inmates who will spend the rest of their lives in prison, managing their health care will become critical. These inmates will eventually need assistance with ADLs, and assisted living facilities will become a necessity. Prison officials will be faced with the problem of finding suitable work and recreational activities so that inmates can pass the time in reasonably good health. Of course, inmates who have spent a greater portion of their lives incarcerated will need intensive discharge planning and community placement orientation. Locating family or community members who will accept aging inmates eligible for parole will be a challenge.

It is impossible to prescribe all the solutions needed in responding to the aging prison population. In recognition of the rapid increase in the older offender population, policymakers and criminal justice officials in each state or jurisdiction will have the responsibility of entering into long-range planning. Effectively meeting these challenges coupled with future court rulings or American Disability Act requirements, limited budgets, overcrowded conditions, pressures to reduce medical costs, and lack of public support for special treatment for inmates will require significant leadership from a variety of stakeholders. The task is a daunting one, and societal forces are in place to provide significant challenges for America's prisons in the 21st century.

REFERENCES

Adams, W. E. (1995). Incarceration of older criminals balancing safety costs and humanitarian concerns. *Nova Law Review, 19,* 465–486.

Adams, W. E. (2000). Elders in the courtroom. In M. B. Rothman, B. D. Dunlop, & P. Entzel (Eds.), *Elders, crime, and the criminal justice system.* New York: Springer.

Aday, R. H. (1994a). Aging in prison: A case study of new elderly offenders. *International Journal of Offender Therapy and Comparative Criminology, 38*(1), 79–91.

Aday, R. H. (1994b). Golden years behind bars: Special programs and facilities for elderly inmates. *Federal Probation*, 58(2), 47–54.

Aday, R. H. (1999). *Golden years behind bars: A ten-year follow-up*. Paper presented at the annual meeting of the Academy of Criminal Justices Sciences, Orlando, FL.

Aday, R. H., & Rosefield, H. A. (1992, Winter). Providing for the geriatric inmate: Implications for training. *Journal of Correctional Training*, 1214–1620.

Alston, L. T. (1986). *Crime and older Americans*. Springfield, IL: Charles C. Thomas.

Anderson, J. C., & Morton, J. B. (1989). Graying of the nation's prisons presents new challenges. *Aging Connection*, 10, 6–7.

Atchley, R. C. (2000). *Social forces and aging*. Belmont, CA: Wadsworth.

Bachand, D. J. (1984). *The elderly offender: An exploratory study with implications for continuing education of law enforcement personnel*. Unpublished doctoral dissertation, University of Michigan, Ann Arbor.

Black, D. (1980). *The manners and customs of the police*. Orlando, FL: Academic Press.

Burnett, C. (1989). Older offenders: Introduction. *Journal of Offender Counseling, Services & Rehabilitation*, 15, 1–17.

Cain, B., & Fontenot, C. (2001). Angola's long-term inmates. *Corrections Today*, 63, 120–124.

Cavan, R. H. (1987). Is special treatment needed for elderly offenders? *Criminal Justice Policy Review*, 2, 213–224.

Champion, D. J. (1988). The severity of sentencing: Do federal judges really go easier on elderly felons in plea-bargaining negotiations compared with their younger counterparts? In B. McCarthy and R. Langworthy (Eds.), *Older offenders: Perspectives in criminology and criminal justice* (pp. 143–156). New York: Praeger.

Chaneles, S. (1987, October). Growing old behind bars. *Psychology Today*, 21, 46–51.

Chaneles, S., & Burnett, C. (1989). *Older offenders: Current trends*. New York: Haworth.

Clark, C., & Mezey, G. (1997). Elderly sex offenders against children: A descriptive study of child sex abusers over the age of 65. *Journal of Forensic Psychiatry*, 8(2), 357–369.

Cohen, F. (1985). Old age as a criminal defense. *Criminal Law Bulletin*, 21(1), 5–36.

Colsher, P. L., Wallace, R. B., Loeffelholz, P., & Sales, M. (1992). Health status of older male prisoners: A comprehensive survey. *American Journal of Public Health*, 82(6), 881–884.

Cullen, F. T., Wozniak, J. F., & Frank, J. (1985). The rise of the elderly offender: Will a "new" criminal be invented? *Crime and Social Justice*, 23, 151–165.

Cutshall, C., & Adams, K. (1983). Responding to older offenders: Age selectivity in the processing of shoplifters. *Criminal Justice Review*, 8, 1–5.

Dickens, B. M. (1969). Shops, shoplifting, and law enforcement. *Criminal Law Review*, 25, 464–472.

Ebersole, P., & Hess, P. (1998). *Toward healthy aging.* St. Louis: Mosby.

Edwards, T. (1998). *The aging inmate population: SLC special series report.* Atlanta: The Council of State Governments.

Ellsworth, T., & Helle, K.A. (1994). Older offenders on probation. *Federal Probation, 58*(4), 43–50.

Fattah, E.A., & Sacco, V.F. (1989). *Crime and victimization of the elderly.* New York: Springer-Verlag.

Federal Bureau of Investigation. (1999). *Uniform crime reports.* Washington, DC: U.S. Government Printing Office.

Feinberg, G. (1984). White haired offenders: An emergent social problem. In W. Wilbanks & P. Kim (Eds.), *Elderly criminals* (pp. 83–108). Lanham, MD: University Press of America.

Feinberg, G. (1988). The role of the elderly defendant in the criminal court: Full dress adversary or reluctant penitent? In B. McCarthy & R. Langworthy (Eds.), *Older offenders: Perspectives in criminology and criminal justice* (pp. 123–142). New York: Praeger.

Feinberg, G., & Kholsa, D. (1985). Sanctioning elderly delinquents. *Trail, 21,* 46–56.

Feinberg, G., & McGriff, M. D (1989). Defendant's advanced age as a prepotent status in criminal case disposition and sanction. *Journal of Offender Counseling, Services & Rehabilitation, 13,* 87–124.

Finkel, S.I., & Macki, I.J. (2000). Impact of the criminal justice process on older persons. In M.B. Rothman, B.D. Dunlop, & P. Entzel (Eds.), *Elders, Crime, and the Criminal Justice System.* New York: Spring.

Flynn, E.E. (1992). The graying of America's prison population. *Prison Journal, 72,* 77–98.

Fyfe, J. (1984). Police dilemmas in processing elderly offenders. In E.S. Newman, D.J. Newman & M.L. Gewirtz. (Eds.), *Elderly criminals* (pp. 97–112). Cambridge, MA: Oelgeschlager, Gunn, & Hain.

Gallagher, E.M. (1990). Emotional, social, and physical health characteristics of older men in prison. *International Journal of Aging and Human Development, 31,* 251–265.

Glugover, S., & Zwetchkenbaum, I. (1980). *Community alternatives to arrest in shoplifting cases.* Broward Senior Intervention and Education Program. Broward County, FL.

Helms, J. (1997). Mandatory sentencing guidelines: The Oregon model. *U.C. Davis Law Review, 25,* 697–714.

Holman, B. (1998). Nursing homes behind bars: The elderly in prison. *Coalition for Federal Sentencing Reform, 2*(1), 1–2.

Jackson, B. (1996). Assessment, threatment & theorizing about sex offenders. *Criminal Justice & Behavior, 23,* 162–195.

James, M.F. (1992). The sentencing of elderly criminals. *American Criminal Law Review, 29,* 1025–1044.

Johnston, W., & Alozie, B.O. (2001). The effect of age on criminal processing: Is there an advantage in being "older"? *Journal of Gerontological Social Work, 35,* 47–62.

Krajick, K. (1979). Growing old in prison. *Corrections Magazine*, 5(1), 32–46.

Krane, J. (1999, April 15). Death and mourning inside the walls: Funerals becoming a part of prison life. *www.apbonline.com/cjsystem/behindbars/oldprisoners*. pp. 1–4.

Kratcoski, P.C. (1990). Circumstances surrounding homicides by older offenders. *Criminal Justice and Behavior*, 17, 420–430.

Lindquist, J.H., White, O.Z., & Chambers, C.D. (1986). Elderly felons: Dispositions of arrests. In C.D. Chambers, J.H. Lindquist, O.Z. White, & M.T. Harter (Eds.), *The elderly: Victims and deviants* (pp. 161–177). Athens, OH: University of Ohio Press.

Malcolm, A.H. (1988, December 24). Aged inmates pose problem for prisons. *The New York Times*, p. 1.

Malinchak, A A. (1980). *Crime and gerontology*. Englewood Cliffs, NJ: Prentice-Hall.

McCarthy, B. & Langworthy, R. (1987). Older offenders on probation and parole. *Journal of Offender Counseling, Services and Rehabilitation*, 11, 136–150.

Mother is Acquitted in Paralyzing Attack (1999, August 7). *New York Times*, p. B1.

Newman, E.S., Newman, D.J., & Gewirtz, M.L. (1984). *Elderly criminals*. Cambridge, MA: Oelgeschlager, Gunn & Hain.

Ogloff, J.R., Roesch, R. & Eaves, D. (1995). International perspectives on mental health research in the criminal justice system. *International Journal of Law and Psychiatry*, 18, 1–25.

Pertierra, C.J. (1995). Do the crime, do the time: Should elderly criminals receive proportionate sentences? *Nova Law Review*, 19, 793–819.

Roesch, R., & Golding, S.C. (1985). Who is competent to stand trial? *Trial*, 2(9), 40–45.

Rosefield, H.A. (1993). The older inmate: "Where do we go from here?" *Journal of Prison and Jail Health*, 12, 51–58.

Roth, E.B. (1992, July–October). Elders behind bars. *Perspectives on Aging*, 21, 25–30.

Sherwin, R. (1990). Employing life expectancy as a guideline in sentencing criminal offenders: Toward a humanistic proposal for change. *Prison Journal*, 70, 125–127.

Shichor, D. (1984). The extent and nature of lawbreaking by the elderly: A review of arrest statistics. In E.S. Newman, D.J. Newman, & M.L. Gewitz (Eds.), *Elderly criminals* (pp. 17–32). Cambridge, MA: Oelgeschlager, Gunn, and Hain.

Shichor, D. (1985). Male-female differences in elderly arrests: An exploratory analysis. *Justice Quarterly*, 2, 399–414.

Shichor, D. (1988). An exploratory study of elderly probationers. *International Journal of Offender Therapy and Comparative Criminology*, 32, 163–174.

Silverman, M., Smith, L.G., Nelson, C., & Dembo, R. (1984). The perception of the elderly criminal when compared to adult and juvenile offenders. *Journal of Applied Gerontology*, 3, 97–104.

Steffensmeier, D. J., & Motivans, M. (2000). Older men and older women in arms of criminal law: Offending patterns and sentencing outcomes. *Journal of Gerontology: Social Sciences, 55B,* 141–151.

Steffensmeier, D. J., Kramer, J., & Ulmer, J. (1995). Age differences in sentencing. *Justice Quarterly, 12,* 583–601.

Stock, R. W. (1996, January 18). Inside prison, too, a population is aging. *New York Times,* 14.

Terry, C. W., & Entzel, P. (2000). Police and elders. In M. B. Rothman, B. D. Dunlop, & P. Entzel (Eds.), *Elders, crime, and the criminal justice system* (pp. 3–18). New York: Springer.

Tucker, M. (1996). *The impact of knowledge and attitudes toward aging on students' perceptions of a geriatric justice system.* Unpublished master's thesis. Murfreesboro: Middle Tennessee State University.

Turner, G. S., & Champion, D. J. (1989). The elderly offender and sentencing leniency. *Journal of Offender Counseling, Services and Rehabilitation, 13,* 125–140.

Turley, J. (1992, November). A solution to prison overcrowding. *USA Today Magazine, 121,* 80–81.

United States Sentencing Commission (1989). Federal sentencing guidelines and policy statements. Washington, D.C.

Vega, M., & Silverman, M. (1988). Stress and the elderly convict. *International Journal of Offender Therapy and Comparative Criminology, 32,* 153–162.

Visher, C. A. (1983). Gender, police arrest decisions, and notions of chivalry. *Criminology, 21,* 5–28.

Walsh, C. E. (1989). The older and long-term inmate growing old in the New Jersey prison system. *Journal of Offender Counseling, Services and Rehabilitation, 13,* 215–247.

Wilbanks, W. (1985, April 25). *Are elderly felons treated more leniently by the criminal justice system?* Paper presented at the Third National Conference on Elderly Offenders, Kansas City, MO.

Wikberg, R. (1988). The longtermers. *Angolite, 13,* 1–14.

Will, G. F. (1998, July 20). A jail break for geriatrics. *Newsweek,* 70.

Williams, G. C. (1989). *Elderly offenders: A comparison of chronic and new elderly offenders.* Unpublished master's thesis. Murfreesboro: Middle Tennessee State University.

Yates, J., & Gillespie, W. (2000). The elderly and prison policy. *Journal of Aging and Social Policy, 11*(2–3), 167–175.

Index

About the Author

RONALD H. ADAY is Director of Aging Studies and Professor of Sociology at Middle Tennessee State University.